Fyodor Dostoevsky

The Biography of the Greatest Russian Novelist

AIMÉE **DOSTOEVSKY**

Discovery Publisher

Fyodor Dostoyevsky, A Study by Aimée Dostoyevsky
New Haven Yale University Press

2021, Discovery Publisher

Author: Aimée Dostoevsky

616 Corporate Way
Valley Cottage, New York
www.discoverypublisher.com
editors@discoverypublisher.com
Proudly not on Facebook or Twitter

New York • Paris • Dublin • Tokyo • Hong Kong

Table of Contents

Fyodor Dostoevsky

The Biography of the Greatest Russian Novelist

AIMÉE **DOSTOEVSKY**

Preface

Russia was preparing to celebrate the centenary of the birth of Fyodor Dostoevsky on October 30, 1921. Our writers and poets hoped to do honour in prose and verse to the great Russian novelist; the Slav peoples had arranged to send deputations to Petrograd, to pay their homage in Czech, Serbian and Bulgarian to the great Slavophil, who was ever faithful to the idea of our future Slav confederation. The Dostoevsky family, in its turn, proposed to mark the occasion by publishing the documents preserved in the Historical Museum of Moscow. My mother was to have given the world her memories of her illustrious husband, and I was to have written a new biography of my father, and to have recorded my childish impressions of him.

It is unlikely that any such festival will take place. A terrible storm has passed over Russia, destroying the whole fabric of our European civilisation. The Revolution, long ago predicted by Dostoevsky, burst upon us after a disastrous war. The gulf which for two centuries had been widening between our peasants and our intellectuals, became an abyss. Our intellectuals, intoxicated by European Utopias, were advancing towards the West, while our people, faithful to the tradition of their ancestors, had set their faces to the East. The Russian Nihilists and Anarchists desired to introduce European atheism into our country, whereas our deeply religious peasantry remained faithful to Christ.

The result of this conflict is now before us. The intellectuals who hoped to reign in Russia in the place of the Tsar, and to govern it according to their fancy, were swept away by our exasperated people as stupid and maleficent beings. Some of them have found shelter in the palaces of our former Embassies, and pretend to govern Russia from the banks of the Thames or the Seine, trying not to notice the sly smiles of the European ambassadors; others gather round the innumerable Russian newspapers, of which some hundred copies a number are printed, and offered gratis to any one who can be induced to read them. Readers, however, become more and more rare. Europeans begin to understand that our intellectuals are dreamers, and that the socialistic and anarchistic *moujik* of whom they speak in their journals has never existed save in the naive imaginations of "the grandfathers and grandmothers of the Russian Revolution."

Far from being an anarchist, the Russian *moujik* is on the way to construct a huge Oriental Empire. He is fraternising with the Mongolians, and establishing friendly relations with India, Persia and Turkey. He keeps Bolshevism like a scarecrow for sparrows, in order to keep off old Europe, and prevent her from meddling in Russian affairs, and hampering the construction of the national edifice. On the day when it is completed, the Russian *moujik* will destroy the scarecrow, which will have served its turn, and astonished Europe will see rising before her a new Russian Empire, mightier and more solid than the old. Our *moujiks* are good architects, and like wise men, which they have always been, they have no idea of inviting the intellectuals to be their architects. They have realised that these sick men could destroy the finest civilisation in the world, but that they are quite incapable of constructing anything in its place.

If Dostoevsky's centenary cannot be celebrated in Russia, I should like to see it commemorated in Europe, for he has long been accepted as a universal writer, one of those beacons which illuminate the path of humanity. I have therefore decided to publish in Europe the biography of my father, which I once hoped to publish in Russia; this is the more expedient, since my entire fortune is in the hands of the Bolsheviks, and I must now work for my living. The new details of my father's life which will be found in my book may suggest to his admirers fresh critical studies of his works, and make them more popular among European and American readers. This will surely be the best way in which to celebrate the centenary of the famous writer.

Aimée Dostoevsky

Fyodor Dostoevsky

The Biography of the Greatest Russian Novelist

AIMÉE **DOSTOEVSKY**

I

Origin of the Dostoevsky Family

"I know our people. I have lived with them in prison, eaten with them, slept with them, worked with them. The people gave me back Christ, whom I learned to know in my father's house, but whom I lost later, when I in my turn became 'a European Liberal.'" —August, 1880.

In reading biographies of my father, I have always been surprised to find that his biographers have studied him solely as a Russian, and sometimes even as the most Russian of Russians. Now Dostoevsky was Russian only on his mother's side, for his paternal ancestors were of Lithuanian origin. Of all lands in the Russian Empire, Lithuania is certainly the most interesting by reason of its transformations and the various influences it has undergone in the course of centuries. The Lithuanian breed is the same mixture of Slavs and Finno-Turkish tribes as the Russian. Yet there is a very marked difference between the two peoples. Russia remained long under the Tatar yoke, and became mongolised. Lithuania, on the other hand, was normanised by the Normans, who traded with Greece by the waterways of the Niemen and the Dnieper. Finding this trade highly profitable, the Normans established vast mercantile dépôts in Lithuania, and placed them under the guard of sentinels. Gradually these dépôts were transformed into fortresses, and the fortresses into towns. Some of these towns exist to this day, as, for instance, the town of Polozk, which was governed by the Norman prince Rogvolod. The whole country was divided into a number of small principalities; the population was Lithuanian, the government Norman. Perfect order reigned in these principalities, and excited the envy of the neighbouring Slav peoples.[1]

1. This envy led the Slavs who inhabited the shores of the Dnieper, and were the ancestors of the Ukrainians and Russians, to desire Norman princes to rule over them in their turn. They sent a deputation to Lithuania to offer Prince Rurik the crown of the Grand Duchy of Kiew. Rurik, probably the brother or the younger son of some Norman prince who was governing a part of Lithuania, accepted

The Normans did not hold aloof from the Lithuanians; the princes and their followers married readily among the women of the country, and were gradually merged with the original inhabitants. Their Norman blood gave such vigour to the hitherto insignificant Lithuanians that they overcame the Tatars, the Russians, the Ukrainians, the Poles, and the Teutonic Knights, their northern neighbours. In the fifteenth century Lithuania had become an immense Grand Duchy, which comprised all Ukrainia and a large part of Russia. It played a very great part among the other Slav countries, had a brilliant, highly civilised Court, and attracted numerous foreigners of distinction, poets and men of learning. The Russian Boyards who opposed the tyranny of their Tsars fled to Lithuania and were hospitably received there. This was the case of the celebrated Prince Kurbsky, the mortal enemy of the Tsar Ivan the Terrible.[1]

The Normans were ruling in Lithuania at the beginning of the Christian era, and perhaps before. We find them still in power in 1392, in the person of the Grand Duke Witold, who, as his name indicates, was a descendant of the Norman princes. It is obvious that Lithuania must have become profoundly normanised in the course of fourteen centuries. To say nothing of the marriages contracted by the princes and the members of their retinue, the numerous merchants and warriors who came to Lithuania from the North readily took to wife young Lithuani-

the crown and went to Kiew with his Norman retinue. The descendants of Rurik reigned in Russia until the seventeenth century, first under the title of Grand Duke, and later under that of Tsar. When the last descendant of Rurik died at Moscow, Russia passed through a period of anarchy, until the Boyards elected as Tsar Mihail Romanoff, whose family was of Lithuanian origin — that is to say, a strongly normanised Slav family. In their turn the Romanoffs reigned for several centuries, loved and venerated by the Russian people. The curious fact that the Russian nation has twice chosen as princes Normans or normanised Slavs, is readily explained by the disputatious character of my countrymen. Interminable talkers and controversialists, capable of holding forth for a dozen hours on end without uttering a single sensible word, the Russians can never agree. The Normans, clear-headed and practical, sparing of words but prolific in deeds, made them live in peace one with another, and kept order in our country.

1. Modern historians who deal with the history of Lithuania and Ukrainia rarely mention the Normans. On the other hand, they often speak of the Varangians, and assert that the latter played an important part in Lithuania, and even in Ukrainia. Now the Varangians are in fact Normans, for the word Varangian means in old Slav "enemy." As the Normans always beat the Slavs, the latter called them the "enemies." Slavs have as a rule but little curiosity, and are not concerned to know the race to which their neighbours belong; they prefer to give them fancy names. Thus when the Russians began to trade with the Germans they called them "Nemzi," which in old Russian means "the Dumb," because the Germans did not understand their language and could not answer their questions. The Russian people still call the Germans "Nemzi." The name German or Teuton is used only by the intellectuals.

ans, who, thanks to their Slav blood, are handsomer and more graceful than the women of Finno-Turkish tribes in general. The offspring of these marriages inherited the Lithuanian type of their mothers, and the Norman brains of their paternal ancestors. Indeed, when *we* examine the Lithuanian character, we recognise its strong resemblance to the Norman character. I recommend to those who wish to study this practically unknown country, *Lithuania, Past and Present*, by W. St. Vidûnas. I shall often have occasion to quote this learned writer, but his excellent study should be read in its entirety. A curious fact in connection with Vidûnas's book is that while he describes the Lithuanian character as essentially Norman, he ignores the Norman blood of his compatriots, and declares ingenuously that they are merely Finno-Turks, who came originally from Asia. The author here adopts the attitude of the majority of the Lithuanians, who, under the influence of some perverted sense of national pride, have always repudiated their Norman ancestors.[1]

Instead of glorying in their descent, as the wise Rumanians glory in their descent from the ancient warriors of Rome, the Lithuanians have always tried to pass off their Norman Grand Dukes as princes of native blood. The Russians have never been deceived on this point. They knew that the Lithuanians were too weak to beat them, and were only able to do so with the help of the Normans. This is why my compatriots have always given all these Gediminas, Algardas and Vitantas their true Norman names of Guedimine, Olguerd and Witold. The Poles and the Germans have done the same, and the Norman princes have passed into history under their real names, to the great annoyance of all the Lithuanophils. Guedimin was the most famous of these princes. He was of the true Norman type, almost without any trace of Finno-Turkish blood. His portraits always remind me of those of Shakespeare; there is a family likeness between these two Normans. Guedimin showed the characteristic Norman indifference and tolerance in religious matters; he protected both Catholic and Orthodox. For his own part, he preferred to remain a pagan.

As Russia and Ukrainia became stronger, they succeeded in severing their connection with Lithuania and recovering their former independence. When they had lost their rich provinces to the east and the south, the Lithuanians were enfeebled, and could no longer struggle against their mortal enemies, the Knights of the Teutonic Order. The Germans

---

1. In their hatred of Russia and of Poland, the Lithuanians have even refused to admit that they have Slav blood in their veins. Yet one has only to look at them to see that they are much more Slav than Finno-Turkish.

conquered Lithuania, and introduced into the country a host of mediaeval institutions and ideas. These the Lithuanians retained for a long time when they had entirely disappeared from the rest of Europe. The Germans forced the Lithuanians to become Protestants. Like all Slavs, the Lithuanians were mystics, and Luther's religion meant nothing to them.[1]

When at a later period Poland had become a powerful state in its turn, and had wrested Lithuania from the Teutonic Knights,[2] the Lithuanians hastened to return to the Catholic or Orthodox faith of their ancestors. The Polish Catholic clergy, especially the Jesuits, warred passionately against the Orthodox monastic houses; but these were protected by many Lithuanian families, who preferred the Orthodox religion. Among these were some very influential personalities, notably Prince Constantine Ostrogesky, the celebrated champion of the Orthodox Church. In face of this determined resistance the Poles were obliged to leave the Orthodox religious houses in the country, placing them, however, under the supervision of noble Catholic families, in order to check Orthodox propaganda. The Jesuits organised excellent Latin schools, forced the nobility of the country to send their sons to them, and in a short time succeeded in latinising all the young nobles of Lithuania. Poland, wishing to attach the Lithuanians to herself definitively, introduced among them many Polish institutions, including the *Schlialiia*, or Union of Nobles. The *Schliahtitchi* (nobles) adopted the custom of rallying to the banner of some great lord of the country in time of war, and lived under his protection in time of peace. These lords allowed the *Schliahtitchi* to adopt their armorial bearings. Later, Russia, who had borrowed numerous institutions from Lithuania, imitated the *Schliahta* by creating the Union of Hereditary Nobles. Among the Russians, this Union was agrarian rather than martial; but in both countries the Unions were above all patriotic.

The Finns, the Esthonians and the Letts, who are Finno-Turks of unmixed race, adopted the Protestant religion with ardour and remained faithful to it. The hostility the Lithuanians have always shown to Protestantism attests their Slav blood more eloquently than all else. The Slavs, who readily embraced the Orthodox or the Catholic faith, have never been able to understand the doctrine of Luther.

The Germans, however, kept a part of Lithuania, which was inhabited by the Lithuanian tribe of the Borussi. They germanised it and christened it Prussia. The Prussians are not Germans, but Lithuanians, first normanised and then germanised. Their strength of character and the important part they have played in Germany are due to their Norman blood. The majority of the Prussian Junkers are the direct descendants of the ancient Norman chiefs.

$*\ *\ *$

My father's ancestors were natives of the Government of Minsk, where, not far from Pinsk, there is still a place called Dostoyeve, the ancient domain of my father's family. It was formerly the wildest part of Lithuania, covered almost entirely with vast forests; the marshes of Pinsk extended as far as the eye could reach. The Dostoevsky were *Schliahtitchi* and belonged to the "grassy Radwan." That is to say, they were nobles, they went to war under the banner of the Lord of Radwan, and had the right to bear his arms. My mother had the Radwan armorial bearings drawn for the Dostoevsky Museum at Moscow. I have seen them, but I cannot describe them, as I have never studied heraldry.

The Dostoevsky were Catholics, very devout and very intolerant, it seems. In the course of our researches into the origin of our family, we found a document, in which an Orthodox monastery placed under the supervision of the Dostoevsky family complained of their harsh treatment of the Orthodox monks. This document proves two things:

That the Dostoevsky must have held a good position in their country, otherwise an Orthodox monastery would not have been placed under their supervision.

That as fervent Catholics, the Dostoevsky must have sent their sons to the Latin schools of the country, and that my father's ancestors must have possessed that excellent Latin culture which the Catholic clergy propagate wherever they go.

When in the eighteenth century the Russians annexed Lithuania, they did not find the Dostoevsky in the country; the family had passed into Ukrainia. What they did there and what towns they inhabited we know not. I have no idea what my great grandfather Andrey may have been, and this for a very curious reason.

The fact is that my grandfather Mihail Andrevitch Dostoevsky was a highly original person. At the age of fifteen he had a mortal quarrel with his father and his brothers, and ran away from home. He left the Ukraine, and went to study medicine at Moscow University. He never spoke of his family, and made no reply when questioned as to his origin. Later, when he had reached the age of fifty, his conscience seems to have reproached him for having thus quitted the paternal roof. He put an advertisement in the papers, begging his father and his brothers to let him hear from them. No notice was ever taken of this advertisement. It is probable that his relations were all dead. The Dostoevsky do not make old bones.

However, my grandfather Mihail must have declared his origin to his children, for I often heard my father and later my uncles say: "We Dostoevsky are Lithuanians, but we are not Poles. Lithuania is a country quite distinct from Poland."

My father told my mother of a certain Episcopus Stepan, who, according to him, was the founder of our *Orthodox* family. To my great regret, my mother did not pay much attention to these words of her husband's, and did not ask him for more precise details. I suppose that one of my Lithuanian ancestors, having emigrated to the Ukraine, changed his religion in order to marry an Orthodox Ukrainian, and became a priest. When his wife died he probably entered a monastery, and later, rose to be an Archbishop.[1]

This would explain how the Archbishop Stepan may have founded our Orthodox family, in spite of his being a monk. My father must have been convinced of the existence of this Episcopus, for he named his second son Stepane in his honour.

At this time Dostoevsky was fifty years old. It is very curious that my grandfather published his advertisement in the newspaper when he reached this age, and that it was also at the age of fifty that my father suddenly remembered the existence of the Archbishop Stepan. Both seem to have felt a wish to strengthen the bonds of union with their ancestors at this period.

It is somewhat surprising to see the Dostoevsky, who had been warriors in Lithuania, become priests in the Ukraine. But this is quite in accordance with Lithuanian custom. I may quote the learned Lithuanian W. St. Vidûnas in this connection:[2]

"Formerly many well-to-do Lithuanians had but one desire: to see one or more of their sons enter upon an ecclesiastical career. They gladly provided the funds necessary to prepare them for such a calling. But they had no sympathy with studies of a more general character, and were averse from the adoption of any other liberal profession by the sons. Even of late years many young Lithuanians have had to suffer greatly from parental obstinacy. Their fathers have refused them the money necessary for advanced secular studies, when they have declined to become ecclesiastics. Thus many lives of the highest promise have been wrecked."

1. In the Orthodox Church only monks — the Black Clergy — may become Archbishops. The White Clergy — married priests — never rise to high rank. When they lose their wives they often become monks, and can then pursue their career.
2. See his *La Lituanie dans le passé et dans le présent*.

These words of Vidûnas probably give the key to the extraordinary quarrel of my grandfather Mihail with his parents, which broke all the ties between our Moscovite family and the Ukrainian family of my greatgrandfather Andrey. The latter perhaps wished his son to pursue an ecclesiastical career, while the young man had a vocation for medicine. Seeing that his father would not pay for his medical studies, my grandfather fled from his home. We must admire the truly Norman energy of this youth of fifteen who entered an unknown city without money or friends, managed to get a superior education, made a good position for himself in Moscow, brought up a family of seven children, gave dowries to his three daughters and a liberal education to his four sons. My grandfather had good reason to be proud of himself, and to quote himself as an example to his children.

Andrey Dostoevsky's wish to see his son a priest was not, indeed, very extraordinary, for the Ukrainian clergy has always been highly distinguished. The Ukrainian parishes enjoyed the right to select their own priests, and naturally only men of blameless life were chosen. As to the higher ecclesiastical dignities, they were nearly always held by members of the Ukrainian nobility, which was very rarely the case in Greater Russia, where the priests are an isolated caste. Stepan Dostoevsky must have been a man of good family and good education or he could not have become an Episcopus. The Archbishop or Episcopus is the highest dignity in the Orthodox Church, for we have no Cardinals. After the abolition of the Patriarchate, the Archbishops managed the affairs of our church, each in turn taking part in the deliberations of the Holy Synod.

We have yet another proof that the Ukrainian Dostoevsky were intellectuals. Friends who had lived in Ukrainia told us that they had once seen there an old book, a kind of Almanach or poetical Anthology published in Ukrainia at the beginning of the nineteenth century. Among the poems in this book there was a little bucolic piece written in Russian and gracefully composed. It was not signed, but the first letters of each line formed the name Andrey Dostoevsky. Was it the work of my great-grandfather or of some cousin? I know not, but it proves two things of great interest to the biographers of Dostoevsky:

First, that his Ukrainian ancestors were intellectuals, for in Ukrainia only the lower and middle classes speak Ukrainian, a pretty and poetic, but also an infantile and somewhat absurd language. The upper classes in Ukrainia habitually spoke Polish or Russian, and accordingly last year, when the country separated from Russia and proclaimed its independence, the new Hetman, Scoropadsky, had to post up eloquent appeals, which said: "Ukrainians I learn your native tongue!" The Hetman himself probably did not know a word of it.

That poetic talent existed in my father's Ukrainian family and was not the gift of his Moscovite mother, as Dostoevsky's literary friends have suggested.

The interesting and varied history of Lithuania had a great influence in the formation of my father's powers. We find in his works traces of all the transformations Lithuania has undergone in the course of centuries. My father's character was essentially Norman: very honest, very upright, frank and bold. Dostoevsky looked danger in the face, never drew back before peril, pressed on to his goal unweariedly, brushing aside all the obstacles in his path. His normanised ancestors had bequeathed to him an immense moral strength which is rarely found among Russians, a young, and consequently a weak race. Other European nations also contributed to the formation of Dostoevsky's genius. The Knights of the Teutonic Order gave to his ancestors their idea of the State and of the family.

In Dostoevsky's works, and still more in his private life, we find innumerable mediaeval ideas. In their turn the Catholic clergy of Lithuania, the leaders of whom came from Rome, taught my father's ancestors discipline, obedience, and a sense of duty, which can hardly be said to exist in the youthful and anarchic Russian nation. The Latin Schools of the Jesuits formed their minds. Dostoevsky learned to speak French very quickly, and preferred it to German, though he knew German so well that he proposed to his brother Mihail that they should collaborate in translating Goethe and Schiller. My father had evidently the gift of languages, which is very rare among the Russians. Europeans generally say: "The Russians can speak all tongues." They do not, however, notice that those among my compatriots who speak and write French and German well all belong to Polish, Lithuanian and Ukrainian families, whose ancestors were latinised by the Catholic clergy. Among the Russians of Great Russia, it is only the aristocrats who have had a European education for several generations who speak the European languages well.

The Russian *bourgeois* find the study of foreign languages enormously difficult. They learn them at school for seven years, and when they leave can barely manage to say a few sentences, and do not understand the simplest books. Their accent is deplorable. The Russian language, which has hardly anything in common with the European tongues, is rather a hindrance than a help to linguistic studies.

The emigration of my ancestors to Ukrainia softened their somewhat harsh Northern character, and awoke the dormant poetry of their hearts. Of all the Slav countries which form the Russian Empire, Ukrainia is certainly the most poetic. When one comes from Petrograd to Kiew, one feels oneself in the South. The evenings are warm, the streets full of pedestrians who sing, laugh, and eat in the open air, at tables on the pavement outside the cafés. We breathe the perfumed air of the South, we look at the moon which silvers the poplars; the heart dilates, one becomes a poet for the moment. Everything breathes poetry in this softly undulating plain bathed in happy sunshine. Blue rivers flow serene and unhasting seawards; little lakes sleep softly, girdled by flowers; it is good to dream in the rich forests of oak. All is poetry in Ukrainia: the costumes of the peasants, their songs, their dances, and above all their theatre. Ukrainia is the only country in Europe which possesses a theatre created by the people themselves and not arranged by the intellectuals to develop the taste of the masses, as elsewhere. The Ukrainian theatre is so essentially popular that it has not even been possible to make a *bourgeois* theatre of it. In early days Ukrainia was in close contact with the Greek colonies on the shores of the Black Sea. Some Greek blood flows in the veins of the Ukrainians, manifesting itself in their charming sunburnt faces and their graceful movements. It may even be that the Ukrainian theatre is a distant echo of the drama so beloved of the ancient Greeks.

Emerging from the dark forests and dank marshes of Lithuania, my ancestors must have been dazzled by the light, the flowers, the Greek poetry of Ukrainia. Their hearts warmed by the southern sunshine, they began to write verses. My grandfather Mihail carried a little of this Ukrainian poetry in his poor student's wallet when he fled from his father's house, and kept it carefully as a souvenir of his distant home. Later, he handed it on to his two elder sons, Mihail and Fyodor. These youths composed verses, epitaphs and poems; in his youth my father wrote Venetian romances and historical dramas. He began by imitating Gogol, the great Ukrainian writer, whom he greatly admired. In Dostoevsky's first works we note a good deal of this naïve sentimental and romantic poetry. It was not until after his imprisonment, when he became Russian, that we find in his novels the breadth of view and depth of thought proper to the Russian nation, the nation of great genius and a great future. And yet it is not right to say that Dostoevsky's powerful realism is essentially Russian. The Russians are not realists; they are dreamers and mystics.

They love to lose themselves in visions instead of studying life. When they try to be realists, they fall at once into Mongolian cynicism and eroticism. Dostoevsky's realism is an inheritance from his normanised ancestors. All writers of Norman blood are distinguished by their profound realism. It was not for nothing that Dostoevsky admired Balzac so heartily, and took him as his model.

The Dostoevsky family was essentially a family of nomads. We find them now in Lithuania, now in Ukrainia, now domiciled in Moscow, now in Petersburg. This is not surprising, for Lithuania is distinguished from other countries by its curious class of "nomad intellectuals." In all other countries it is the proletariat which emigrates. In Russia, the *moujiks*, who cross the Ural Mountains in hordes every year and are absorbed by Asia; in Europe, the peasants and lower middle classes who go to seek their fortune in America, Africa and Australia. In Lithuania, the populace remained in the country; only the intellectuals emigrated. As long as Lithuania was a brilliant Grand Duchy attracting European poets and learned men, the Lithuanian nobility stayed at home. But when the splendour of Lithuania began to wane, the intellectuals[1] soon felt themselves circumscribed in their forests and swamps and emigrated to neighbouring nations. They entered the service of the Poles and the Ukrainians, and helped to build up their civilisation. A great number of famous Poles and Ukrainians are of Lithuanian origin.[2]

Later, when Russia annexed Lithuania, a horde of Lithuanian families descended upon our large towns. At the beginning of the nineteenth century the Poles in their turn entered the service of Russia, but my compatriots very soon noted the difference between the Polish and the Lithuanian "sky."[3]

Though the Poles lived and grew rich in Russia, they remained Catholics, spoke Polish among themselves, and treated the Russians as barbarians. The Lithuanians, on the other hand, forgot their mother-tongue, adopted the Orthodox faith, and thought no more of their native land.[4]

1. Critics may accuse me of confounding the words "noble" and "intellectual," which are not always synonymous. But they must remember that in the good old times education was impossible for the proletariat and the middle classes. The Catholic and Orthodox clergy, who were the principal educationists of Lithuania, were only interested in the sons of the nobility, the future legislators and governors of their country.

2. It is thought that the great Polish poet Mickiewicz was a Lithuanian. One of his poems begins: "Lithuania, my country."

3. "Sky" is the termination of the names of the Polish and Lithuanian nobility.

4. Among the great Russian families of Lithuanian origin, we must note more especially the Romanoffs, the ancestors of the late reigning family, who belonged

This migration of the intellectuals, and their facility in amalgamating with the nations of their adoption, is the most characteristic feature bequeathed by the Normans to their Lithuanian posterity. The Normans alone among the nations of antiquity possessed a nomad nobility. The young men of the highest families rallied to the banner of some Norman prince, and sailed in their light vessels to seek new homes. It is generally asserted that all the aristocracies of northern Europe were founded by the Normans. There is nothing surprising in this: when the young Norman nobles appeared among some primitive people, they naturally became the chiefs of the wild and ignorant aborigines. Their descendants, accustomed to govern, continued to do so throughout successive centuries. The Normans, as we have already seen, did not hold aloof from the nations they conquered; they married the women of the country, and adopted its ideas, its costume and its beliefs. Two centuries after their arrival in Normandy, the Normans had forgotten their native tongue, and spoke French to each other. When William the Conqueror landed in England with his warriors, the culture he brought to the English was a Latin, and not a Norman culture. When the Norman family of the Comtes d'Hauteville conquered Sicily, they adopted the Byzantine and Saracen culture they found in that country with amazing rapidity. In Lithuania there was a complete fusion of invaders with invaded; the Normans gave the Lithuanians their moral strength, and bequeathed to them the mission of civilising neighbouring peoples. All the nomad intellectuals of Lithuania are, in fact, but Normans in disguise. They continue the great work of their ancestors with unfailing courage, patience and devotion.

It is obvious that poor Lithuania, who gives the flower of her race to others, can never become a great state again. She understands and regrets this herself. "The Lithuanians must be accounted in general a most intelligent race," says Vidûnas; "that in spite of this, Lithuania has exercised no influence on European civilisation, is to be explained by the fact that Lithuanian intelligence has been perpetually at the service of other nations, and has never been able to put forth all its powers in its native land." Vidûnas is no doubt right when he deplores the emigration of the Lithuanian intellectuals, but he is mistaken when he says that Lithuania has had no influence on European civilisation. No country, indeed, has done so much for the civilisation of the Slav states as Lith-

to the tribe of the Borussi; the Soltikoffs, whose Lithuanian name was Saltyk; and the Golitzins, the descendants of Duke Guedimin. In Poland, the majority of the aristocratic families were of Lithuanian origin, as well as the royal house of Jagellon.

uania. Other peoples worked for themselves alone, for their own glory; Lithuania has devoted the gifts of her intelligence to the service of her neighbours. Poland, Ukrainia and Russia do not understand this yet, and are unjust. But the day will come when they will see clearly what a huge debt they owe to modest and silent Lithuania.

The Dostoevsky were such wanderers, they had such a thirst for new ideas and new impressions, that they tried to forget the past, and refused to talk to their children of their forbears. But while thus renouncing the past, they had a desire to link their wandering family by a kind of Ariadne's thread. This thread, which enables us to trace them throughout the centuries, is their family name Andrey. The Catholic Dostoevsky of Lithuania habitually gave this name to one of their sons, generally to the second or the third; and the Orthodox Dostoevsky have kept up the custom till the present. In each generation of our family there is always an Andrey, and, as before, this name is borne by the second or the third son.

II

The Childhood of Fyodor Dostoevsky

After completing his medical studies at Moscow, my grandfather Mihail entered the army as a surgeon, and in this capacity served during the war of 1812. We may assume that he was well skilled in his profession, for he was soon appointed superintendent of a large State hospital in Moscow. About this time he married a young Russian girl, Marie Netchaïev. She brought a sufficient dowry to her husband, but the marriage was primarily one of mutual love and esteem. The young couple, indeed, lacked nothing, for in those days government appointments were fairly lucrative. If salaries were not very high, the State made amends by providing its functionaries with all the requisites of a comfortable existence. Thus, in addition to his income, my grandfather Mihail was lodged in a Crown building, a small house of one storey, built in the bastard Empire style which was adopted for all our Crown buildings in the nineteenth century. This house was situated close to the hospital and was surrounded by a garden. In this little house Fyodor Dostoevsky was born on October 30, 1821.

My grandfather was allowed the services of the servants attached to the hospital, and a carriage to visit his patients in the town. He must have had a good practice, for he was soon able to buy two estates in the government of Tula, 150 versts from Moscow. One of these properties, called Darovoye, became the holiday residence of the Dostoevsky. The whole family, with the exception of the father, spent the summer there. My grandfather, who was kept in the city by his medical duties, only joined them for a few days in July. These annual journeys, which in those pre-railway days were made in a *troika* (a carriage with three horses), delighted my father, who was devoted to horses in his childhood.

A few years after the birth of his elder sons, my grandfather had himself registered together with them in the book of the hereditary nobility of Moscow.[1] My father was five years old at the time. It is strange that my

1. No one could be registered in the books of the nobility unless they possessed titles of hereditary nobility. The Russian nobles willingly admitted to their un-

grandfather, who had all his life held aloof from the Moscovites, should have wished to place his family under the protection of the Russian nobility. It is probable that he recognised in it the Lithuanian *Schliahta* of which the Russian Union of Nobles is, in fact, an imitation.[1] As of old his ancestors had placed their sons under the banner of the united Lithuanian nobility, so my grandfather hastened to place his children under the protection of the united Russian nobility.

As a Moscovite noble my grandfather remained morally a Lithuanian *Schliahtitch*—proud, ambitious, and very European in many of his ideas. He was economical almost to the verge of niggardliness; but in the matter of the education of his sons he did not grudge expense. He began by placing his two boys in the French school of Suchard. As Latin was not taught in this establishment, my grandfather undertook the Latin lessons himself. When they came home, his sons prepared their French lessons, and in the evening did Latin exercises with their father. They never ventured to sit down in his presence, and conjugated their verbs standing, trying not to make mistakes, and greatly in awe of their teacher. My grandfather was very severe; but his children never received corporal punishment. This is the more remarkable, as the little Moscovites of the period were very vigorously chastised. Tolstoy has told us in his recollections of childhood how he was beaten at the age of twelve. It is evident that my grandfather Mihail had European ideas of education. Thanks to their proximity to Poland and Austria, Lithuania and Ukrainia were much more civilised than Russia. In later years, when Dostoevsky recalled his childhood, he would say to his younger brothers, Andrey and Nicolai, that their parents were remarkable people, more advanced in their ideas than the majority of their contemporaries.

Like many Lithuanians whose ancestors were latinised by the Catholic clergy, my grandfather had an affection for the French tongue. He talked French with his wife, and encouraged his children to express themselves in that language. To please him, my grandmother made his sons and daughters write their good wishes on their father's birthday in French. She corrected their mistakes on the rough drafts, and the children then made fair copies on ornamental sheets of paper. On the day of the anniversary, they marched up to their father in turns, and blushingly presented the rolls of paper, tied up with a coloured ribbon. My grand-

ions Polish, Lithuanian, Ukrainian, Baltic and Caucasian nobles.
1. In the eighteenth century the Russians still called their hereditary nobility *Schliahetstvo*. This word is no longer current, and the majority of the Russian nobles are unaware that their institution of hereditary nobility is of Lithuanian origin.

father unfolded them, read the artless congratulations aloud with emotion, and kissed the little writers. Later, his elder sons were not content with good wishes; to please their father they learned French poems by heart and recited them to their parents in the presence of their brothers and sisters. My father once recited a fragment of the *Henriade* at a family festivity. Dostoevsky inherited his father's liking for French; French phrases occur frequently in his novels and newspaper articles.[1] He read a great deal of French, and very little German, although he knew the language well. At that period, German was not fashionable in Russia. But my father did not forget it; German must have been retained intact in some cell of his brain, for as soon as he passed the Prussian frontier he at once began to speak German, and, according to my mother, he spoke it fluently.

When his elder sons had finished their course at the Suchard school, my grandfather placed them at the preparatory school of Tchermack, the best private school in Moscow, an expensive establishment frequented by the sons of the intellectuals of the city. In order that they might prepare their lessons under the superintendence of their teachers, my grandfather sent them as boarders, and they came home only on Sundays and festivals. The Moscovite nobles of this period preferred to send their children to private schools, for in the Crown institutions the most severe corporal punishment was inflicted. The school of Tchermack was of a patriarchal character, and the arrangements were modelled on those of family life. M. Tchermack dined with his pupils, and treated them kindly, as if they were his sons. He got the best masters in Moscow to give lessons in his school, and the work done there was of a high order.

My grandfather dreaded the brutality of the Moscovite lower orders, and never allowed his children to walk in the streets. "We were sent to school in our father's carriage, and fetched home in the same way," my uncle Andrey once told me. My father knew so little of his native city that there is not a single description of Moscow in any of his novels. Like many Poles and Lithuanians, my grandfather despised the Russians, and was prejudiced enough to look upon them as barbarians. The only Moscovites he received in his house were his wife's relations. Later,

---

1. The writer Stralioff, a great friend of my father's, says in his reminiscences that he preferred talking of serious things to Dostoevsky, and did not like to hear his jests, for, according to him, Dostoevsky always jested *à la française*. The play of words and images which is the essence or French wit is not appreciated by my compatriots, who like more solid pleasantries. Strahoff considered that Dostoevsky jested *à la française* not only in conversation, but in his writings. This was, no doubt, the result of a certain hereditary latinisation of the mind in Dostoevsky.

widen my father went from Petersburg to Moscow, he met only his relatives. There were no friends of childhood, no old comrades of his father's to visit.

If my grandfather distrusted Russian civilisation, he was careful not to say so before his children. He brought them up after the European fashion; that is to say, he strove to awaken and foster patriotism in their hearts. In his *Journal of the Writer*, Dostoevsky relates that when he was a child his father was fond of reading episodes of Karamzin's Russian history aloud in the evenings and explaining them to his young sons.[1] Sometimes he would take his children to visit the historic palaces of the Kremlin and the cathedrals of Moscow. These excursions had all the importance of great patriotic solemnities in the eyes of his sons.

It is also possible that in thus holding aloof from the Moscovites, my grandfather gave way to that segregating instinct so characteristic of the Lithuanians. "The Lithuanian is attracted by solitude," wrote Vidûnas; "he likes to live to himself. Solitude is a refuge to him." This curious shyness of the Lithuanians is probably a growth of their soil. The Russians and Ukrainians, inhabitants of vast plains, have been able to found large villages, to go to market in the neighbouring towns, to meet other villagers, to enter into relations with them and so to become sociable and hospitable. The great forests and wide marshes of Lithuania have prevented the development of large villages. The few houses it was possible to build on an oasis of firm ground formed but a single family, which, owing to the impracticable roads, was unable to visit the inhabitants of the adjacent oases. Living thus in isolation, the Lithuanians became unsociable. These temperamental defects, the growth of centuries, take centuries to correct, even in those who have long lived in a different country and under different conditions.[2]

The Lithuanians are as a rule excellent husbands and fathers. They are only happy in their homes; but loving it so dearly, they are apt to become jealous of their wives and children, and to wish to withdraw them from outside influences. My grandfather, when he shut up his sons in a kind of artificial Lithuania in the heart of Moscow, did not realise how difficult such an education would make life for the boys, who, after all,

1. Karamzin's *History of Russia* was my father's favourite book. He read and re-read it in his childhood till he finally knew it by heart. This was very remarkable, for in Russia not only the children but the grown-up persons know very little of the history of their country.

2. The Lithuanians never forget their forests; they continue to adore them even when they have quitted them for generations. In his *Journal of the Writer* Dostoevsky says: "All my life I have loved the forest, with its mushrooms, its fruits, its insects, its birds and its squirrels; I revelled in the scent of its damp leaves. Even at this moment I write I can smell the aroma of the birches."

were Russians, and had to work among their compatriots. Happily, my grandfather at least provided good companions for his children in their domestic prison; in the evenings of the festivals, all the family assembled in the drawing-room and read the works of the great Russian writers aloud in turns. At the age of fifteen my father was familiar with the majority of our masterpieces. The children were accustomed to recite the poems they had learnt. Sometimes competitions in recitation were arranged between the boys. My father and his brother Mihail learned Russian poems by heart, and the parents decided which of them had recited best. My grandmother took a great interest in her children's reading. She was a pretty, gentle creature, devoted to her family, and absolutely submissive to her husband. She was delicate; her numerous confinements had greatly exhausted her.[1] She had to lie in bed for days together, and loved then to hear her sons recite her favourite poems. The two elder boys, Mihail and Fyodor, worshipped her. When she died, while still a young woman, they mourned most bitterly, and composed her epitaph in verse. My grandfather had her effigy carved on the marble monument he erected to her memory.

In accordance with the fashion of the day, my grandfather had portraits of himself and his wife painted by a Moscow artist. My grandmother is represented in the costume and head-dress of 1830, young, pretty and happy. Her father was a Russian of Moscow, yet she has the Ukrainian type. Possibly her mother was a Ukrainian.[2] It was, perhaps, her origin which first attracted my grandfather and led to his marriage with this daughter of Moscow. His portrait shows him in a gala uniform, richly embroidered with gold. At this period, everything in Russia was militarised. Doctors in the service of the State were not allowed to dress in mufti, but had to wear uniform and a sword. In Dostoevsky's memory, his father figured as a military man, the more so because my grandfather, who had begun life as an army surgeon, always retained the military bearing of an officer. He had the characteristic Lithuanian type; his four sons were all very like him. My father's eyes, however, were brown, true Ukrainian eyes, and he had the kindly smile of his Russian mother. He

1. My grandparents had eight children, four sons and four daughters. One of these, twin-sister to my aunt Vera, was stillborn. My grandmother had only been able to nurse one of her children, her eldest son Mihail, whom she loved above all the rest. The remaining children were suckled by nurses chosen among the peasant-women of the country round Moscow.

2. She belonged to the family of Kotelenitsky, a name which is often met with in Ukrainia. They were a family of intellectuals; my grandmother's uncle, Vassil Kotelenitsky, was a professor at the University of Moscow. He had no children, was very fond of his great-nephews, and often invited my father and his brothers to spend long days in his house at Novinskoye.

was livelier, more passionate and more enterprising than his brothers. His parents called him "the hothead." He was not proud, and had none of that disdain for the proletariat which is often shown by Poles and Lithuanians. He loved the poor, and felt a keen interest in their lives. There was an iron gate between my grandfather's private garden and the great garden of the hospital, where the convalescents were sent to walk. The little Dostoevsky were strictly forbidden to go to this gate; my grandparents distrusted the manners and behaviour of the lower class Moscovites. All the children obeyed the injunction, with the exception of my father, who would steal up to the gate and enter into conversation with the convalescent peasants and small tradespeople, braving the wrath of his father. During the summer visits to Darovoye, my father made friends with the serfs belonging to his parents. According to my uncle Andrey, his brother Fyodor's greatest pleasure was to make himself useful to the poor peasant-women who were working in the fields.

My grandparents were very religious. They often went to church, taking their children with them. My father recalls in his works the immense impression made upon him by the readings from the Bible which he heard in church. My grandfather's faith had little in common with the mystical, hysterical and tearful faith of the Russian intellectuals. My compatriots complain incessantly of the trials life brings to all; they accuse God of harshness, revile Him, and shake their fists at Heaven, like foolish children. The Lithuanian faith of my grandfather was that of a mature people which had suffered and struggled. The Jesuits, perhaps, and also the Teutonic Knights taught the Lithuanians to respect God and bow to His will. Their descent from pious Ukrainians, who looked upon the ecclesiastical career as the noblest and most dignified of human callings, inclined the Dostoevsky family to love God, and made them eager to draw near to Him. It was with such ideals as these that my grandfather brought up his young wife and his sons and daughters. A childish memory was deeply impressed on my father's mind. One spring evening at Moscow the door of the drawing-room where all the family was assembled was thrown open, and the bailiff of the Darovoye estate appeared on the threshold. "The domain has been burnt," he announced in a tragic voice. At the first moment my grandparents believed that they were entirely ruined; but instead of lamenting, they knelt down before the icons and prayed God to give them strength to bear the trial He had sent them. What an example of faith and resignation they gave their children, and how often my father must have remembered this scene during the course of his stormy and unhappy life!

III

Adolescence

When his elder sons had finished their term at Tchermack's preparatory school, my father took them to Petersburg. He did not intend to make doctors of them; he wished them to embark on a military career, which at this period had brilliant possibilities for the intelligent. In Russia every official had a right to ask for free education for his sons at one of the State schools. My grandfather, a practical man, chose the School of Military Engineers, with a double end in view: on leaving, a pupil might become an officer in a regiment of the Imperial Guard, and have a splendid career, or he might become a civil engineer and amass a considerable fortune. My grandfather Mihail was very ambitious for his sons, and perpetually reminded them that they must work incessantly. "You are poor," he would say; "I cannot leave you a fortune; you have only your own powers on which to rely; you must work hard, be strict in your conduct, and prudent in your words and deeds."

At this time my father was sixteen, and my uncle Mihail seventeen. Brought up as they had been always under the paternal eye, knowing nothing of life, and possessing no friends of their own age, they were nothing but two big children, artless and romantic. There was a passionate affection between the two brothers. They lived in a world of dreams, reading a great deal, exchanging their literary impressions, and ardently admiring the works of Pushkin, their common ideal. When they started for Petersburg they did not realise that their childhood was over, that they were entering a new world.[1]

1. My uncle Andrey tells us in his reminiscences that my grandfather never allowed his sons to go out alone and never gave them any money. He watched over their conduct most jealously; no flirtation, even of the most innocent kind, was tolerated. These young Puritans never dared to speak of women save in verse. Of course, their modesty must have been a source of great amusement to their comrades in the School of Engineers, for the amorous adventures of the young Russian begin early. Dostoevsky, for his part, must have suffered a good deal from the cynicism of his young comrades. When in *The Brothers Karamazov* my

During the journey from Moscow to Petersburg, which lasted several days,[1] the young Dostoevsky continued to dream. "My brother and I," says my father, "dreamed of the great and the beautiful. These words sounded magnificent to us. We used them without irony. How many fine words of the same order we repeated in those days! We had a passionate belief in I know not what, and, although we knew all the difficulties of mathematical examinations, we could only think of poetry and poets. My brother wrote poems, and I was writing a Venetian romance."

A great misfortune awaited the young dreamers at Petersburg. Though he had obtained two nominations for his sons at the School of Engineers, my grandfather was only able to place his son Fyodor there. Mihail was pronounced too delicate to study in the capital, and the authorities sent him with some other youths to Reval, where the School of Engineers had a kind of annexe. My father's despair at this separation from his adored brother was immeasurable. He suffered the more because, when his father had returned to Moscow he was left utterly alone, without friends or relations. He was a boarder, and, as he knew no one in the city, he had to spend all his holidays at school.[2]

The School of Engineers was in the ancient palace of Paul, where the unhappy Emperor had been murdered. It is in the best quarter of the town, opposite the Summer Garden, on the banks of the Fontanka river. The rooms are large and light, full of air and sunshine. One could have wished no better domicile for one's children; as a doctor my grandfather realised the important part played by space and light in the physical education of young people. Nevertheless, my father was not happy at the Engineers' Castle.[3] He disliked the life in common with the other pupils, and the mathematical sciences he had to study were repellent to his poetic soul. Obedient to his father's wishes, he did his work conscientiously, but his heart was not in it. He spent his spare time seated in the

father described Aliosha stopping his ears in order not to hear the obscene talk of his schoolfellows, he was probably drawing on his own experiences.

1. There were no railways in those days. Travellers went by the stage-coach, or in a *troika*, which often took nearly a week to get from Moscow to Petersburg.

2. When he placed his son at school in Petersburg, my grandfather had counted on the kindness of his relative, General Krivopichin, who held an important administrative post. But Krivopichin disliked his Moscow kinsman, and would do nothing for his son. However, after the death of my grandfather, the General remembered his obligations; he went to see my father at the School of Engineers, and invited him to his house. Dostoevsky, who was eighteen by this time, soon became a favourite with all the Krivopichin family, of whom he speaks affectionately in his letters to his brother Mihail.

3. This was the name by which the School of Engineers was known in Petersburg. The Palace of Paul does, in fact, look like an ancient castle.

embrasure of a window, watching the flowing river, admiring the trees of the park, dreaming and reading… Scarcely had he quitted his father's house, when the Lithuanian unsociability took possession of him; he felt himself attracted by solitude. His new companions did not attract him. They were for the most part the sons of colonels[1] and generals, who were commanding the garrisons in the various provincial towns. At this period there was little reading in the provinces, and even less thinking. It was difficult to find a serious book there, though one could always reckon on a bottle of champagne of a good brand. People drank a great deal, played very high, flirted, and, above all, danced with passion. The parents paid very little attention to their children, and left them to the care of servants. My father's new companions were like young animals, full of gaiety, loving to laugh, and run, and play. They made fun of the serious airs of their Moscow schoolfellow, and his passion for reading. Dostoevsky, for his part, despised them for their ignorance; they seemed to him to belong to another world. This was not surprising. My father was several centuries ahead of his Russian companions. "I was struck by the foolishness of their reflections, their games, their conversation and their occupations," he wrote later. "They respected nothing but success. All that was righteous, but humiliated and persecuted, called forth their cruel mockery. At the age of sixteen, they talked of nice little lucrative situations. Their vice amounted to monstrosity." As he observed his schoolfellows, Dostoevsky felt his father's Lithuanian disdain for the Russians awaking in his heart, the contempt of a civilised individual for brutes and ignoramuses.[2]

My father, however, found a friend at last. This was the young Grigorovitch, who, like himself, was only half a Russian; his maternal grandmother was a Frenchwoman. She took a great interest in her grandson's education, and made him a well-informed young man. Gay and sociable as the French generally are, Grigorovitch was ready enough to play with his schoolfellows, but he preferred the society of my father. There was a

1. My grandfather's position at Moscow was equivalent to that of a colonel.
2. Although he despised them, my father never cast off his companions. Former pupils at the School of Engineers remember that he was always ready to protect new pupils when they arrived, helping them with their lessons, and defending them against the tyranny of the elder boys. General Savélieff, who at this period was a young officer acting as superintendent of the classrooms, states in his recollections that the school authorities considered Dostoevsky a young man of high culture, with great strength of character and a deep sense of personal dignity. He obeyed the orders of his superiors readily enough, but declined to bow to the decrees of his elder comrades, and held aloof from all their demonstrations. This was a very characteristic trait, for in Russian schools boys as a rule show more deference to their elders than to their masters.

bond of union between them: both were writing in secret, and dreaming of becoming novelists.[1]

His friendship with young Grigorovitch did not make my father forget his brother Mihail. They corresponded constantly; some of their letters have been published. In these they speak of Racine, Corneille, Schiller and Balzac, recommend interesting books to each other, and exchange their literary impressions. My uncle took advantage of his term at Reval to study the German language thoroughly. Later he translated several of the works of Goethe and Schiller, and his translations were much appreciated by the Russian public.

Letters from the young Dostoevsky to their father have also been published. They are very respectful, but as a rule contain nothing but requests for money. My grandfather was not loved by his children. This Lithuanian, who had so many good qualities, had also one great defect: he was a hard drinker, violent and suspicious in his cups. As long as his wife was there to intervene between him and the children all was well; she had considerable influence over him, and prevented him from drinking to excess. After her death my grandfather gave way to his weakness, became incapable of working, and resigned his appointment. Having placed his younger sons, Andrey and Nicolai, at Tchermack's school, and having married his eldest daughter Barbara to a native of Moscow, he retired to Darovoye and devoted himself to agriculture. He took his two younger daughters, Vera and Alexandra, with him, and led them a terrible life. At this time it was usual to bring up girls under the superintendence of their parents. The instruction given them was not very extensive: French, German, a little piano-playing and dancing, fancy needlework. Only the daughters of the poor worked. The girls of noble families were destined for marriage, and their virginity was carefully guarded. My grandfather never allowed his pretty daughters to go out alone, and accompanied them himself on the rare occasions when they went to visit their country neighbours. The jealous vigilance of their father offended the delicacy of my aunts. Later they remembered with horror how their father used to visit their bedrooms at night to make sure that they had not hidden some lover under the bed. My aunts at this time were pure and innocent children.

My grandfather's avarice increased as his drinking habits became more

1. My father had another friend at this period, the young Schidlovsky, his former schoolfellow at Tchermack's. For some reason unknown to me, Schidlovsky travelled a great deal, going sometimes to Reval, sometimes to Petersburg. He acted as bearer of dispatches to the young Dostoevsky. Schidlovsky was a poet, an idealist and a mystic. He had a great influence on my father. He was probably of Lithuanian origin.

confirmed. He sent so little money to his sons that they were in want of everything. My father could not indulge in a cup of tea when he came in from drill, which was often carried on in a downpour of rain; he had no change of boots, and, worst of all, no money to give to the orderlies who waited on the engineer cadets. Dostoevsky rebelled against the privations and humiliations to which his father's meanness subjected him; a meanness for which there was no excuse, for my grandfather owned land and had money put away for the dowry of his daughters. My father considered that, as my grandfather had chosen a brilliant and distinguished school for him, he ought to have given him enough money to live in the same manner as his comrades.

This state of friction between the father and his sons did not long continue. My grandfather had always been very severe to his serfs. His drunkenness made him so savage, that they finally murdered him. One summer day he left his estate Darovoye to visit his other property, Tchermashnia, and never returned. He was found later half-way between the two, smothered under the cushions of his carriage. The coachman had disappeared with the horses; several of the peasants of the village disappeared at the same time. When interrogated by the Court, other serfs of my grandfather's admitted that the crime was one of vengeance.

My father was not at home at the time of this horrible death. He no longer went to Darovoye, for in summer the pupils of the School of Engineers had to carry out manoeuvres in the neighbourhood of Petersburg. The crime committed by the peasants of Darovoye, of whom he had been so fond as a child, made a great impression upon his adolescent imagination.[1] He thought of it all his life, and pondered the causes of this dreadful end deeply. It is very remarkable that the whole of my grandfather's family looked upon his death as a disgrace, never mentioned it, and prevented Dostoevsky's literary friends, who knew

1. According to a family tradition, it was when he heard of his father's death that Dostoevsky had his first epileptic fit. We can only conjecture what his state of mind must have been, for all the correspondence with his brother Mihail which might have thrown some light on this period of his life has been destroyed. Later, the brothers never mentioned their father in their letters; the subject was probably too painful to both of them. From certain sentences in the last letter before the murder of his father, we may infer that Dostoevsky knew various circumstances of his life in the country. "Poor father!" he wrote to his brother Mihail, "what an extraordinary character. Ah! what misfortunes he has had! What a pity it is that I cannot console him! But do you know, our father has no idea of life. He has lived for fifty years, and has still the same idea of men as when he was thirty." As always, Dostoevsky's prescience made him divine the principal cause of his father's misfortunes. My grandfather indeed lived all his life as a Lithuanian, and never troubled to study the Russian character. He paid dearly for his ignorance.

the details of his life, from speaking of it in their reminiscences of my father. It is evident that my uncles and aunts had a more European idea of slavery than the Russians of the period. Crimes of vengeance committed by peasants were very frequent at the time, but no one blushed for them. The victims were pitied, the murderers denounced with horror. The Russians had a naive belief that masters might treat their serfs like dogs, and that the latter had no right to revolt. The Lithuanian family of my grandfather looked at the matter from a very different point of view.

I have always thought that Dostoevsky had his father in mind when he created the type of old Karamazov. It is not, certainly, an exact portrait. Fyodor Karamazov is a buffoon; my grandfather was always a dignified person. Karamazov was a profligate; Mihail Dostoevsky loved his wife and was faithful to her. Old Karamazov forsook his sons, and took no interest in them; my grandfather gave his children a careful education. But certain traits are common to both. When creating the type of Fyodor Karamazov, Dostoevsky perhaps remembered his father's avarice, which caused his young sons so much suffering and indignation at school, his drunkenness, and the physical disgust it provoked in his children. When he says that Aliosha Karamazov did not share this disgust, but pitied his unhappy father, Dostoevsky probably recalls the moments of pity which succeeded to those of disgust in his own youthful heart. The great psychologist in embryo must have divined at times that his father was, after all, but a diseased and unhappy being. It must be understood that this likeness between my grandfather and the old Karamazov is merely a supposition on my part, for which there is no documentary evidence. Yet it may not be simply a coincidence that Dostoevsky has given the name of Tchermashnia[1] to the village where old Karamazov sent his son Ivan just before his death. I am the more inclined to think this, because it is a tradition in our family that my father portrayed himself in the person of Ivan Karamazov. Thus did he conceive of himself at the age of twenty. It is curious to note Ivan's religious beliefs, his poem, *The Grand Inquisitor*, and his immense interest in the Catholic Church. It must not be forgotten that only some three or four generations intervened between Dostoevsky and the Catholicism of his ancestors. The Catholic faith must have been still alive in his soul. It is still more curious to note that Dostoevsky gave his own name, Fyodor, to old Karamazov, and made Smerdiakov say to Ivan: "You are the most like your father of all his sons." It is probable that Dostoevsky was haunted all his life by the

---

1. As we have seen above, it was on his way to his property of Tchermashnia that my grandfather was murdered.

bloody spectre of his father, and that he analysed his own actions minutely, fearing that he might have inherited his father's vices. This was far from being the case; Dostoevsky's character was totally different. He did not like wine, and it disagreed with him, as with all persons of nervous temperament. He was kind and affectionate to every one around him, and far from being suspicious, was rather simple and confiding. Dostoevsky has often been reproached for his inability to keep money. He could never refuse those who asked him for it, and gave all he possessed to others. He was moved to do so by charity, but also, no doubt, by dread of developing the avarice of his father. He feared this the more, because he saw this vice reproduced in his sister Barbara, and gradually taking the form of a veritable mania. Dostoevsky, no doubt, said to himself that avarice, that moral malady, was hereditary in his family, and that each of them might be attacked by it if he were not careful.

The alcoholism of my grandfather ravaged the lives of nearly all his children. His eldest son Mihail and his youngest son Nicolai inherited his disease. My uncle Mihail, though he drank, was at least able to work; but the unhappy Nicolai, after a brilliant course of study, was never able to do anything, and remained a burden on his family all his life. My father's epilepsy, which caused him so much suffering, was probably due to the same cause. But the most miserable of the family was certainly my aunt Barbara. She married a well-to-do man, who left her considerable house- property in Moscow. The houses brought in a good income; my aunt's children were comfortably settled in life, and lacked nothing. She had therefore all that was necessary to ensure her comfort in her old age; but the unhappy woman was the victim of a sordid and diseased avarice. She opened her purse with a kind of despair; the smallest expenditure was torture to her. She finally dismissed her servants, to avoid paying their wages. She had no fires in her apartments and spent the winter wrapped in a cloak. She did no cooking; twice a week she went out and bought a little bread and milk. There was a great deal of gossip in the district where she lived about her inexplicable avarice. It was said that she must have a great deal of money, and that, like all misers, she kept it in her house. This gossip worked upon the mind of a young peasant, who acted as porter to my aunt's tenants. He came to an understanding with a vagabond who was prowling about in the neighbourhood; one night they got into the poor mad woman's dwelling and murdered her. The crime was committed long after my father's death.

I conclude that my grandfather's alcoholism must have been hereditary, for his personal drunkenness could not have caused such disaster in our family. The disease persisted in my uncle Mihail's family; the second and third generation were victims to it. My aunt Barbara's son was so stupid that his folly verged on idiocy. My uncle Andrey's son, a young and brilliant savant, died of creeping paralysis. The whole Dostoevsky family suffered from neurasthenia.

IV

First Steps

When he had completed his studies at the Castle of the Engineers, Dostoevsky obtained an appointment in the Department of Military Engineering. He did not keep it long and hastened to resign. His father was no longer there to force him to serve the State; he had no taste for military service, and longed more than ever to be a novelist. Young Grigorovitch followed his example. They determined to live together, set up in bachelors' quarters, and engaged a servant. Grigorovitch received money from his mother, who lived in the provinces. My father had an allowance from his guardian at Moscow, who sent him enough to live modestly. Unfortunately, my father always had very fantastic ideas concerning economy. All his life he was a Lithuanian *Schliahtitchi*, who spent the money that was in his pocket without ever asking himself how he was to live the next day. Age failed to correct this. I remember a journey we made all together towards the end of his life, going to the Ukraine to spend the summer with my uncle Jean. We had to stay at Moscow a few days *en route*, and here, to the great indignation of my mother, Dostoevsky insisted on putting up at the best hotel in the town, and took a suite of rooms on the first floor, whereas at Petersburg we had a very modest domicile. My mother protested in vain; she never succeeded in curing her husband of his prodigality. When we had relations coming to dinner on some family festival, my father always offered to go and buy the *hors d'œuvre*, which play such an important part in a Russian dinner, the fruit, and the dessert. If my mother were imprudent enough to consent, Dostoevsky went to the best shops in the town and bought of all the good things he found there. I always smile when I read how Dmitri Karamazov bought provisions at Plotnikov's, before starting for Mokroé. I seem to see myself at Staraya Russa, in that selfsame shop, where I sometimes went with my father, and observed with all the interest of a greedy child his original manner of providing for himself. When I went with my mother, she would come out carrying a modest parcel in her hand. When I accompanied my father, we left the shop empty-handed, but several small boys preceded or followed us to our house, gaily bearing big baskets and reckoning on a good tip. Like a true *Schliahtitchi*, my father never asked himself whether he was rich or poor. Formerly, in Poland and in Lithuania, the native nobility starved at home, and arrived at all public gatherings in gilt coaches and magnificent velvet coats. They lived crippled by debts, paying back only a tithe of what they had borrowed, never thinking of their financial position, amusing themselves, laughing and dancing. These racial defects take centuries to eradicate; many a descendant of Dostoevsky's will yet have to suffer for the mad prodigality of their ancestors. There was, however, one important difference between my father and the Lithuanian *Schliahtitchi*. They thought only of living merrily, and cared little for others. He gave alms to all the poor he encountered, and was never able to refuse money to those who came to tell him of their misfortunes and beg him to help them. The tips he gave to servants for the smallest services were fabulous and exasperated my poor mother.

It is obvious that living in this manner my father spent more than his guardian could send him from Moscow. He got into debt, and, wishing to escape from the importunities of his creditors, he proposed to his guardian to barter his birthright for a comparatively small sum of ready money. Knowing nothing of newspapers or of publishers, Dostoevsky ingenuously hoped to make a living by his pen. His guardian agreed to the bargain, which he ought never to have entertained. My aunts argued that their brother Fyodor knew nothing of business, and that he could be made to accept the most disadvantageous terms. They tried to repeat the process later on, when the Dostoevsky family inherited some further property, and the struggle on which my father was forced to enter with his sisters darkened the close of his life. I shall speak of this business more fully in the final chapters of my book.

Having paid his debts, Dostoevsky soon spent the little money he had left. He tried to make translations,[1] but of course this brought in very little. At this juncture his aunt Kumanin came to his assistance and made him an allowance. She was a sister of his mother's, who had made a rich marriage, and lived in a fine house in Moscow, surrounded by a horde of devoted servants, and waited on and amused by a number of lady companions, poor women who trembled before her, and gave way to all the caprices of their wealthy despot. She patronised her nephews and nieces, and was particularly well disposed to my father, who was

1. It was at this time that he made an excellent translation of Eugénie Grandet.

always her favourite. She alone of all the family appreciated his powers, and was always ready to come to his aid. My father was very fond of his old aunt Kumanin, though he made fun of her a little, like all her young nephews. He painted her in *The Gambler*, in the person of the old Moscow grandmother, who arrives in Germany, plays roulette, loses half her fortune and goes back to Moscow as suddenly as she came. At the time when roulette was flourishing in Germany, my great-aunt was too old to travel. It may be, however, that she played cards at Moscow, and lost large sums of money. When he depicted her as coming to Germany and playing roulette at his side, Dostoevsky perhaps meant to show us whence came his passion for gaming.

It must not be supposed, however, that because my father spent a good deal of money he was leading a profligate life. Dostoevsky's youth was studious and industrious. He went out very little, and would sit all day at his writing-table, talking to his heroes, laughing, crying, and suffering with them. His friend Grigorovitch, more practical than he, while working at his writing, tried to make acquaintances useful to his future career, got himself introduced into literary society, and then introduced his friend Dostoevsky. Grigorovitch was handsome, gay and elegant; he made love to the ladies, and charmed every one. My father was awkward, shy, taciturn, rather ugly; he spoke little, and listened much. In the drawing-rooms they frequented the two friends met the young Turgenev, who had also come to embark upon the career of a novelist at Petersburg. My father admired him greatly. "I am in love with Turgenev," he wrote ingenuously to his brother Mihail, who, having completed his military studies was serving at Reval as an officer. "He is so handsome, so graceful, so elegant!" Turgenev accepted my father's homage with an air of condescension. He considered Dostoevsky a nonentity.

Grigorovitch succeeded in making the acquaintance of the poet Nekrassov, who proposed to start a literary review. Grigorovitch was eager to be connected with this review in one way or another. His first works were not quite finished — he was rather too fond of society — but he knew that my father had written a novel and was perpetually correcting it, fearing he had not been very successful. Grigorovitch persuaded him to entrust the manuscript to him and took it to Nekrassov. The latter asked Grigorovitch if he were familiar with the work of his comrade, and hearing that he had not yet found time to read it, proposed that they should go through two or three chapters together, to see if it were worth anything. They read this first novel of my father's through at a sitting.[1] Dawn was stealing in at the windows when they finished it. Nekrassov was astounded. "Let us go and see Dostoevsky," he proposed; "I want to tell him what I think of his work." "But he is asleep, it is not yet morning," objected Grigorovitch. "What does it matter? This is more important than sleep!" And the enthusiast set off, followed by Grigorovitch, to rouse my father at five o'clock in the morning, and inform him that he had an extraordinary talent.

Later on the manuscript was submitted to the famous critic Belinsky, who, after reading it, desired to see the young author. Dostoevsky entered his presence trembling with emotion. Belinsky received him with a severe expression. "Young man," he said," do you know what you have just written? No, you do not. You cannot understand it yet."

Nekrassov published *Poor Folks* in his Review, and it had a great success. My father found himself famous in a day. Everybody wished to know him. "Who is this Dostoevsky?" people were asking on every side. My father had only recently began to frequent literary society, and no one had noticed him particularly. The timid Lithuanian was always retiring into a corner, or the embrasure of a window, or lurking behind a screen. But he was no longer allowed to hide himself. He was surrounded and complimented; he was induced to talk, and people found him charming. In addition to the literary *salons*, where those who aspired to be novelists, or those who were interested in literature were received, there were other more interesting *salons* in Petersburg where only famous writers, painters and musicians were admitted. Such were the *salons* of Prince Odoevsky, a distinguished poet, of Count Sollohub, a novelist of much taste, who has left us very penetrating descriptions of Russian life in the first half of the nineteenth century, and of his brother-in-law, Count Vieillegorsky, a russianised Pole. All these gentlemen hastened to make Dostoevsky's acquaintance, invited him to their houses and received him cordially. My father enjoyed himself more especially with the Vieillegorsky, where there was excellent music. Dostoevsky adored music. I do not think, however, that he had a musical ear, for he distrusted new compositions, and preferred to hear the pieces he knew already. The more he heard them, the more they delighted him.

1. It was called *Poor Folks*. Before writing it my father began a tragedy, *Mary Stuart*, which he laid aside in order to write a drama, *Boris Godunov*. The choice of these subjects is very significant. It is probable that in Dostoevsky's early youth, the Norman blood of his paternal ancestors was at war in his heart with the Mongolian blood of his Moscow ancestors. But the Slav strain was the strongest and overcame the Norman and Mongolian atavisms. Dostoevsky abandoned *Mary Stuart* and *Boris Godunov*, and gave us *Poor Folks*, which is full of the charming Slav sentiment of pity.

Count Vieillegorsky was a passionate lover of music; he patronised musicians, and was accustomed to hunt them out in the most obscure corners of the capital. It is probable that some strange type, some poor, drunken, ambitious, jealous violinist, discovered by Count Vieillegorsky in a garret, and induced to play at his receptions, struck my father's imagination, for Count Vieillegorsky's house is the scene of his novel *Netotchka Xesvanova*. In this Dostoevsky achieved a true masterpiece of feminine psychology, though, in his youthful inexperience, he may not have sufficiently explained it to his public. It is said that Countess Vieillegorsky was born Princess Biron. Now the Princes Biron, natives of Courland, always claimed to belong to the sovereigns, rather than to the aristocracy of Europe. If we read *Netotchka Nest-anova* attentively, we shall soon see that Prince S., who had offered hospitality to the poor orphan girl, is merely a man of good education and good society, whereas his wife is very haughty, and gives the air of a palace to her home. All those around her speak of her as of a sovereign. Her daughter Katia is a regular little "Highness," spoilt and capricious, now terrorising her subjects, now making them her favourites. Her affection for Netotchka becomes at once very passionate, even slightly erotic. The Russian critics rebuked Dostoevsky very severely for this suggestion of eroticism. Now my father was perfectly truthful, for these poor German princesses, who can never marry for love, and are always sacrificed to interests of State, often suffer from such passionate and even erotic feminine friendships. The disease is hereditary among them, and might well have declared itself in their descendant, the little Katia, a precocious child. The Vieillegorsky had no daughter; the type of Katia was entirely created by my father, who depicted it after studying the princely household. In the portrait of this little neurotic Highness Dostoevsky shows a knowledge of feminine psychology very remarkable in a shy young man, who scarcely dared to approach women. His talent was already very great at this period. Unfortunately, he lacked models. Nothing could have been paler or less distinctive than the unhappy natives of Petersburg, born and bred in a swamp. They are mere copies and caricatures of Europe. "These folks have all been dead for a long time," said the Russian writer, Mihail Saltikov. "They only continue to live because the police have forgotten to bury them."

Dostoevsky's friends, the young novelists who were beginning their literary careers, had not the strength of mind to accept his unexpected success. They became jealous, and were irritated by the idea that the timid and modest young man was received in the salons of celebrities, to which aspirants were not yet admitted. They would not appreciate his novel. *Poor Folks* seemed to them wearisome and absurd. They parodied it in prose and verse, and ridiculed the young author unmercifully.[1] To injure him in public opinion they invented grotesque anecdotes about him. They asserted that success had turned his head, that he had insisted that each page of his second novel, which was about to appear in Nekrassov's Review, should be enframed in a border to distinguish it from the other works in the Review. This was, of course, a lie. *The Double* appeared without any frame. They scoffed at his timidity in the society of women, and described how he had fainted with emotion at the feet of a young beauty to whom he had been presented in some drawing-room. My father suffered greatly as he lost his illusions concerning friendship. He had had a very different idea of it; he imagined artlessly that his friends would rejoice at his success, as he would certainly have rejoiced at theirs. The malice of Turgenev, who, exasperated at the success of *Poor Folks* did his utmost to injure Dostoevsky, was particularly wounding to my father. He was so much attached to Turgenev, and admired him so sincerely. This was the beginning of the long animosity between them, which lasted all their lives, and was so much discussed in Russia.

When we pass in review all the friends my father had during his life we shall see that those of his early manhood differ very markedly from those of his maturity. Until the age of forty Dostoevsky's relations were almost exclusively with Ukrainians, Lithuanians, Poles and natives of the Baltic Provinces. Grigorovitch, half Ukrainian, half French, was his earliest friend, and found a publisher for his first novel. Nekrassov, whose mother was a Pole, gave him his first success; Belinsky, Polish or Lithuanian by origin, revealed his genius to the Russian public. It was Count Sollohub, the descendant of a great Lithuanian family, and Count Vieillegorsky, a Pole, who received him cordially in their *salons*. Later, in Siberia, we shall find Dostoevsky protected by a Swede and natives of the Baltic Provinces. It seems that all these people recognised in him a European, a man of Western culture, a writer who shared their Slavo-Norman ideas. At the same time, all the Russians were hostile to him. His comrades in the School of Engineers ridiculed him cruelly; his young literary friends hated him, despised him, tried to make him a laughing-stock. It was as if they recognised in him something opposed to their Russian ideals.

After the age of forty, when Dostoevsky had definitively adopted the

---

1. Turgenev wrote a burlesque poem, in which he made my father cut a ridiculous figure.

Russian attitude, the nationality of his friends changed. The Slavo-Normans disappeared from his life. The Russians sought his friendship and formed a body-guard around him. After his death they continued to guard him as jealously as in the past. Whenever I mention the Lithuanian origin of our family, my compatriots frown, and say: "Do forget that wretched Lithuania! Your family left it ages ago. Your father was Russian, the most Russian of Russians. No one ever understood the real Russia as he did."

I smile when I note this jealousy, which is, in its essence, love. I think that after all the Russians are right, for it was they who gave Dostoevsky his magnificent talent. Lithuania formed his character and civilised his mind; Ukrainia awoke poetry in the hearts of his ancestors; but all this fuel, gathered together throughout the ages, kindled only when Holy Russia fired it with the spark of her great genius.

My father's first novel was certainly very well written, but it was not original. It was an imitation of a novel of Gogol's, who in his turn had imitated the French literature of his day. *Les Misérables*, with its marvellous Jean Valjean, is at the bottom of this new literary movement. It is true that *Les Misérables* was written later; but the type of Valjean, a convict of great nobility of mind, had begun to appear in Europe. The democratic ideas awakened by the French Revolution, led writers to raise poor folks, peasants, and small tradespeople to the rank occupied by the nobles and the intellectuals of the upper middle class. This new trend in literature was very pleasing to the Russians, who, having never had any feudal aristocracy, were always attracted by democratic ideas. Russian writers, who at this period were polished and highly educated persons, would no longer describe the drawing-room; they sought their heroes in the garret. They had not the least idea what such people were really like, and instead of describing them as they were in reality, illiterate and brutalised by poverty, they endowed their new heroes with chivalrous sentiments, and made them write letters worthy of Madame de Sévigné. It was false and absurd, nevertheless, these novels were the origin of that magnificent nineteenth-century literature which is the glory of our country. Writers gradually perceived that before describing a new world, one must study it. They set to work to observe the peasants, the clergy, the merchants, the townsfolk; they gave excellent descriptions of Russian life, which was very little known. But this was much later. At the period of which I am writing, Russian novelists drew on their imagination, and have left us works full of absurdities.

My father no doubt realised how false these novels were, for he tried to break away from this new literary *genre* in his second work. *The Double* is a book of far higher quality than *Poor Folks*. It is original, it is already "Dostoevsky." Our alienists admire this little masterpiece greatly, and are surprised that a young novelist should have been able to describe the last days of a madman so graphically, without having previously studied medicine.[1]

Yet this second novel was not so successful as the first. It was too new; people did not understand that minute analysis of the human heart, which was so much appreciated later. Madmen were not fashionable; this novel without hero or heroine was considered uninteresting. The critics did not conceal their disappointment. "We were mistaken," they wrote; "Dostoevsky's talent is not so great as *we* thought." If my father had been older, he would have disregarded the critics, he would have persisted in his new *genre*, would have imposed it on the public, and would have produced very fine psychological studies even then. But he was too young; criticism distressed him. He was afraid of losing the success he had achieved *with* his first novel, and he went back to the false Gogol manner.

But this time he was not content to draw on his imagination. He studied the *new* heroes of Russian literature, went to observe the inhabitants of garrets in the little *cafés* and drinking shops of the capital. He entered into conversation with them, watched them, and noted their manners and customs carefully. Feeling shy and uncertain how to approach them, Dostoevsky invited them to play billiards with him. He was un-familiar with the game, and not at all interested in it, and he naturally lost a good deal of money. He did not regret this, for he was able to make curious observations as he played, and to note many original expressions.[2]

After studying this curious society, of which he had known nothing, for some months, Dostoevsky began to describe the lower orders as they really were, thinking this would interest the public. Alas! He was even less successful than before. The Russian public was ready to take an in-

1. Dostoevsky thought very highly of *The Double*. In a letter to his brother Mihail, written after his return from Siberia, my father said: "It was a magnificent idea; a type of great social importance which I was the first to create and present."

2. My father's friends relate in their reminiscences that he often invited strangers to visit him among those he met in the *cafés*, and that he would spend whole days listening to their conversation and stories. My father's friends could not understand what pleasure he could take in talking to such uneducated people; later, when they read his novels, they recognised the types they had encountered. It is evident that, like all young men of talent, he could only paint from nature at this period. Later he did not need models, and created his types himself.

terest in the wretched, if they were served up *à la* Jean Valjean. Their real life, in all its sordid meanness, interested no one.

Dostoevsky began to lose confidence in his powers. His health gave way, he became nervous and hysterical. Epilepsy was latent in him, and before declaring itself in epileptic seizures, it oppressed him terribly.[1] He now avoided society, would spend long hours shut up in his own room, or wandering about in the darkest and most deserted streets of Petersburg. He talked to himself as he walked, gesticulating, and causing passers-by to turn and look at him. Friends who met him thought he had gone mad. The colourless, stupid city quenched his talent. The upper classes were mere caricatures of Europeans; the populace belonged to the Finno-Turkisk tribe, an inferior race, who could not give Dostoevsky any idea of the great Russian people. He had not enough money to go to Europe, the Caucasus or the Crimea; travelling was very costly at this period. My father languished in Petersburg and was only happy with his brother Mihail, who had resigned his commission and settled in the capital, meaning to devote himself to literature. He had married a German of Revai, Emilie Dibmar, and had several children. My father was fond of his nephews; their childish laughter banished his melancholy.

It is astonishing to find no woman in the life of Dostoevsky at this period of early youth, which is the age of love for most men. No betrothed, no mistress, not even a flirtation! This extraordinary virtue can only be explained by the tardy development of his organism, which is not rare in Northern Russia. Russian law allows women to marry at the age of sixteen; but quite recently, a few years before the war, Russian savants had begun to protest against this barbarous custom. According to their observations the Northern Russian woman is not completely developed until the age of twenty-three. If she marries before this, childbearing may do her great harm and ruin her health permanently. It is to this evil custom that our doctors attribute the hysteria and nervous complaints that ravage so many Russian homes. If the savants are right, we must place the complete development of the Northern Russian male organism in the twenty-fifth year, as men always come to maturity later than

---

1. Dr. Janovsky, whom my father liked very much, and consulted about his health, says that long before his convict-life Dostoevsky already suffered from a nervous complaint, which was very like epilepsy. As I have mentioned above, my father's family declared that he had had his first attack when he heard of the tragic death of my grandfather. It is evident that he was already suffering from epilepsy at the age of eighteen, although it did not assume its more violent form until after his imprisonment.

women. As to abnormal organisms, those of epileptics, for instance, they must mature even more slowly. It is possible that at this age, Dostoevsky's senses were not yet awakened. He was like a schoolboy who admires women from afar, is very much afraid of them, and does not yet need them. My father's friends, as we have seen, ridiculed his timidity in the society of women.[1] His romantic period began after his imprisonment, and he showed no timidity then.

The heroines of Dostoevsky's first novels are pale, nebulous, and lacking in vitality. He painted only two good feminine portraits at this period—those of Netotchka Nesvanova and the little Katia, children of from ten to twelve years old. This novel is, if we except *The Double*, his best work of this period. It has but one fault, which is common to all the novels written by Dostoevsky before his imprisonment: the heroes are too international. They can live under any skies, speak all tongues, bear all climates. They have no fatherland, and, like all cosmopolitans, are pale, vague and ill-defined. To make them live, it was necessary to create a nationality for them. This Dostoevsky was about to do in Siberia.

---

1. Dr. Riesenkampf, who knew my father well at this period of his life, wrote in his reminiscences: "At the age of twenty young men generally seek a feminine ideal, and run after all young beauties. I never noticed anything of the sort with Dostoevsky. He was indifferent to women, had even an antipathy to them." Riesenkampf adds, however, that Dostoevsky was much interested in the love-affairs of his comrades, and was fond of singing sentimental songs. This habit of singing songs that pleased him he retained to the end of his life. He generally sang in a low voice when he was alone in his room.

V

The Petracheysky Conspiracy

It was at this unhappy period of his life that my father was involved in the Petrachevsky conspiracy. Those who were familiar with Dostoevsky's monarchic principles in later life could never understand how he came to associate himself with revolutionaries. It is, indeed, inexplicable if my father's Lithuanian origin be ignored. He plotted against the Tsar, because he did not yet understand the real meaning of the Russian monarchy. At this period of his life Dostoevsky knew little of Russia. He had spent his childhood in a kind of artificial Lithuania created by his father in the heart of Moscow. In his adolescence at the Castle of the Engineers he held aloof as far as possible from his Russian comrades. When he became a novelist he frequented the literary society of Petersburg, the least stable in the whole country. At that time Russia was practically unknown; our geographers and historians hardly existed as yet. Travelling was difficult and expensive. There were neither railways nor steamers in the country. The peasant-serfs worked their land and kept silence; the *moujik* was called "a sphynx." The Russian writers lived only by the mind of Europe, read only French, English and German books, and shared all the ideas of Europeans concerning liberty. Instead of informing Europe as to Russian ideas, our writers ingenuously asked Europe to explain to them what Russia was. Now if my compatriots knew little of Russia, Europe knew nothing of it. European writers, scientists, statesmen and diplomatists did not learn the Russian language, did not travel in Russia, did not take the trouble to go and study the *moujik* in his home. They were content to get their information from the political refugees who inhabited their towns. All these Jews, Poles, Lithuanians, Armenians, Finns and Letts could not even speak Russian, and talked the most terrible jargon. This did not prevent them from addressing Europe in the name of the Russian people. They assured Europeans that the *moujiks* were groaning under the yoke of the Tsars, and were waiting impatiently for the nations of Europe to come and deliver them, in order to give them that European republic of which (according to the refugees) the *moujik* was dreaming day and night. Europe took their word for it. It has only been in our own days, when Europeans have seen "Tsarism" replaced by Bolshevism and *défaitisme*, that they have begun to understand how they have been deceived. It will be a long time yet before they understand the true Russia. Meanwhile the Russian Colossus has many rude awakenings and unpleasant surprises in store for them.

At the time of the Petrachevsky conspiracy my father was more Lithuanian than Russian, and Europe was dearer to him than his fatherland. The novels he wrote before his imprisonment were all imitations of European works: Schiller, Balzac, Dickens, Georges Sand and Walter Scott were his masters. He believed in the European newspapers as one believes in the Gospels. He dreamed of going to live in Europe, and declared that he could only learn to write well there. He talked of this project in his letters to his friends, and lamented that lack of means prevented him from carrying it out. The thought that it might be well to go east instead of west, in order to become a great Russian writer, never entered his head. Dostoevsky hated the Mongolian strain in the Russians; he was a true Ivan Karamazov at this time of his life.

The emancipation of the serfs was then imminent. Everyone was talking of it, and every one realised the necessity for it. Our government, true to its tradition, hesitated to make the reform. The Russians, who understood their own slow and indolent national character knew that they had only to wait patiently for a year or two and they would obtain it. The Poles, the Lithuanians and the natives of the Baltic Provinces did not understand this delay, and believed that the Tsar would never give liberty to his people. They proposed to overthrow him in order to secure it themselves for the peasants. Dostoevsky shared their misgivings. He knew nothing of Oriental indolence; all his life he was active and energetic. When an idea seemed right to him he at once put it into practice; he could not understand the dilatoriness of the Russian bureaucracy. He could not forget his father's tragic death, and he ardently desired the abolition of a system which made the masters cruel and incited the slaves to crime. In his then state of mind, the meeting with Petrachevsky was bound to have fatal results. Petrachevsky, as his name indicates, was of Polish or Lithuanian origin, and this was a bond of union between him and Dostoevsky stronger than all the rest. Petrachevsky was eloquent and adroit; he drew all the young dreamers in Petersburg around him and inflamed them. The idea of sacrificing oneself to the happiness of others is very attractive to young and generous hearts, especially when their own lives are as sad as was my father's at that time. During his lonely wanderings in the dark streets of Petersburg, he must often have said to himself that it would be better to die in a noble cause than to drag out a useless existence.

The Petrachevsky trial is one of the most obscure of all Russian political trials. The secret documents which have been published give but a very commonplace picture of a political gathering, where young people met to repeat truisms about the new ideas which were arriving from Europe, to lend each other books forbidden by the Censor, and to declaim incendiary fragments from revolutionary pamphlets. Nevertheless, my father always maintained that it was a political plot, the object of which was to overthrow the Tsar, and set up a republic of intellectuals in Russia. It is probable that Petrachevsky, while preparing an army of volunteers, confided the secret aims of the enterprise only to a chosen few. Appreciating Dostoevsky's mind, courage and moral force, Petrachevsky probably intended him to play a leading part in the future republic.[1] My uncle Mihail, was also interested in the society, but as he was married, and the father of a family, he thought it wise not to frequent the Petrachevsky gatherings too assiduously. He took advantage, however, of the library of forbidden books. My uncle was at this time a great admirer of Fourier, and a fervid student of his romantic theories. My uncle Andrey also attended the meetings. At this period he was a very young man, and had only just begun his higher courses of study. He was many years younger than his two elder brothers, and looked upon them rather as parents than as equals. The older men in their turn, treated him as a little boy. Such relations do not exist among Russians, but they are often found in Polish and Lithuanian families. My father never discussed politics with his younger brother, and my uncle Andrey was unaware of the part he was playing in Petrachevsky's society. Andrey Dostoevsky had none of the literary talent of his brothers; but the family readings which my grandfather Mihail continued for the benefit of his younger sons gave him a great interest in literature. Later, when serving the State

1. One of the members of the Petrachevsky association gave it as his opinion that Dostoevsky was the only one of the band who was a typical conspirator. He was silent and reserved, not given to opening his heart to every one after the Russian fashion. This reticence persisted all his life. He maintained it even towards my mother, and in the early days of their marriage she found it very difficult to make him speak of his past life. Later, however, when Dostoevsky realised how devoted his second wife *was* to him, he opened his heart to her, and had no more secrets from her.

in various provincial towns, he always managed to draw all the intellectuals of the place round him. Having heard of the interesting gatherings that took place at Petrachevsky's house, he begged one of his comrades to introduce him. He attended several meetings without encountering my father. One evening, when my uncle Andrey was passing from group to group, listening with great interest to the political discussions of the young men, he suddenly found himself confronted by his brother Fyodor, whose face was white and drawn with anger.

"What are you doing here?" he asked in a terrible voice. "Go away, go away at once, and let me never see you in this house again."

My uncle was so alarmed by his elder brother's anger that he left Petrachevsky's reception immediately, and never returned. When the police discovered the plot later on, all three Dostoevsky brothers were arrested. My uncle Andrey's ingenuous replies made it evident to the judges that he knew nothing of the conspiracy, and he was soon released. The anger of his brother had saved him. My uncle Mihail was kept in prison for some weeks. Dostoevsky said later in the *Journal of the Writer*, that Mihail knew a great deal. It is probable that my father had no secrets from him. My uncle also knew how to hold his tongue, and he confessed nothing. He was able to prove easily that he rarely visited Petrachevsky and only went to his house to borrow books. He was eventually released, and Prince Gagarin, who was looking into his case, knowing the affection that existed between the two brothers, hastened to let my father know that his brother had been liberated, and that he need have no further fears on his account. My father never forgot this generous action on the part of Prince Gagarin, and he spoke of it later in the *Journal of the Writer*.

Dostoevsky was treated more harshly than his brothers. He had been sent to the Peter-Paul fortress, the terrible prison of political conspirators. Here he spent the most miserable months of his life. He did not like to speak of them; he tried to forget. Strange to say, *The Little Hero*, the novel he wrote in prison, is the most poetic, the most graceful, the youngest and freshest of all his works. As we read it we might suppose that Dostoevsky was trying to evoke in his dark prison the scent of flowers, the poetic shade of the great parks with their centenarian trees, the joyous laughter of children, the beauty and grace of young women. Summer was reigning in Petersburg, but the sun barely glanced on the damp walls of the old fortress.

The Petrachevsky trial dragged on as was usual in Russia. Autumn had already come when the Governor at last made up his mind to deal seriously with the conspirators. Our political cases were nearly always tried by the military courts; the chief among the generals who had to enquire into the Petrachevsky affair was General Rostovzov. Later, he was appointed President of the Commission for the emancipation of the serfs, and conducted a vigorous struggle with the great landowners who wished to emancipate the serfs, but to keep all the land for themselves. Rostovzov, supported by Alexander II, who had a great regard for him, gained the victory, and the peasants received their portions of land. General Rostovzov was an ardent patriot, and looked upon all political conspiracies as crimes. He carefully studied all the documents the police had seized in the dwellings of Petrachevsky and of the young men who belonged to his party, and was probably surprised at the weakness of the evidence against them. Knowing something of Dostoevsky's intellect and talent, he suspected him of being one of the leaders of the movement, and resolved to make him speak. On the day of the trial he was amiable and charming to my father. He talked to Dostoevsky as to a young author of great gifts, a man of lofty European culture, who had unfortunately been drawn into a political plot without very well knowing the gravity of what he was doing. The General was obviously indicating to Dostoevsky the part he ought to play to avoid severe punishment. My father was always very ingenuous and very confiding. He did not understand all this, was much attracted by the General, who treated him not as a criminal, but as a man of the world, and answered all his questions readily. Rostovzov must have let slip some unguarded word, for my father suddenly realised that he was being invited to buy his own liberty by selling his comrades. He was deeply indignant that such a proposal should have been made to him. His sympathy for Rostovzov changed to hatred. He became stubborn and cautious, fencing with each question put to him. The young man, though nervous and hysterical, and exhausted by long months of imprisonment, was stronger than the General. Seeing that his stratagem was detected, Rostovzov lost his temper; he quitted the court, leaving the interrogatory to the other members of the tribunal. Occasionally he opened the door of an adjoining room where he had taken refuge and asked: "Have they finished examining Dostoevsky? I won't come back into the court until that hardened sinner has left it."

My father could never forgive Rostovzov's hostile attitude. He called him a mountebank, and spoke of him with contempt all his life. He despised him the more, because at the time of the trial, Dostoevsky believed himself to be in the right, and considered himself as a hero eager to save his country. The anguish my father endured during his examination made a deep impression on his mind. Later it found expression in Raskolnikov's duel with Porfiry, and Dmitri Karamazov's duel with the magistrates who came to interrogate him at Mokroé.

The Generals, headed by Rostovzov, presented the death-sentence to Nicholas I. He refused to sign it. The Emperor was not cruel, but he was narrow-minded, and had no idea of psychology. This science was, indeed, very little known in Russia at this period. The Emperor did not desire the death of the conspirators, but he wished "to give the young men a good lesson." His advisers proposed a lugubrious comedy. The prisoners were told to prepare for death. They were taken to a public place, where the scaffold had been erected. They were made to mount it. One of the conspirators was bound to a post with his eyes bandaged. The soldiers made as if they were about to shoot the unhappy prisoners... At this moment a messenger arrived and announced that the Emperor had changed the death-sentence into that of hard labour. Memoirs of the time state that for fear of accidents the soldiers rifles were not even loaded, and that the messenger who was supposed to have come from the Palace was actually on the spot before the arrival of the conspirators. All this was, no doubt, true; but the unfortunate young men knew nothing of it, and were making ready to die. If Nicholas I had been more subtly constituted, he would have realised that it would have been more generous to shoot the conspirators than to make them undergo such anguish. However, the Emperor acted in accordance with the manners of his time; our grandfathers had a great liking for scenes of false sentiment. Nicholas no doubt thought he would confer a great joy on the young men by giving them back their lives on the scaffold itself. Few among them were able to bear this joy; some lost their reason, others died young. It is possible that my father's epilepsy would never have taken such a terrible form but for this grim jest.

Ill and enfeebled as he was, Dostoevsky had mounted the scaffold boldly and had looked death bravely in the face. He has told us that all he felt at this moment was a mystic fear at the thought of presenting himself immediately before God, in his unprepared state. His friends who were gathered round the scaffold say he was calm and dignified. My father has described his emotions at this moment in *The Idiot*. Though he paints the anguish of one condemned to death, he tells us nothing of the joy he felt on learning his reprieve. It is probable that when the first rush of animal joy was over he felt a great bitterness, a deep indignation at the thought that he had been played with and tortured so cruelly. His pure soul, which was already aspiring heavenwards, perhaps regretted that it had to sink to earth again, and plunge once more into the mud in which we are all struggling.

My father returned to the fortress. A few days later he left for Siberia in company of a police officer. He quitted Petersburg on Christmas Eve. As he passed in a sleigh through the streets of the capital, he looked at the lighted windows of the houses and said to himself: "At this moment they are lighting up the Christmas tree in my brother Mihail's house. My nephews are admiring it, laughing and dancing round it, and I am not with them. God knows if I shall ever see them again!" Dostoevsky regretted only his little nephews as he turned his back on that cold-hearted city.

On arriving in Siberia my father had a visit at one of the first halts from two ladies. They were the wives of "Dekabrists,"[1] whose self-appointed mission it was to meet newly arrived political prisoners, in order to say a few words of comfort to them, and give them some advice about the life that awaited them as convicts. They handed my father a Bible, the only book allowed in prison. Taking advantage of a moment when the police officer's back was turned, one of the ladies told my father in French to examine the book carefully when he was alone. He found a note for 25 roubles stuck between two leaves of the Bible. With this money he was able to buy a little linen, soap and tobacco, to improve his coarse fare, and get white bread. He had no other money all the time he was in exile. His brothers, his sisters, his aunt and his friends had all basely deserted him, terrified by his crime and its punishment.

---

1. Persons implicated in a political plot against Nicholas I at the beginning of his reign. They made their attempt to overthrow autocratic rule in the month of December, whence their name of "Dekabrists." They were sent to a convict station; their wives followed them. They enjoyed more liberty than their husbands, who at the time of the Petrachevsky conspiracy, had already served their sentence, but had still to remain in Siberia under police surveillance. The "Dekabrists" had wished to introduce an aristocratic republic in Russia, and apportion power among those who belonged to the union of hereditary nobles. The nobles always had a great respect for the "Dekabrists" and considered them martyrs.

VI

Prison Life

When a man is suddenly uprooted and finds himself obliged to spend years in a strange world, with people whose coarseness and lack of education are bound to distress him, he thinks out a plan by means of which he may avoid the worst blows to his susceptibilities, adopts an attitude, and resolves on a certain course of conduct. Some entrench themselves in silence and disdain, hoping to be left in peace; others become flatterers, and seek to purchase their repose by the basest adulation. Dostoevsky, condemned to live for years in prison, in the midst of a redoubtable band of criminals, who, having nothing to lose, feared nothing and were capable of anything, chose a very different attitude; he adopted a tone of Christian fraternity. This was no new part to him; he had already essayed it when, as a child, he had approached the iron gate in his father's private garden and, risking a punishment, had entered into conversation with the poor patients of the hospital; again, when he had talked with the peasant-serfs of Darovoye, and tried to gain their affection by helping the poor women in their field-work. He adopted the same fraternal tone later when he studied the poor of Petersburg in the small cafés and drink-shops of the capital, playing billiards with them, and offering them their choice of refreshments the while he tried to surprise the secrets of their hearts. Dostoevsky realised that he would never become a great writer by frequenting elegant drawing-rooms, full of polite people in well-cut coats, with fashionable cravats, empty heads, anæmic hearts and colourless souls. Every writer depends on the people, on the simple souls who have never been taught the art of hiding their sufferings under a veil of trivial words. The moujiks of Yasnaia Poliana taught Tolstoy more than his Moscow friends could teach him. The peasants who accompanied Turgenev on his sporting expeditions gave him more original ideas than his European friends. Dostoevsky in his turn depended on poor people, and from his childhood, instinctively sought a means of approaching them. This science, which he had already acquired to some extent, was to prove of the greatest service to him in Siberia.

Dostoevsky has not concealed from us his method of making himself beloved by his fellow-convicts. In his novel, *The Idiot*, he describes his first steps in detail. Prince Mishkin, the descendant of a long line of ancestors of European culture, is travelling on a cold winter's day. He is a Russian, but having spent all his youth in Switzerland, he knows little of his fatherland. Russia interests and attracts him greatly; he longs to enter into her soul and discover her secrets. As the Prince is poor, he travels third class. He is no snob; his coarse, common fellow-travellers inspire no disgust in him. They are the first real Russians he has seen; in Switzerland he met only our intellectuals, who aped Europeans, and political refugees, who, speaking a horrible jargon they called Russian, posed as the representatives of the sacred dreams of our nation. Prince Mishkin realises that hitherto he had seen only copies and caricatures, he longs to know the originals at last. Looking sympathetically at his third-class companions, he waits only for the first sentence to enter into conversation with them. His fellow-travellers observe him with curiosity; they had never seen such a bird at close quarters before. The Prince's polite manners and European dress seemed ridiculous to them. They entered into conversation with him to make a fool of him, that they might have some fun at his expense. They laughed rudely, nudging each other, at the Prince's first words; but gradually, as he went on speaking, they ceased to laugh. His charming courtesy, his freedom from snobbishness, his ingenuous manner of treating them as his equals, as people of his own world, made them realise that they were in the presence of an extremely rare and curious creature — a true Christian. The youthful Rogogin feels the attraction of this Christian kindness, and hastens to pour out the secret of his heart to this distinguished unknown, who listens to him with so much interest. Though illiterate, Rogogin is very intelligent; he understands that Prince Mishkin is morally his superior. He admires and reverences him, but he sees clearly that the poor Prince is but a big child, an artless dreamer, who has no knowledge of life. He knows how malicious and relentless the world is. The idea of protecting this charming Prince enters Rogogin's noble heart. "Dear Prince," he says, when he takes leave of him in the station at Petersburg, "Come and see me. I will have a good pelisse made for you, and I will give you money and magnificent clothes, suitable to your rank."

Dostoevsky arrived in Siberia on a cold winter's day. He travelled third-class, in company with thieves and murderers, whom the mother-country was sending away from her to the different convict-stations of Siberia. He observed his new companions with curiosity. Here it was at last, the real Russia which he had vainly sought in Petersburg! Here they were, those Russians, a curious mixture of Slavs and Mongolians, who had conquered a sixth part of the world! Dostoevsky studied the gloomy faces of his fellow-travellers, and that second sight which all serious writers have more or less, enabled him to decipher their thoughts and read their child-like hearts. He looked sympathetically at the convicts who were walking by his side, and entered into conversation with them at the first opportunity. The convicts, for their part, glanced at him enquiringly, but not with friendliness. Was he not a noble, did he not come of that accursed class of hereditary tyrants, who treated their serfs like dogs, and looked upon them as slaves, condemned to toil all their lives that their masters might live riotously? They entered into conversation with Dostoevsky, hoping to laugh at him, and to amuse themselves at his expense. They nudged each other and mocked at my father, when they heard his first words; but gradually, as he went on speaking, the jeers and laughter ceased. The *moujiks* saw before them their ideal — a true Christian, a wise and modest man, who placed God above all, who sincerely believed that neither rank nor education could open any real gulf between men, that all were equal before God, and that he who is so fortunate as to possess culture should seek to spread it round him, instead of priding himself upon it. This was the *moujiks'* idea of true nobles, true *baré;* but alas! they very seldom encountered any of this type. At each word Dostoevsky spoke, the eyes of his companions opened more widely.

When Dostoevsky wishes to draw his own portrait in the person of one of his heroes, and to relate an epoch of his own life, he gives that hero all the ideas and sensations he himself had at the period. It seems somewhat strange that Prince Mishkin (in *The Idiot),* who was not a criminal and had never been tried and sentenced should, on his arrival at Petersburg, talk of nothing but the last moments of a man condemned to death. We feel that he is entirely possessed by the idea. Dostoevsky explains this eccentric behaviour by telling us that the director of the sanatorium to which the poor Prince had been sent by his family, had taken him to Geneva to see an execution. These Swiss seem to have had a strange idea of the treatment suitable for a nervous patient; it is not surprising that they were not able to cure the Prince. My father made use of this somewhat far-fetched explanation in order to hide from the general public that Prince Mishkin was, in reality, no other than that unhappy convict, the political conspirator, Fyodor Dostoevsky,[1] who, throughout the first year of his prison life, was hypnotised by his recollection of the scaffold, and could think of nothing else. In *The Idiot*, Prince Mishkin describes all the impressions of the condemned man to the servant of the Epantchin family. When they question him later about the execution, the Prince replies: "I have already told your servant my impressions; I cannot talk about it any more." The Epantchin have great difficulty in making Mishkin speak on the subject. This was precisely Dostoevsky's attitude; he described his sufferings to the convicts and refused to discuss them subsequently with the intellectuals of Petersburg. In vain they would question him eagerly; Dostoevsky would frown and change the subject.

It is remarkable that Prince Mishkin, who falls in love with Nastasia Philipovna, does not become her suitor, and says to a young girl who loves him and is willing to marry him: "I am ill, I can never marry." This was probably Dostoevsky's conviction in early manhood; he did not change his opinion until after his imprisonment. The resemblance between Dostoevsky and his hero extends to the smallest details.

Thus Prince Mishkin arrives at Petersburg without a portmanteau, carrying a small parcel containing a little clean linen. He has not a kopeck, and General Epantchin gives him *twenty-five roubles*. Dostoevsky arrived in Siberia with a little parcel of linen which the police had allowed him to bring away; he had not a kopeck, and the wives of Dekabrists brought him twenty-five roubles, concealed between the pages of a Bible.

His good reputation followed him to prison; those of his travelling companions who were imprisoned with him at Omsk spoke to their new companions of this strange man, Dostoevsky, who was to serve his sentence among them. Certain good-natured convicts were already considering how they could protect this young, sickly fellow, this dreamer, who had been so busy thinking of the heroes of his novels that he had had no time to study real life. The convicts said to themselves that if life was hard to them, inured as they were from childhood to fatigue and privation, how much harder it must be to Dostoevsky, bred in comfort, and above all, thanks to his social position, accustomed to be treated with respect by everyone. They tried to console him, telling him that

1. It is hardly necessary to say that in identifying himself with a prince, Dostoevsky had no snobbish intention. He wanted to show what an immense moral influence a man of lofty hereditary culture might have upon the masses if he behaved to the people as a brother and a Christian, and not as a snob.

life is long, that he was still young, that there was happiness in store for him after his release. They showed a delicacy of feeling peculiar to the Russian peasants. In *The House of the Dead* my father has described how when he was wandering sadly about the prison, the convicts would come and ask him questions about politics, foreign countries, the Court, the life in large cities. "They did not seem to take much interest in my replies," says my father; "I could never understand why they asked for such information." The explanation was, however, a very simple one; a kind- hearted convict noticed Dostoevsky walking alone, in a kind of dream, staring into space. He was anxious to distract his thoughts. It seemed to his rustic mind impossible that a gentleman should be interested in vulgar things, and the ingenuous diplomatist accordingly spoke to my father of lofty subjects: politics, government, Europe. The answers did not interest him, but he attained his end. Dostoevsky was roused, he talked with animation, his melancholy was exorcised.

But the convicts saw more in my father than a sad and suffering young man. They divined his genius. These illiterate *moujiks* did not know exactly what a novel was, but with the infallible instinct of a great race they perceived that God had sent this dreamer on earth to accomplish great things. They realised his moral greatness and did what they could to tend him. Dostoevsky has told in his Memoirs how one day, when the convicts were sent to bathe, one of them asked to be allowed to wash my father. This he did most carefully, supporting him like a child, lest he should slip on the wet boards. "He washed me as if I had been made of china," says Dostoevsky, much astonished at all this care. My father was right. He was, in fact, a precious object to his humble comrades. They felt that he would render great services to the Russian community, and they all protected him. One day, exasperated by the bad food they were given, they made a demonstration, and demanded to see the Governor of the Fortress of Omsk. My father thought it his duty to take part in the manifestation, but the convicts would not allow him to join them.[1] "Your place is not here," they cried, and they insisted on his returning to the prison. The convicts knew that they risked incurring a severe punishment for their protest, and they wished to spare Dostoevsky. These humble *moujiks* had chivalrous souls. They were more generous to my father than his Petersburg friends, the mean and jealous writers who did all in their power to poison his youthful success.

1. I have mentioned above that Dostoevsky took no part in any demonstrations at the Castle of the Engineers. In associating himself with that of the convicts, he showed that he had more respect for them than for the Russian nobles and intellectuals.

If the convicts protected my father, he, for his part, must have exercised a great moral influence over them. He is too modest to speak of this himself, but Nekrassov has proclaimed it. The poet was a man of great discrimination. In *Poor Folks*, which Nekrassov published so readily in his Review, he recognised Dostoevsky's genius. When he made the young novelist's acquaintance he was struck by his purity of heart and nobility of mind. The narrow, jealous, intriguing circle in which the Russian writers of the period lived prevented Nekrassov from becoming my father's friend, but he never forgot him. When Dostoevsky was sent to Siberia, Nekrassov often thought of him. This poet was distinguished from others by his profound knowledge of the souls of the peasants. He spent all his childhood on his father's small estate, and in later life went there every summer. Knowing the Russian people and knowing Dostoevsky, he asked himself what the relations between the convicts and the young novelist would be. Poets think in song, and Nekrassov has left us an excellent poem, *The Wretched*, in which he depicts Dostoevsky's life among the criminals. He does not mention him by name—the Censorship, which was very strict at this period, would not have permitted this—but he told his literary friends, and later Dostoevsky himself, who his hero was.

The story is put into the mouth of a convict, formerly a man in good society, who had killed a woman in a fit of jealousy. In prison he associates with the vilest of the criminals, drinks and gambles with them in spite of his contempt for them. His attention is attracted by a prisoner who is unlike the rest. He is very weak, and has the voice of a child; his hair is light and fine as dawn.[1] He is very silent, lives isolated from the others, and fraternises with no one. The convicts dislike him, because he has "white hands," that is to say, he cannot do heavy work. Seeing him toiling all day, but achieving little on account of his weakness, they jeer at him and call him "the Mole." They amuse themselves by hustling him, and laugh when they see him turn pale and bite his lips at the brutal orders of the warders. One evening in prison the convicts are playing cards and getting drunk. A prisoner who has been ill a long time, is dying; the convicts deride him and sing blasphemous requiems to him. "Wretches! Do you not fear God?" cries a terrible voice. The convicts look round in amazement. It is "the Mole" who spoke, and who now looks like an eagle. He orders them to be silent, to respect the last moments of the dying man, speaks to them of God, and shows them the

---

1. In the description of Prince Mishkin, Dostoevsky says he was very thin and looked ill, and that his hair was so fair that it was almost white.

abyss into which they are slipping. From this day forth he becomes the master of those whose conscience is not quite dead. They surround him in a respectful crowd, drinking in his words eagerly. This prisoner is a man of learning; he talks to the convicts of poetry, of science, of God, and, above all, of Russia. He is a patriot who admires his country, and foresees a great future for her. His speeches are not eloquent and are not distinguished by beauty of style; but he has the secret of speaking to the soul and touching the hearts of his pupils. In the poem the prisoner dies, surrounded by the respect and admiration of the convicts. They nurse him devotedly during his illness; they make a sort of litter, and carry him out daily into the prison yard that he may breathe the fresh air and see the sun he loves. After his death his grave becomes a place of pilgrimage for all the inhabitants of the district.

When my father came back from Siberia Nekrassov showed the poem to him and said: "You are the hero of it." Dostoevsky was greatly touched by these words; he admired the poem very much, but when his literary friends asked him if Nekrassov had described him faithfully he answered smilingly: "Oh, no! he exaggerated my importance. It was I, on the contrary, who was the disciple of the convicts."

It is difficult to say which was right, Nekrassov or Dostoevsky. The poem may have been only a poetic dream, but it shows what Nekrassov's opinion of my father was. When he spoke of Dostoevsky as he did in *The Wretched*, Nekrassov avenged him for all the base calumnies of his literary rivals. It is strange that none of Dostoevsky's Russian biographers, save Nicolai Strahoff, have mentioned Nekrassov's poem, although they have faithfully reported all the ignoble slanders invented by young writers after the success of *Poor Folks*. Yet they cannot have been unaware that he was the hero of the poem, for Dostoevsky himself recorded his conversation with Nekrassov on the subject in his *Journal of the Writer*. It is almost as if they had wished to conceal the Russian poet's conception of the novelist from the public.

VII

What the Convicts Taught Dostoevsky

Dostoevsky had some reason to declare that the convicts had been his teachers. As a fact, they taught him what it was above all things important for him to learn; they taught him to know and to love our beautiful and generous Russia. When he found himself for the first time in his life in a truly national centre, he felt his mother's blood speaking more and more loudly in his heart. My father began to recognise that Russian charm which is indeed the strength of our country. It is not by fire and sword that Russia has conquered her enemies; it is the heart of Russia that has formed the vast Russian Empire. Our army is weak, our poor soldiers are often beaten, but wherever they pass they leave imperishable memories. They fraternise with the vanquished instead of oppressing them; open their hearts to them; treat them as comrades; and the vanquished, touched by this generosity, never forget them. "Where the Russian flag has once flown, it will always fly," we say in Russia. My compatriots are conscious of their charm.

The Russian peasant, dirty, wild and ragged, is in fact, a great charmer. His heart is gentle, tender, gay and childlike. He has no education, but his mind is broad, clear and penetrating. He observes a great deal and meditates on subjects that would never come into the head of a European *bourgeois*. He works all his life, but cares nothing for profit. His material wants are few, his moral needs much more extensive. He is a dreamer, his soul seeks for poetry. Very often he will leave his fields and his family to visit monasteries, to pray at the tomb of saints, or to travel to Jerusalem. He belongs to the Oriental race that gave the world a Krishna, a Buddha, a Zarathustra, a Mahommed. The Russian peasant is always ready to leave the world and go to seek God in the desert. He lives more in the beyond than in this world. He has a strong sense of justice: "Why quarrel and dispute? We should live according to the truth of God." Such phrases may often be heard from Russian peasants. This "truth of God" is much in their minds; they try to live according to the

Gospel. They love to caress little children, to comfort weeping women, to help the aged. It is not often one meets a "gentleman" in Russian cities, but there are plenty in our villages.

Studying his convict companions, Dostoevsky did justice to the generosity of their hearts and the nobility of their souls, and learned to love his country as she deserves to be loved. Russia conquered Dostoevsky's Lithuanian soul through the poor convicts of Siberia, and conquered it forever. My father could do nothing by halves. He gave himself heart and soul to Russia, and served the Russian flag as faithfully as his ancestors had served the flag of the Radwan. Those who wish to understand the change in Dostoevsky's ideas should read his letter to the poet Maikov, written from Siberia shortly after his release. It is a fervid hymn to Russia. "I am Russian, my heart is Russian, my ideas are Russian," he repeats in every line. When we read this letter it is easy to understand what was taking place in his heart. Every serious and idealistic young man tries to become a patriot, for only patriotism can give him strength to serve his country well. A young Russian is instinctively patriotic, but a Slav, whose paternal family comes from another country and who has been brought up in a different atmosphere, cannot possess this instinctive patriotism. Before offering his services to Russia, the young Lithuanian wished to know what her aims were. On leaving the School of Engineers, Dostoevsky sought this explanation in the society of Petersburg, and failed to find it. In the drawing-rooms of Petersburg he found only people who were seeking their material advantage, or intellectuals who hated their fatherland and blushed to acknowledge that they were Russians. These languid and listless people could give my father no idea of the greatness of Russia. In the novel, *The Adolescent*, Dostoevsky has drawn a curious type, the student Kraft, a Russian of German origin, who commits suicide because he is persuaded that Russia can play but a secondary part in human civilisation. It is very possible that in his youth Dostoevsky had himself suffered from Kraft's disease, a disease to which all Russians of foreign extraction are more or less subject. My father often told his friends that he was on the verge of suicide, and that his arrest saved him. But if Petersburg could not teach Dostoevsky patriotism, the Russian people he met in prison soon taught him the great Russian lesson of Christian fraternity, that magnificent ideal which has gathered so many races under our banners. Dazzled by its beauty, my father wished to follow their example. Was he the first Slavo-Norman who gave himself heart and soul to Russia? No. All the Moscovite Grand Dukes who founded Great Russia, who defended the Orthodox

Church and fought valiantly against the Tartars, were also Slavo-Normans, the descendants of Prince Rurik. Thanks to their Norman perspicacity, these first Russian patriots understood our great Idea better even than the Russians themselves in their national infancy. It often happens that young nations serve their national idea instinctively, without understanding it very well, and thus their patriotism is never very profound. It is only when they mature that nations fully realise the idea they have been building up, and, understanding at last the services their ancestors have rendered to humanity, become proud of their country. Among races which are growing old, patriotism reaches its apogee, and often dazzles them. It is at this stage that Napoleons and Williams make their appearance; inordinately proud of their national culture, they desire to impose it on others.

Having at last understood the Russian Idea, Dostoevsky eagerly followed the example of the illustrious Slavo-Normans whose history he knew so well, having studied it in his childhood in the works of Karamzin. Like the Moscovite Grand Dukes of old, Dostoevsky explained the Russian Idea to his compatriots; like them, he cherished all that was original in Russia: our ideas, our beliefs, our customs and our traditions. He inaugurated his patriotic services by renouncing his republicanism. It had seemed very beautiful to him once, when he had expounded it in Petersburg drawing-rooms to an enthusiastic crowd of Poles, Lithuanians, Swedes from Finland, Germans from the Baltic Provinces, and young Russians. In Siberia, where he was in daily contact with representatives of the Russian people from every point of our huge country, the thought of introducing the institutions of modern Europe into Holy Russia struck him as absurd. He saw that the Russian people were still in the stage of Byzantine culture, which had been arrested in its development by the Turkish conquest of Byzantium. The Orthodox clergy, who had propagated this culture among the peasants, had been unable to develop it, and the Russian people continue to live in the fifteenth century, retaining all the ingenuous mystical ideas of that period. It is obvious that the introduction of the European ideas of the nineteenth century among persons so ill-prepared to receive them could only produce a terrible anarchy, in which all the European civilisation introduced at immense cost by the descendants of Peter the Great would be submerged. When he took part in Petrachevsky's conspiracy, my father dreamed of substituting a republic of intellectuals for the monarchy. He now saw that this would be impossible, because the people hated the *baré* (nobles or intellectual *bourgeois*) with a fierce and implacable hatred. The peasants could not forget the cruelty of their masters, and they distrusted all nobles and all educated persons. Dostoevsky realised that the only republic possible in Russia would be a peasant republic, that is to say, a reign of ignorance and brutality which would cut off our country from Europe more than ever. The Russians dislike Europeans, and reserve all their sympathies for Slavs and the Mongolian tribes of Asia, to which they are akin. The introduction of a republican *régime* would tend to transform Russia into a Mongolian country, and all the work of our Tsars and nobles would perish. At this period of his life Dostoevsky loved Europe too much to wish to separate Russia from European influences. Rather than drag down his country into a gulf of ignorance and violence, he renounced his political ideas. This did not happen all at once. This is what Dostoevsky says himself in the *Journal of the Writer:* "Neither imprisonment nor suffering broke us.[1] Something else changed our hearts and our ideas: union with the people, fraternity in misery. This change was not sudden; on the contrary, it came about very gradually. Of all my political comrades, I was the one to whom it was easiest to embrace the Russian Idea, for I came of a patriotic and deeply religious stock. In our family we had been familiar with the Gospel from childhood. By the time that I was ten years old, I knew all the principal episodes of Karamzin's Russian history, which my father read aloud to us every night. Visits to the Kremlin and to the cathedrals of Moscow were always solemn events to me."

Recognising that the European institutions of the nineteenth century were unsuitable to the Russian people, my father considered other means of ameliorating the civilisation of our country. He thought it would be well to work for the development of the Byzantine culture, which had taken root in the hearts and minds of our peasants. In its day, Byzantine culture had been of a higher order than the average culture of Europe. It was only when the Greek men of learning, fleeing from the Turks, had sought asylum in the great European towns, that the culture of Europe began to emerge from the mists of the Middle Ages. If Byzantine civilisation had helped to develop European culture, it might well do the same for Russia. Dostoevsky accordingly began to study our Church, which had guarded this civilisation, and preserved it as it had been received from Byzantium. The last of the Moscovite patriarchs, more learned than their forerunners, were already beginning to develop this civilisation on Russian lines, when their work was interrupted by

1. When he says "us" my father refers to comrades of the Petrachevsky circle, some of whom also changed their political opinions after their imprisonment.

Peter the Great. At first my father had taken little interest in the Orthodox Church. There is no mention of it in any of the novels he wrote before his imprisonment. But after this the Church figures in every new book; Dostoevsky's heroes speak of it more and more, and in his last novel, *The Brothers Karamazov*, the Orthodox monastery dominates the whole scene. My father now saw what an important part religion plays in Russia, and he began to study it with passion. Later, he visited the monasteries and talked with the monks; he sought to be initiated into the traditions of the Orthodox religion; he became its champion and was the first who dared to say that our Church had been paralysed since the time of Peter the Great, to demand its independence, and to desire to see a Patriarch at its head. The Russian clergy hastened to meet his advances. Accustomed to being treated with scorn by Russian intellectuals, as a senile and senseless institution, they were touched by Dostoevsky's sympathy, called him the true son of the Orthodox Church, and remain faithful to his memory.

My father also studied the Russian monarchy, and at last realised that the Tsar, the so-called Oriental despot, was in the eyes of the Russian people simply the head of their great community, the only man in the whole country who is inspired by God. According to Orthodox belief, the coronation is a sacrament; the Holy Spirit descends on the Tsar, and guides him in all his acts. Formerly all Europe shared such convictions; but as atheistical opinions gained ground they gradually disappeared, and now Europeans smile at them. The Russians, who are yet in the fifteenth century, still hold this faith religiously. Profoundly mystical, they need divine help and cannot live without it. The Russians will only obey a man crowned in a cathedral of Moscow by an Archbishop or a Patriarch. However intelligent a President of the Russian Republic might be, in the sight of our peasants he would be simply a ridiculous chatterer; the halo of the coronation would always be lacking to him. The people would distrust him; they are, unhappily, well aware how easy it is to buy a Russian official. It would be useless for our Presidents to sign treaties and promise the aid of Russian troops to Europeans; they would never be able to honour their own drafts. It would only be necessary to spread a rumour that the President had been bought by Europe to provoke an epidemic of *défaitisme*.

Realising the immense part played by the Tsar in Russia, and his moral power among the peasantry, thanks to his coronation, seeing that he alone could keep them united and preserve them from the anarchy which is always lying in wait for Mongolian races, my father became a monarchist. Great was the indignation of all our writers, of all the intellectual society of Petersburg which was hostile to Tsarism when they learned that Dostoevsky had abjured his revolutionary creed. While my father had been studying the Russian people in prison, these gentlemen had been talking in drawing-rooms, drawing their knowledge of Russia from European books, and looking upon our peasants as idiots, who could be made to accept all laws and all institutions without discussion or question. The intellectuals could never understand the reasons for Dostoevsky's change of mind, and could never forgive what they called "his betrayal of the holy cause of liberty." They hated my father throughout his life and continued to hate him after his death. Each new novel of Dostoevsky's was greeted, not with the impartial criticism which analyses a work and gives its author the wise counsels eagerly looked for by a writer, but by attacks like those of a pack of mad dogs, throwing themselves on my father's masterpieces, and, under pretence of criticising, biting, tearing their prey, insulting and offending him cruelly. The moral influence exercised by my father on the students of Petersburg, which grew ever greater as his talents matured, infuriated the Russian writers. When Tretiakov[1] wished to include a portrait of my father in his collection of "Great Russian Writers," and commissioned a famous artist to paint it, the rage of Dostoevsky's political enemies knew no bounds. "Go to the exhibition and look at the face of this madman," they shrieked to the readers of their newspapers, "and you will realise at last who it is you love and listen to and read."

This ferocious and implacable hatred wounded my father deeply. He wished to live in peace with other writers, and to work in concert with them, for the glory of his country. He could not retract opinions based on his profound study of the Russian people, begun in prison and continued throughout his life. He felt that he had no right to hide the truth from Russia; he was constrained to show them the abyss to which the Socialists and anarchists of Petersburg drawing-rooms were leading them. The sense of duty accomplished gave him strength to struggle, but his life was very hard. Dostoevsky died without having been able to demonstrate that he was right. It is we, the hapless victims of the Russian Revolution, who now see all his predictions fulfilled, and have to expiate the irresponsible chatter of our Liberals.

✳ ✳ ✳

1. A rich merchant of Moscow, who bequeathed a fine gallery of national pictures to his native town.

It was not only the Russian soul that my father studied in prison. He also made an earnest study of the Bible. We all profess to be Christians, but how many of us are familiar with the Gospels? Most of us are content to hear them in church, and to retain some vague idea of their preparation for their first communion. Possibly my father in his youth knew the Bible after the fashion of the young men of his world—that is to say, very superficially. He says as much in the autobiography of Zossima,[1] which is to some extent his own: "I did not read the Bible," says Zossima, speaking of his youthful years, "but I never parted with it. I had a presentiment that I should want it some day." According to his letters to his brother Mihail, Dostoevsky began the study of the Bible at the Peter-Paul fortress. He continued it in Siberia, where for four years it was his only book. He studied the precious volume the wives of the Dekabrists had presented to him, pondered every word, learned it by heart and never forgot it. No writer of his time had had so profound a Christian culture as Dostoevsky. All his works are saturated with it, and it is this which gives them their power. "What a strange chance that your father should have had only the Gospels to read during the four most important years of a man's life, when his character is forming definitively," many of his admirers have said to me. But was it a chance? Is there such a thing as chance in our lives? Is not everything foreseen? The work of Jesus is not finished; in each generation He chooses His disciples, signs to them to follow Him, and gives them the same power over the human heart that He gave of old to the poor fishermen of Galilee.

Dostoevsky would never be without his old prison[2] Testament, the faithful friend that had consoled him in the darkest hours of his life. He always took it with him on his travels and kept it in a drawer of his writing-table, within reach of his hand. He acquired a habit of consulting it in important moments of his life. He would open the Testament, read the first lines he saw, and take them as an answer to his doubts.

Dostoevsky wrote nothing while in his Siberian prison.[1] And yet he left Omsk a much greater writer than he had been when he arrived. The young Lithuanian, who certainly loved Russia but understood very little about her, was transformed into a real Russian in prison. If all his life he retained the Lithuanian characteristics and culture of his forefathers, he only loved Russia the more deeply for this. He judged her from the

1. *The Brothers Kamarazov.*
2. All he did was to make a few notes of curious words and expressions used by the convicts, which were introduced by him later in *The House of the Dead.* He wrote them in a little book he made himself, which is now in the Dostoevsky Museum at Moscow.

standpoint of a benevolent Slav, conquered by the charm of Russia. Our faults did not alarm him; he saw that they arose from the youthfulness of the nation, and believed they would disappear in time. A son of little Lithuania, which has had her hour of glory, but will probably have no more, Dostoevsky wished to devote his talents to the service of Great Russia. Perhaps he felt that it was his mother's blood that had given them, and that therefore Russia had more right to these than Lithuania or Ukrainia. Moreover, the idea of breaking Russia up into a number of little countries, which finds so much favour at present, was non-existent then, and in working for Russia Dostoevsky thought he would also be working for Lithuania and Ukrainia.

A reverent admirer and passionate disciple of Christ, with a beloved country to serve, Dostoevsky was better equipped for his lofty work than before his imprisonment. It was no longer necessary for him to imitate the European novelists; he had only to draw his subjects from Russian life, and to recall the confessions of the convicts, the ideas and beliefs of our *moujiks*. This Lithuanian at last understood the Russian ideal, revered the Russian Church, and forgetting Europe, gave himself up wholeheartedly to painting the Slavo-Mongolian manners of our great country.

VIII

Dostoevsky a Soldier

Dostoevsky's last year in prison was more tolerable than the first three. The brute who commanded the fortress of Omsk and poisoned the convicts was at last superseded. The new Commandant was an educated man of European culture. He took an interest in my father and tried to be of service to him. He was legally empowered to employ the literary convicts on the work of his Chancellory. He sent for my father, who passed through the town escorted by a soldier. The Commandant gave him some easy work to do, ordered good meals to be served to him, brought him books, showed him the newspapers, which my father devoured eagerly.[1] He had seen no newspaper for three years, and he knew nothing of what was happening in the world. He seemed to be born anew; he was soon to leave his "House of the Dead." What a blessed moment!" he exclaims in describing his release in his memoirs.

Dostoevsky's political comrade, Durov, was released at the same time. But alas! the poor fellow had not the strength to rejoice in his liberty. "He went out like a candle," says my father. "He was young and handsome when he went into captivity. He came out half dead, grey-haired, bent, scarcely able to stand."

And yet Durov was not an epileptic, like my father, and he was in excellent health at the time of his arrest. How, then, are we to explain the different manner in which these two conspirators faced the world after four years of prison life? We must, I think, look for this explanation in their nationality. Durov was a Russian; he belonged to a nation still young, which soon expends its strength, loses courage at the first obstacle, and cannot sustain a struggle. Dostoevsky was a Lithuanian, a scion of a much older race, and had Norman blood in his veins. Resistance has always been a joy to the Lithuanians. Vidûnas, who knew his people

1. My father never made any public reference to this Commandant, fearing to injure him in the sight of the Government, but he often talked of him to his relations. Though Dostoevsky hated to speak of the sufferings he had endured during his captivity, he loved to recall those who had been good to him in his trials.

so thoroughly, has spoken thus on this point: "Whatever may befall a Lithuanian, he is not discouraged. This is not to say that he is indifferent to his fate. His sensibility is too lively for this, but it has an elasticity and resilience of a remarkable quality. He can bear the inevitable with courage, and face new experiences steadily. The Lithuanian aspires involuntarily to the mastery of the different elements of life. This becomes very evident when he has to grapple with a difficulty. The tension of his mind is manifested in a very characteristic fashion; the greater the difficulty, the more he is disposed to accept all with serenity, and even with gaiety and jest."

Dostoevsky probably began this struggle for life on the very first day of his captivity. He struggled against despair by studying with interest the characters of the convicts, their manners, habits, ideas and conversation. Seeing in them the future heroes of his novels, he carefully noted all the precious indications they were able to give him; no foreigner can form any idea of the just, penetrating and observant mind of the Russian peasant. When, on holidays, the convicts got drunk and were reduced to a state of bestiality, Dostoevsky sought solace for his disgust in the Gospel. "I cannot see his soul; perhaps it is nobler than mine," he would say to himself, as he looked at some drunken convict reeling about, and shouting obscene songs. He soon realised that hard labour was an excellent remedy for despair. He looked upon it as a kind of sport, and set about it with the passionate energy he brought to bear on everything that interested him. In certain chapters of *The House of the Dead* we see clearly what pleasure he took in outdoor work or in grinding alabaster.[1]

Obliged to conceal from the convicts the anger, contempt and disgust certain of their acts excited in him, Dostoevsky learned to discipline his nervous temperament. Reality, harsh and implacable, cured him of his imaginary fears. "If you imagine that I am still nervous, irritable and obsessed by the thought of illness, as I used to be at Petersburg, you must get rid of this idea. There is not a vestige of that left," he wrote to his brother Mihail shortly after his release.

Another and loftier idea sustained and consoled Dostoevsky during his sojourn in the fortress. Deeply religious as he had always been, he must often have asked himself why God had punished him, the innocent martyr of a noble theory, so severely. At that time he considered himself a hero, and was very proud of the Petrachevsky conspiracy. The

---

1. Speaking of some work allotted to him in prison, he says: "I was obliged to turn the wheel; it was difficult, but it served as an excellent gymnastic." Later he describes how he had to carry bricks on his back, and declares that he liked this work, because it developed his physical strength.

thought that this conspiracy was a crime which might have plunged Russia into anarchy, the thought that a handful of young dreamers had no right to impose their will on an immense country never entered his head till much later, some ten years perhaps after his release. Believing himself blameless, knowing himself to be free from vice and inspired only by pure and lofty thoughts, he must have asked in bewilderment how he could have deserved his terrible sufferings, by what action he could have incurred the wrath of a God he had always loved and reverenced. He then said to himself that God must have sent these miseries upon him not to punish, but to strengthen him and to make him a great writer, useful to his country and his people. The ignorant public often confounds the man of talent with his talent and cannot distinguish between them. But such men themselves do not fall into this error. They know that their talent is a gift apart which belongs to the community rather than to themselves. If he be in any degree a believer, each writer, musician, painter or sculptor feels himself a Messiah, and accepts his cross. He has a very definite sense that in giving him a talent God did not mean to place him above the crowd, but rather to sacrifice him to the good of others, and make him the servant of humanity. The greater his gift, the more illuminating is this sense of sacrifice in the eyes of its possessor. Sometimes he rebels, and thrusts aside the bitter cup which destiny prepares for him. At other moments he is exalted by the thought that he has been chosen to make known the ways of God to men. As the man of genius meditates on his mission his anger and rebellion disappear. He soars above the crowd; he feels himself nearer to God than other mortals, and his zeal for his mission increases daily. "Make me suffer, if so my talent and my influence may be increased," he prays courageously. "Spare me not! I will bear all if only the work Thou sentest me to do be well done." When the man of genius has reached this stage of resignation nothing can terrify him any more, and his devotion to the cause of humanity has no limits. Later, after his return to Petersburg, Dostoevsky said to his friends who denounced his punishment as unjust: "No, it was just. The people would have condemned us. I realised that in prison. And then, who knows, perhaps God sent me there that I might learn the essential thing, without which there is no life, without which we should only devour each other, and that I might bring that essential thing to others, even if but to a very few, to make them better, even if but a very little better. This alone would have made it worthwhile to go to prison."

✳ ✳ ✳

According to Russian law, Dostoevsky's punishment was not at an end when he was released. He had to serve as a soldier in a regiment at the small Siberian town of Semipalatinsk until the time when he should have gained his commission as an officer and be restored to his status as a free man. But military service was almost liberty in comparison with what he had endured in the fortress. The officers of his regiment treated him rather as a comrade than as a subordinate. At this period the Siberians had a great respect for political prisoners. The Dekabrists, who belonged to the best families of the country, and who bore their punishment without complaint, and with much dignity, prepared the ground for the Petrachevsky conspirators. My father would have been received with open arms by the whole town, even if he had not been a writer. His novels, which were very much read in the provinces, increased the sympathy of the inhabitants of Semipalatinsk for him. My father, for his part, sought their friendship. The close intimacy in which he had been obliged to live with the convicts had cured him of his Lithuanian aloofness. He no longer felt any Lithuanian scorn for the ignorant Moscovites; he knew that lack of culture in the Russian is often combined with a heart of gold. He went into society, took part in the amusements of Semipalatinsk, and made himself beloved by the whole town. The joy of life filled his being. Whereas poor Durov went out like a candle and died shortly after his release, Dostoevsky took up life at the point where he had left it at the moment of his condemnation. He hastened to resume amicable relations with his kinsfolk at Moscow and Petersburg.[1] He generously forgave them for having forsaken him in his prison; in his joy at being at last free, he called his sisters, who had been so cold-hearted to him, "the angels." He wrote to his literary friends in Petersburg, sent for their works, and showed much interest in what they had been doing during "my death." He formed friendships with officers and soldiers of his regiment.[2]

On the occasion of the departure of one of his new friends, named Vatihanov, Dostoevsky was photographed with him by the unskillful practitioner of Semipalatinsk. To this circumstance we owe the only existing portrait of Dostoevsky as a young man.

1. My father was able to send his first letters to his brother Mihail, and receive a little money from him before his release, thanks to the kindness of the Commandant.

2. Dostoevsky tells us later, in the journal, *The Citizen*, that he liked to read aloud to his comrades, the soldiers, in the evening when they were all assembled in the barrack-room. He admits that these readings and the discussions that followed them gave him great pleasure.

A few months after his release, Dostoevsky met at Semipalatinsk a man of his own world, the young Baron Wrangel, who had come to Siberia on business connected with his ministry. He was a native of the Baltic Provinces, of Swedish descent, but completely russified, and a great admirer of my father's works. He proposed that they should live together, and Dostoevsky accepted his offer. It is curious that each time Dostoevsky agreed to live with a comrade, it should have been with Russians of European origin: Grigorovitch, a Frenchman, and Wrangel, a Swede. It is probable that my father could never have endured the semi-Oriental habits of the true Russians, who sleep all day after playing cards all night. He wanted a regular life with a well-bred companion, who would respect his hours of work and meditation. He was happy with young Wrangel. They spent the winter in the town, and in summer they rented a rustic dwelling in the form of a villa, and amused themselves by growing flowers, of which they were both very fond.

Later, Baron Wrangel changed his ministry, and devoted himself to diplomacy. He was our *chargé d'affaires* in the Balkans, lived there a long time, and knew many remarkable people. Nevertheless, at the close of his life he dwelt solely upon his friendship with Dostoevsky. My compatriots who knew him in his last post as Russian Consul at Dresden used to tell me that whenever a Russian made his acquaintance, Baron Wrangel would always begin by telling him that he had been the friend of the great Dostoevsky, and describing their life together at Semipalatinsk. "It became a veritable mania," said the Russians naïvely. They would have understood his enthusiasm had its object been a Duke or a Marquis — but a writer! That was not much to boast of. The Baltic noble was more intelligent and more civilised than my snobbish compatriots. In his old age, looking back on his career, Baron Wrangel realised that the most beautiful page of his life had been the friendship of the great writer, and his greatest service to humanity the few months of tranquillity his delicacy and refinement had secured for a suffering man of genius, neglected by his friends, who needed rest after the terrible trial he had undergone.

Baron Wrangel published his reminiscences of my father. He could not describe the intimate life of Dostoevsky, for my father only spoke of this to his relatives or to friends of many years standing and of proved fidelity, but he gives an excellent account of the society of Semipalatinsk and of the part my father played in the little town. Baron Wrangel's reminiscences are the only record we possess of this period of Dostoevsky's life.

Dostoevsky's first marriage

The labour my father had to perform in prison was very hard, but it did him good by developing his body. He was no longer a sick creature, or an adolescent whose development had been arrested. He had become a man, and he longed for love. Any woman rather more adroit than the rustic beauties of Semipalatinsk could have won his heart. Such an one was to appear a few months after his release. But what a terrible woman fate had allotted to my poor father!

Among the officers of the Semipalatinsk regiment there was a certain Captain Issaïeff, a good fellow not overburdened with brains. He was in wretched health, and had been given up by all the doctors in the town. He was charming to my father, and often invited him to his house. Maria Dmitrievna, his wife, received Dostoevsky with much grace, and exerted herself to please him and to tame him. She knew that she would soon be a widow and would have no means beyond the meagre pension which the Russian Government gave to the widows of officers, a sum barely sufficient to feed her and her son, a boy of seven years old. Like a good woman of business, she was already looking about for a second husband. Dostoevsky seemed to her the most eligible *parti* in the town; he was a writer of great talent, he had a rich aunt in Moscow, who had again begun to send him money from time to time. Maria Dmitrievna played the part of a poetic soul, misunderstood by the society of a small provincial town, and yearning for a kindred spirit, a mind as lofty as her own. She soon took possession of the ingenuous heart of my father, who, at the age of thirty-three, fell in love for the first time.

This sentimental friendship was suddenly interrupted. The captain was ordered to Kusnetzk, a little Siberian town where there was another regiment belonging to the same division as that of Semipalatinsk. He took away his wife and child, and died a few months afterwards at Kusnetzk of the phthisis from which he had long been suffering. Maria Dmitrievna wrote to announce her husband's death to Dostoevsky, and kept up a lively correspondence with him. While waiting for the Government to grant her little pension she was living in great poverty, and complained bitterly to my father. Dostoevsky sent her nearly all the money he received from his relatives. He pitied her sincerely and wished to help her, but his feeling for her was rather sympathy than love. Thus when Maria Dmitrievna wrote that she had found a suitor at Kusnetzk and was about to marry again, he rejoiced; far from being heartbroken, he was delighted to think that the poor woman had found a protector. He even made interest with his friends to procure for his rival some coveted appointment. In fact, Dostoevsky did not look upon Maria Dmitrievna's future husband as a rival. At this period my father was not very sure that he should ever be able to marry, and considered himself in some degree an invalid. The epilepsy which had so long been latent in him began to declare itself. He had strange attacks, sudden convulsions which exhausted him and made him incapable of work. The regimental doctor who was treating him hesitated to diagnose the malady; it was not until much later that it was pronounced to be epilepsy. Meanwhile everybody—doctors, comrades, relatives, his friend Baron Wrangel, his brother Mihail—advised him not to marry, and Dostoevsky resigned himself sadly to celibacy. He accepted the part of Prince Mishkin, who, though he loves Nastasia Philipovna, allows her to go away with Rogogin and keeps up amicable relations with his rival.

Meanwhile Maria Dmitrievna quarrelled with her lover, and left the town of Kusnetzk. She had at length received her pension, but this pittance was quite insufficient for a capricious, idle and ambitious woman. My father was now an officer, and she came back to her first idea of a marriage with him. In the letters she now wrote with increasing frequency, she exaggerated her poverty, declared that she was weary of the struggle, and threatened to put an end to herself and to her child. Dostoevsky became very uneasy; he wanted to see her, talk to her, and make her listen to reason. As a former political prisoner he had no right to quit Semipalatinsk.[1] His brother-officers, to whom he confided his desire to go to Kusnetzk, arranged to send him thither "on regimental business." The division which had its headquarters at Semipalatinsk

1. Dostoevsky, however, was often detailed to escort scientific missions travelling in Siberia by order of the Government. Thus in one letter my father describes a visit to Barnaoul, a small town between Semipalatinsk and Kusnetzk, which he made in the company of M. P. Semenov and his friends, members of the Geographical Society. On hearing of their arrival, General Gerngross, governor of the town, invited all the mission to a ball at his house, and was particularly polite to my father. In the sight of this Baltic general Dostoevsky, who had only just left a prison, was not a convict but a famous writer.

dispatched to its regiment at Kusnetzk a wagon-load of ropes, which was bound by law to be escorted by armed soldiers and officers. It was not customary to send Dostoevsky on such expeditions—he was always secretly protected by his officers—but this time he was glad enough to take advantage of the pretext, and he travelled some hundreds of versts seated upon the ropes which he was supposed to be guarding. Maria Dmitrievna received him with open arms and quickly regained her old influence over him, which had been somewhat weakened by a long separation. Touched by her complaints, her misfortunes, and her threats of suicide, Dostoevsky forgot the counsels of his friends; he asked her to marry him, promising to protect her and to love her little Paul. Maria Dmitrievna accepted his offer eagerly. My father returned to Semipalatinsk in his wagon, and asked his commanding officer's permission to get married. It was granted, together with leave for a few weeks. He returned to Kusnetzk more comfortably, in a good post-chaise this time, meaning to bring back in it the new Madame Dostoevsky and his future stepson. My father's leave was limited—the Government did not like to have its political prisoners circulating freely in the country—and he was obliged to be married a few days after his arrival at Kusnetzk. How joyful he was as he went to church! Happiness seemed at last about to smile on him, fate was about to compensate him for all his sufferings by giving him a gentle and loving wife, who would perhaps make him a father. While Dostoevsky was dreaming thus, of what was his bride thinking? The night before her marriage Maria Dmitrievna had spent with her lover, a handsome young tutor, whom she had discovered on her arrival at Kusnetzk, and whose mistress she had long been in secret.[1]

This woman was the daughter of one of Napoleon's Mamelukes, who had been taken prisoner during the retreat from Moscow, and brought to Astrakhan on the Caspian Sea, where he changed his name and his religion in order to marry a young girl of good family who had fallen desperately in love with him. She made him join the Russian army; he eventually became a colonel, and commanded a regiment in some provincial town. My father never knew him. By some freak of Nature, Maria Dmitrievna inherited only the Russian type of her mother. I have seen her portrait. Nothing about her betrayed her Oriental origin. On

---

1. It is probable that the Kusnetzk suitor, whose name I do not know, had broken off his engagement with Maria Dmitrievna on discovering her clandestine intrigue with the tutor. My father, who had only paid two short visits to Kusnetzk and knew no one there, had no opportunity of discovering the liaison, more especially as Maria Dmitrievna always played the part of the serious and virtuous woman in his presence.

the other hand, her son Paul, whom I knew later, was almost a mulatto. He had a yellow skin, black glossy hair, rolled his eyes as negroes do, gesticulated extravagantly, and was malicious, stupid and insolent.

At the time of his mother's second marriage he was a pretty, lively little boy whom my father petted to please Maria Dmitrievna. Dostoevsky had no suspicion of the African origin of his wife, who concealed it carefully; he only discovered it much later. Cunning like all the women of her race, she played the model wife, gathered all the lettered society of Semipalatinsk round her and organised a kind of literary *salon*. She passed herself off as a Frenchwoman, spoke French as if it had been her mother-tongue, and was a great reader. She had been well educated in a Government establishment for the daughters of the nobility. The society of Semipalatinsk took the newly married Madame Dostoevsky for a woman of high character. Baron Wrangel speaks of her with respect in his memoirs, and says she was charming. And she continued to pay secret evening visits to her little tutor, who had followed her to Semipalatinsk. It amused her vastly to deceive the world and her poor dreamer of a husband. Dostoevsky knew the young man, as one knows every one in a small town. But the handsome youth was so perfectly insignificant that it never entered my father's head to suspect a rival in him. He thought Maria Dmitrievna a faithful wife, entirely devoted to him. She had, however, a terrible temper, and gave way to sudden paroxysms of fury. My father attributed these to her bad health—she was somewhat consumptive—and forgave the violent scenes she was constantly making. She was a good housekeeper, and knew how to make a home comfortable. After the horrors of his prison, his house seemed a perfect paradise to Dostoevsky. In spite of the forebodings of his friends and relatives, marriage suited him. He put on flesh, became more cheerful, and seemed happy. The Semipalatinsk photograph mentioned above shows us a man full of strength, life and energy. It is not in the least like the portrait of Prince Mishkin in *The Idiot*, nor that of the convict-prophet in Nekrassov's poem. My father's epilepsy, which had at last declared itself, had calmed his nerves. He suffered greatly during his attacks, but on the other hand his mind was calmer and more lucid when they passed off. The sharp, dry, healthy air of Siberia, military service, which took the place of gymnastics, the peaceful life of a little provincial town, all combined to improve Dostoevsky's health. As always, he was absorbed by his novels. He performed his military duties conscientiously, but his heart was not in them. My father was longing for the moment when he might resign his commission and become a free and independent writer once more. During his sojourn at Semipalatinsk, Dostoevsky wrote two books, *The Uncle's Dream* and *Selo Stepantchikovo*. The heroes of these new novels are no longer cosmopolites, as in his earlier works. They bear no resemblance to the pallid citizens of Petersburg; they inhabit the country or small provincial towns, they are very Russian and very vital. Reading these first works written after his release, we see that Dostoevsky had finally broken with the tradition of Gogol, and had returned to the idea of *The Double*. In these new novels he paints abnormal types; Prince K., a degenerate, who becomes imbecile, and Foma Opiskin, an adventurer who possesses a great hypnotic power. The books are gay and ironical, whereas those written before the author's imprisonment are nearly all melodramatic. It is evident that Dostoevsky had arrived at that period of his existence when man no longer takes a tragic view of life, when he can jest a little at it, when he can look at it with a certain detachment, beginning to understand that it is but an episode in the long series of existences which the soul has to pass through. This irony increases as Dostoevsky's talent matures, and as he learns to know men and life more fully. It never becomes bitter or malicious, for love of humanity, and admiration for the Christian fraternity of the Gospel grows stronger and ever stronger in his heart.

My father received permission to publish these two novels, but he was obliged to leave the manuscript of *The House of the Dead* in his portfolio. He had been working at it for a long time, fully conscious of its value, but it was impossible to publish it on account of the Censorship, which was very strict in all matters relating to the prisons. He was now at liberty to live in any town in Siberia, but not to go back to Russia. Nevertheless, my father's one idea was to return to Petersburg, a place he hated. The nomad intellectuals of Lithuania have this strange peculiarity; they cannot live in the country or in the provinces; they must be on the spot where they can feel the pulses of civilisation beating most strongly. The great reforms which shed lustre on the reign of Alexander II were in preparation at Petersburg. My father longed to be there amongst the other Russian writers. He feared that if he remained in Siberia he would not be in touch with the new ideas which were agitating our country. He sought feverishly for means of obtaining permission to return to Russia. He wrote innumerable letters, applied to all his former friends, and at last discovered a protector. The Crimean War had just come to an end. Everybody was talking of General Todleben, who had greatly distinguished himself, and had been created a Count. My father remembered the brothers Todleben, whom he had known at

the School of Engineers. He wrote to them, begging them to intercede
with the Government on his behalf. The Todlebens remembered their
former comrade very well. He had never seemed so strange to them as
to his Russian schoolfellows; they came from Courland, and their ancestors must have often encountered those of Dostoevsky on the banks
of the Niemen. They begged their distinguished brother to plead my
father's cause. The Russian Government could refuse nothing to Count
Todleben, whom every one called "The Defender of Sebastopol." Dostoevsky soon received permission to live anywhere in Russia, with the
exception of the two capital cities. My father chose the town of Tver on
the Volga, a station on the railway line between Petersburg and Moscow.
He resigned his commission joyfully, said farewell to his comrades and
to the kindly people of Semipalatinsk who had received him so hospitably, and set out for Russia with his wife and stepson. To make this
long journey Dostoevsky bought a carriage which he sold on arriving
at Tver; this was the way in which people travelled in those days. How
happy he was as he traversed, free and independent, the road which ten
years before he had passed along in custody of a police officer. He was
about to see his brother Mihail again, to return to that literary world
where he would be able to exchange ideas with his friends, to present his
dear wife, who loved him, to his family. While Dostoevsky was dreaming thus in his post-chaise, the handsome tutor, whom his mistress was
bringing along with her like a pet dog, was following them in a *britshka*
one stage behind. At every halt she left him a hasty love-letter, informing him where they were to stay for the night, and ordering him to halt
at the preceding station and not to overtake them. She must have been
immensely amused on the way to note the naïve delight of her poor
romantic husband.

When he was settled at Tver, my father soon became intimate with
Count Baranov, the Governor. His wife, *née* Vassiletchikov, was a cousin
of Count Sollohub, the writer, who had formerly had a literary *salon* in
Petersburg. My father, who had been one of the habitués of this *salon*
had been presented to Mlle. Vassiletchikov at the time of the success
of his *Poor Folks*. She had never forgotten him, and when he arrived at
Tver, she hastened to renew their acquaintance. She often invited him
to her house, and induced her husband to interest himself in my father's
affairs. Count Baranov did his utmost to obtain permission for Dostoevsky to live at Petersburg. Having heard that the Minister of Police,
Prince Dolgoruky, was opposed to this, the Count advised my father
to write a letter to the Emperor. Like many other enthusiasts, Dostoev-

sky was at this time full of admiration for Alexander II. He composed some verses on the occasion of his coronation, and hoped great things from his reign. He wrote a simple and dignified letter to the Emperor, recounting the miseries of his life, and asked his leave to return to Petersburg. The letter pleased the Emperor and he granted my father's request. Happy at the thought of being able at last to live in the literary world near his brother Mihail, Dostoevsky at once set out for Petersburg with his wife and his stepson, whom he placed in a cadet school. He soon obtained permission to publish *The House of the Dead*. The times of Nicolas I were at an end. Those in power no longer feared the light; on the contrary, they sought it. The book had an immense success, and placed Dostoevsky in the first rank of Russian writers. He never lost this proud position; each new work tended to confirm it. Life began to smile on my father. But fate had a new and cruel trial in store for him.

The change of climate had not suited Maria Dmitrievna. The damp, marshy climate of Petersburg developed the disease which had long been lying in wait for her. In great alarm, she returned to Tver, which is healthier. It was too late; the malady followed its normal course, and in a few months she had become unrecognisable. This woman, coughing and spitting blood, soon disgusted her young lover, who had hitherto followed her everywhere. He fled from Tver, leaving no address. This desertion infuriated Maria Dmitrievna. My father had remained at Petersburg, busy with the publication of his novel, but he often went to visit his wife at Tver. In one of the scenes she made for his benefit, she confessed everything, describing her love-affair with the young tutor in great detail. With a refinement of cruelty she told Dostoevsky how much it had amused them to laugh at the deceived husband, and declared that she had never loved him and had married him for mercenary motives. "No self-respecting woman," said this hussy, "could love a man who had worked for four years in a prison as the companion of thieves and murderers."

My poor father listened with anguish to the outpourings of his wife. This, then, was the love and happiness in which he had been believing for years! It was this fury whom he had cherished as a loving and faithful wife! He turned from Maria Dmitrievna with horror, left her, and fled to Petersburg, seeking consolation from his brother, and among his nephews and nieces. He had arrived at the age of forty without having ever been loved. "No woman could love a convict," he said to himself, remembering the ignoble words of his wife. It was a thought worthy of the daughter of a slave, which could find no echo in the heart of a noble-minded European. But Dostoevsky knew little of women at this period of his life. The thought that he would never have children or a home made him very unhappy. He put all his bitterness as a betrayed husband into the novel *The Eternal Husband*, which he wrote later. It is curious to note that he painted the hero of this story as a contemptible creature, old, ugly, vulgar and ridiculous. It is possible that he despised himself for his credulity and simplicity, for not having discovered the intrigue and punished the treacherous lovers. In spite of his sufferings and despair, Dostoevsky continued to send money to Maria Dmitrievna, placed confidential servants with her, wrote to his sisters at Moscow, begging them to visit her at Tver, and later went himself several times to see if his wife had all she needed. Their marriage was shattered, but the sense of duty towards her who bore his name remained strong in Dostoevsky's Lithuanian heart. Maria Dmitrievna was not softened by this generosity. She hated my father with the rancour of a true negress. Those who nursed her told later how she would pass long hours motionless in an arm-chair, lost in painful meditation. She would get up and walk feverishly through her rooms. In the drawing-room she would stand in front of Dostoevsky's portrait, staring at it, shaking her fist at it, and exclaiming: "Convict, miserable convict!" She hated her first husband too, and spoke of him contemptuously. She hated her son Paul and refused to see him. She had always been very ambitious, and she had greatly desired to place her son in the most aristocratic school in Petersburg. My father did what he could, but only succeeded in obtaining a nomination for the Cadet Corps, to which the boy was entitled as the son of an officer. Seeing that Paul was idle and would not work, Maria Dmitrievna was deeply mortified, and this mortification changed to hatred. Dostoevsky interceded in vain for the child; his mother refused to see him, and my father was obliged to send him to spend his holidays with my uncle Mihail's family.

X

A Passionate Episode

O n his return from Siberia my father found his brother Mihail surrounded by a group of remarkable young writers. My uncle had distinguished himself in Russian literature by his excellent translations of Goethe and Schiller, and he loved to gather the authors of the period round him in his house. Seeing this, my father proposed that he should edit a newspaper. He was burning to reveal to our intellectuals the great Russian Idea which he had discovered in prison, but to which Russian society was deaf and blind. The paper was christened *Vremya* (Time), and the work was divided between the two brothers; my uncle undertook the editorial and financial business, my father the literary interests. He published his novels and his critical articles in *Vremya*. The paper was very successful; the new idea pleased its readers. The brothers invited the collaboration of very good writers, earnest men who appreciated my father. Instead of jeering at him, like his youthful literary associates of old, they became his friends and admirers. Two among them deserve special mention: the poet Apollo Maikov (whom Dostoevsky had known shortly before his imprisonment), and the philosopher Nicolaï Strahoff. Both remained faithful to Dostoevsky all his life and were with him at his death.

After *The House of the Dead* my father published *The Insulted and Injured*, his first long novel, which also had a great success. Dostoevsky was much courted and complimented in the literary *salons* of Petersburg, which he again began to frequent. He also appeared in public. During his sojourn in Siberia, the Petersburg students, male and female, began to play an important part in Russian literature. In order to help their poorer comrades, they organised literary evenings, at which famous writers read extracts from their own works. The students rewarded them with frantic applause, and advertised them enormously, a service the ambitious sought to obtain by flattering the young people. My father was not of the number; he never flattered the students; on the contrary, he never hesitated to tell them unpleasant truths. But the students respected him for it, and applauded him more than any of the other writers. Dostoevsky's popularity was remarked by a young girl named Pauline N. She represented the curious type of the "eternal student," which exists only in Russia. Pauline N. came from one of the Russian provinces, where she had rich relations; they allowed her enough money to live comfortably in Petersburg. Every autumn regularly she enrolled herself as a student at the University,[1] but she never presented herself for examination, and pursued no course of study. However, she frequented the University assiduously, flirting with the students, visiting them in their rooms, preventing them from working, inciting them to revolt, getting them to sign protests, and taking part in all political manifestations, when she would march at the head of the students, carrying a red flag, singing the *Marseillaise*, abusing and provoking the Cossacks, and beating the horses of the police. She in her turn was beaten by the police, and would spend the night in a police cell. On her return to the University she was borne aloft in triumph by the students, and acclaimed as the glorious victim of "Tsarism." Pauline attended all the balls and all the literary soirées given by the students, danced and applauded with them and shared all the new ideas which were agitating youthful minds. Free love was then fashionable. Young and attractive, Pauline adopted this new fashion ardently, passing from one student to another, and serving Venus in the belief that she was serving the cause of European civilisation. Seeing Dostoevsky's success, she hastened to share this latest passion of the students. She hovered about my father, making advances which he did not notice. She then wrote him a declaration of love. Her letter was preserved among my father's papers; it is simple, naïve and poetic. She might have been some timid young girl, dazzled by the genius of the great writer. Dostoevsky read the letter with emotion. It came at a moment when he needed love most bitterly. His heart was torn by the treachery of his wife; he despised himself as a ridiculous dupe; and now a young girl, fresh and beautiful, offered him her heart. His wife had been wrong then! He might still be loved, even after having worked in prison with thieves and murderers. Dostoevsky grasped at the consolation offered him by fate. He had no idea of Pauline's easy morals. My father knew the lives of the students only from the rostrum whence he addressed them. They surrounded him in a respectful throng, talking

---

1. At this period there were no higher courses for young girls in Russia. The Government allowed them provisionally to study at the University together with the male students.

of God, of the fatherland, of civilisation. The idea of initiating this distinguished writer, revered by all, into the squalid details of their private conduct was never entertained. Later, if they noticed Dostoevsky's love for Pauline they were careful not to enlighten him as to her character. He took Pauline for a young provincial, intoxicated by the exaggerated ideas of feminine liberty which were then reigning in Russia. He knew that Maria Dmitrievna was given up by the doctors, and that in a few months he would be free to marry Pauline. He had not the strength to wait, to repulse this young love, which offered itself freely, careless of the world and its conventions. He was forty years old, and no woman had ever loved him...

The lovers decided to spend their honeymoon abroad. My father had long been dreaming of a journey in Europe. Ivan Karamazow, the portrait of my father at twenty, also dreams of foreign travel. According to him, Europe is merely a vast cemetery; but he wished to make obeisance at the tombs of the mighty dead. Now that Dostoevsky had at last money enough, he hastened to realise this dream of long standing. The date of departure drew near; at the last moment my father was detained in Petersburg by business connected with the newspaper *Vremya*. My uncle Mihail's drinking bouts were becoming more and more frequent, and Dostoevsky was obliged to look after the whole of the work. Pauline started alone, promising to await him in Paris. A fortnight later he received a letter from her, in which she informed him that she loved a Frenchman whose acquaintance she had just made in Paris. "All is over between you and me!" she wrote to my father. "It is your fault: why did you leave me so long alone?" After reading this letter, Dostoevsky rushed off to Paris like a madman. He, on this his first journey in Europe, passed through Berlin and Cologne without seeing them. Later, when he visited the banks of the Rhine again, he begged pardon of the Cathedral of Cologne for not having noticed its beauty. Pauline received him coldly; she declared that she had found her ideal, that she did not intend to return to Russia, that her French lover adored her and made her perfectly happy. My father always respected the liberty of others, and made no distinction on this point between men and women. Pauline was not his wife. She had made no vows; she had given herself freely and therefore was free to take back her gift. My father accepted her decision and made no further attempt to see her or speak to her. Feeling that there was nothing for him to do in Paris, he went to London to see Alexander Herzen. In those days people went to England to see Herzen just as later they went to Yasnaïa Poliana to see Tolstoy. My father was far from sharing Herzen's revolutionary ideas. But he was interested in the man, and he took this opportunity of making his acquaintance. He found London much more absorbing than Paris. He stayed there some time, studying it thoroughly, and was enthusiastic over the beauty of young Englishwomen. Later, in his reminiscences of travel, he says that they represent the most perfect type of feminine beauty. This admiration of Dostoevsky's for young Englishwomen is very significant. The Russians who visit Europe are, as a rule, more attracted by French, Italian, Spanish and Hungarian women. Englishwomen generally leave them cold; my countrymen consider them "too thin." Dostoevsky's taste was evidently less Oriental, and the beauty of young Englishwomen touched some Norman chord in his Lithuanian heart.[1]

My father at last went back to Paris, and having heard that his friend, Nicolas Strahoff, was also going abroad, he arranged to meet him at Geneva, and proposed that they should make a tour in Italy together. There is a curious phrase in this letter: "We will walk together in Rome, and, who knows, perhaps we may caress some young Venetian in a gondola." Such phrases are extremely rare in my father's letters. It is evident that at this period Dostoevsky was longing for a romance of some sort with a woman to rehabilitate himself in his own eyes, to prove that he too could be loved. And yet there was no "young Venetian in a gondola" during this journey of the two friends; Dostoevsky's heart was with Pauline. Yet he refused to return with Strahoff to Paris, where he might have encountered her, and went back alone to Russia. He described his impressions of this first journey to Europe in *Vremya*.

Towards the spring, Pauline wrote to him from Paris, and confided her woes to him. Her French lover was unfaithful to her, but she had not the strength to leave him. She implored my father to come to her in Paris. Finding that Dostoevsky hesitated to take this journey, Pauline threatened to commit suicide, the favourite threat of Russian women. Much alarmed, he at last went to Paris and tried to make the forsaken fair one listen to reason. Finding Dostoevsky too cold, Pauline had recourse to heroic measures. One morning she arrived at my father's bedside at seven o'clock, and brandishing an enormous knife she had just bought, she declared that her French lover was a scoundrel, and that she intended to punish him by plunging this knife into his breast; that she was on her

1. Dostoevsky made a curious prediction as to the future of England. He thought the English would eventually abandon the island of Great Britain. "If our sons do not witness the exodus of the English from Europe, our grandsons will," he prophesied.

way to him, but that she had wished to see my father first, to warn him of the crime she was about to commit. I do not know whether he was deceived by this vulgar melodrama. In any case, he advised her to leave her big knife in Paris, and to go to Germany with him. Pauline agreed; this was just what she wanted. They went to the Rhineland, and established themselves at Wiesbaden. There my father played roulette with passionate absorption, was delighted when he won, and experienced a despair hardly less delicious when he lost.[1] Later, they went on to Italy, which had fascinated my father before, and visited Rome and Naples. Pauline flirted with all the men they encountered, and caused her lover much anxiety. My father described this extraordinary journey later in *The Gambler.* He placed it in other surroundings, but gave the name of Pauline to the heroine of the novel.

 Considering this phase of Dostoevsky's life, we ask ourselves in amazement how it was that a man who had lived so irreproachably at twenty could have committed such follies at forty. It can only be explained by his abnormal physical development. At twenty my father was a timid schoolboy; at forty he passed through that youthful phase of irresponsibility, which most men experience. "He who has committed no follies at twenty will commit them at forty," says the proverb, which proves that this curious transposition of ages is not so rare as we suppose. In this escapade of Dostoevsky's there was the revolt of an honest man, of a husband who had been faithful to his wife, while she had been laughing at him with her lover. My father apparently wished to demonstrate to himself that he too could be unfaithful to his wife, lead the light life of other men, play with love, and amuse himself with pretty girls. There are many indications that this was the case. In *The Gambler*, for instance, Dostoevsky depicts himself in the character of a tutor. Rejected by the young girl he loves, this tutor goes at once in search of a courtesan whom he despises, and travels with her to Paris, in order to avenge himself on the young girl, whom he nevertheless continues to love.

 But apart from the vengeance of a deceived husband, there was also real passion in this romance of Dostoevsky's. Hear the hero of *The Gambler* speaking of Pauline: "There were moments when I would have given half my life to be able to strangle her. I swear that could I have plunged a knife into her breast I would have done so exultantly. And yet I swear,

---

1. Dostoevsky had made acquaintance with roulette during his first journey to Europe, and even won a considerable sum of money. At first gambling did not attract him much. It was not until his second visit with Pauline that he developed a passion for roulette.

too, by all that is sacred to me, if, at the summit of the Schlangenberg she had said to me: 'Throw yourself over that precipice,' I would have obeyed her, and even obeyed her joyfully."

Yet while avenging himself with Pauline on Maria Dmitrievna, Dostoevsky took all possible precautions to prevent his sick wife from hearing anything of the matter. He wanted to restore his own self-respect, but he did not wish to inflict pain on the unhappy sufferer. His precautions were so effectual, that only his relations and a few intimate friends knew anything of this episode. But it explains the characters of many of Dostoevsky's capricious and fantastic heroines. Aglac in *The Idiot*, Lisa in *The Possessed*, Grushcnka in the *Brothers Karamazov* and several others arc more or less Paulines. It is in this love-story of my father's, I think, that we shall find the explanation of the strange hatred-love of Rogogin for Nastasia Philipovna.

Dostoevsky returned to Petersburg in the autumn and learned that his wife's illness had reached its final stage. Full of pity for the unhappy woman,[1] my father forgot his anger, started for Tver, and persuaded his wife to come with him to Moscow, where she could have the best medical care. Maria Dmitrievna's agony lasted all the winter. My father remained with her and tended her unceasingly. He went out very little, for he was engrossed by his novel, *Crime and Punishment*, which he was writing at this time. When Maria Dmitrievna died in the spring, Dostoevsky wrote a few letters to his friends to announce her death, mentioning her with respect. He admitted that he had not been happy with her, but pretended that she had loved him in spite of their disagreements. The honour of his name was always dear to Dostoevsky, and led him to conceal his wife's treachery from his friends. Only his relatives knew the truth of this sad story. My father was further anxious to hide the truth on account of his stepson Paul, whom he had brought up in sentiments of respect for his dead parents. I remember on one occasion at a family dinner Paul Issaïeff spoke contemptuously of his father, declaring that he had been nothing but a "wet rag" in the hands of his wife. Dostoevsky became very angry; he defended the memory of Captain Issaïeff, and forbade his stepson ever to speak of his parents in such a manner.

As I have already said, Dostoevsky had intended to marry Pauline on the death of his wife. But since their travels in Europe his ideas about his mistress had undergone a change. Moreover, Pauline was not at all

---

1. Throughout his liaison with Pauline, Dostoevsky never ceased to provide for his sick wife. When he was travelling in Italy, he often wrote to his brother Mihail, requesting him to send her the money due to him for articles in *Vremya*.

inclined towards this marriage, and wished to keep her liberty as a pretty girl. It was not my father she cared for, but his literary fame, and, above all, his success with the students. Directly Dostoevsky ceased to be the fashion, Pauline abandoned him. My father soon began the publication of *Crime and Punishment*. As before, the critics fell upon the first chapters of this masterpiece, and barked their loudest. One of them announced to the public that Dostoevsky had insulted the Russian student in the person of Raskolnikov.[1]

This absurdity, like most absurdities, had a great success in Petersburg. The students who had been Dostoevsky's fervent admirers turned against him to a man. Seeing that my father was no longer popular, Pauline did not want him any more. She declared that she could not forgive his outrage on the Russian student, a being sacred in her eyes, and she broke with him. My father did not remonstrate; he had no longer any illusions as to this light of love.

1. In his celebrated work Dostoevsky showed most striking clairvoyance. A few days before the publication of the first.

XI

A Literary Friendship

With Pauline N. the period of passion in Dostoevsky's life closed. It lasted altogether but ten years, from the age of thirty-three to that of forty-three. The African love of Maria Dmitrievna and the somewhat Oriental passion of Pauline N. had left no very pleasant memories, and in his maturity my father returned to the Lithuanian ideals of his forefathers. He began to seek for a pure and chaste young girl, a virtuous woman, who would be a faithful life companion. His two later romances were romances of the affections, and not of the senses. Let us consider the first of these.

At the period in question a rich landowner, M. Korvin-Kronkovsky, was living in the heart of Lithuania. He belonged to the Lithuanian nobility, and claimed to be a descendant of Corvinus, the somewhat mythical King of heathen Lithuania. He was married and had two daughters whom he had educated very carefully. The younger of the two, Sophie, afterwards married M. Kovalevsky, and was Professor of Mathematics at the University of Stockholm, the first woman who had been admitted to such a position.[1] The elder, Anna, a pretty girl of nineteen, preferred literature. She was a great admirer of my father's, and had read all his works. The novel *Crime and Punishment* made a great impression upon her. She wrote Dostoevsky a long letter about it which pleased him very much. He replied promptly, and a correspondence followed, which extended over some months. Anna then begged her father to take her to Petersburg that she might make the acquaintance of her favourite writer. The whole family arrived in Petersburg and took a furnished flat. They at once invited my father to visit them, and were charming to him. Dostoevsky was often at their hospitable house, and finally made an offer of marriage to Anna Kronkovsky. He was a widower, and tired of living alone. Maria Dmitrievna had accustomed him to a well-kept home and

---

1. At the time of which I am writing Sophie was but fourteen, and she played no part in Dostoevsky's life.

the material comfort only a woman can give to a house. He longed for children, and recognised with terror that he was leaving the years of his youth behind him. He was not in love with Anna, but he liked her as a well-brought-up, lively and amiable girl. Her Lithuanian family pleased him. Mlle. Kronkovsky, on her side, did not love my father, but she had a great admiration for his talent. She consented joyfully to become his wife, but their engagement was, nevertheless, very brief. Their political opinions differed widely. Dostoevsky was becoming more and more a Russian patriot and a monarchist; Anna Kronkovsky was a cosmopolite and an anarchist. As long as they talked literature, all was well; but as soon as they got on to political questions they began to quarrel and dispute. This often happens in Russia, where people have not yet learnt to talk politics calmly. The betrothed couple saw in time that their marriage would be an inferno, and they determined to break off their engagement. But they were not so ready to give up their friendship. After returning to the country, Anna continued to write to my father, and he replied as before. The following winter the Kronkovskys came to Petersburg again, and Dostoevsky was once more a frequent visitor at their house. My father's affection for Mlle. Kronkovsky was at bottom but a literary friendship as necessary to a writer as love itself. When Dostoevsky became engaged to my mother, Anna Kronkovsky was the first to congratulate him heartily. Shortly after his marriage, she went abroad with her parents and met in Switzerland a Frenchman, M. J., an anarchist like herself. They spent delightful hours together, destroying the whole world and reconstructing it on more harmonious lines. This occupation was so congenial to both that they ended by marrying. An opportunity for putting their anarchist theories into practice soon presented itself. The Franco-Prussian war broke out, Paris was besieged, and the Commune established.

The two J.'s took an active part in its proceedings.

After having set fire to a precious art collection, which it was apparently necessary to destroy for the good of humanity, Madame J. fled from Paris. Her husband was arrested and imprisoned. Moved by the despair of his daughter, who adored her husband, M. Korvin-Kronkovsky sold part of his estate and went to Paris, where he managed to procure his son-in-law's escape by spending 100,000 francs. For a long time the couple could not return to France. They settled at Petersburg, where Madame J. continued to be my father's friend. Out of consideration for his former *fiancée*, Dostoevsky received her Communard husband cordially, though he had nothing in common with him. Madame J. in her turn became a friend of my mother's. Her only son, Georges J. was one of my childish play fellows.

I think my father portrayed Mlle. Kronkovsky in Katia, Dmitri Karamazov's *fiancée*. Katia is not Russian; she is a true Lithuanian girl, proud, chaste, and holding lofty ideas as to family honour, sacrificing herself to save that of her father, faithful to her engagement and to her mission of saving Dmitri Karamazov by correcting the faults of his character. Russian girls are much simpler. Oriental passion or Slav pity triumphs over all other considerations with them.

XII

Dostoevsky as Head of His Family

About the time of the publication of my father's famous novel. *Crime and Punishment*, my uncle Mihail's affairs began to be much involved. The publication of the newspaper *Vremya* was prohibited on account of a political article which had been misunderstood by the Censorship. A few months later, Mihail Dostoevsky obtained permission to bring out a new journal under the name *Epoha*, but, as often happens in Russia, the second venture was not so successful as the first, though my uncle secured the collaboration of the same writers. *Epoha* appeared for a few months, and finally became extinct for want of readers. It was a terrible blow for Mihail Dostoevsky. His health, already undermined by alcoholism, gave way, and he died after a short illness. Like most of his compatriots, my uncle had lived lavishly, and had saved nothing, hoping to leave his children a newspaper which would bring in a handsome income. His sons were still very young, and had not finished their education. They could not therefore help their mother. My uncle left large debts. According to Russian law, these debts were cancelled by his death; his family, having inherited nothing, were not obliged to pay them. Every one was therefore greatly astonished when my father informed Mihail Dostoevsky's creditors that he considered himself responsible for all his brother's liabilities, and that he was going henceforth to work hard in order to pay them off as soon as possible. He further promised his sister-in-law to support her and her four children until her sons could earn their living. My father's friends were very much alarmed when they heard of his resolve; they did their best to dissuade him from paying his brother's debts, for which he was not legally responsible. Dostoevsky thought they were urging him to commit an infamous action. They failed to understand each other. My father's literary comrades argued as Russians, Dostoevsky thought as a Lithuanian. Much as he had learnt to admire Russia, he continued to live after the Lithuanian tradition. Reverence for the family was one of the ideas derived by his forefathers from the Teutonic Knights. In their more chivalrous age the family was a larger conception than with us. All who bore the same name were considered as members, and were responsible one for the other. The honour of the family was their supreme ideal; men and women lived entirely for this. On the death of the father the eldest son became the head of the family and ruled it. In the event of his premature death, the second son took his place and inherited all his obligations. Not for nothing did Dostoevsky admire the Gothic beauty of Cologne Cathedral; his own soul was Gothic! He thought it quite a matter of course that he should sacrifice himself for his brother's family, and assume responsibility for all his debts. On their side, my father's friends naturally looked upon such conduct as fantastic, for in the Byzantine civilisation of Russia the idea of the family is almost nonexistent. People exert themselves more or less on behalf of their children, but they are generally indifferent to the fate of their brothers and sisters. "I did not incur these debts, why should I pay them?" every Russian would have said in my father's place, and every Russian would have considered his determination romantic to the verge of absurdity. Far from thinking himself in any way ridiculous, my father took his duties as head of the family very seriously. If he sacrificed his life to the memory of his brother Mihail, he expected that his nephews and nieces, for their part, should look up to him as their guide and protector and follow his advice. This attitude exasperated my uncle's children. They were quite ready to live at their uncle's expense, but were by no means inclined to obey him. They laughed at Dostoevsky behind his back, and deceived him. One of his nieces, his favourite, had a student lover, a somewhat insignificant young man, who hated Dostoevsky, "because he had insulted the Russian student in the person of Raskolnikov." One day when discussing political questions, he spoke most disrespectfully to my father. Dostoevsky was very angry, and desired his sister-in-law not to receive the impertinent youth at her house in future. They pretended to obey, but they entertained the young man secretly. As soon as he had finished his studies at the University and obtained a post in one of the Ministries, he hastened to marry my cousin. The ungrateful girl took a delight in getting married clandestinely, without inviting my father to the wedding, at a time when Dostoevsky was working like a slave to support her family. When she met him later at her mother's house, the bride laughed in his face, and treated him as an old imbecile. My father was cut to the heart by this ingratitude. He loved his niece Marie as if she had been his own daughter, caressing and amusing her when she was little, and later showing great pride in her musical talent[1] and in her girlish triumphs. Marie's husband soon realised the mistake he had made in quarrelling with the distinguished writer. Six or seven years later, when my parents came back from abroad, he tried to re-establish friendly relations, and to interest my father in his numerous children. Dostoevsky consented to receive his niece, but he could not give her back his affection, which was dead.

The second girl of the family grieved Dostoevsky still more deeply. She fell in love with a scientist of some repute, who had been forsaken by his wife. This woman, although she loved another man, would never agree to a divorce, which would have released her injured husband.[2] My cousin braved public opinion and became the mistress, or, in the language of the day, "the civil wife" of the *savant*, who could not marry her. She lived with him till his death, over twenty years, and was looked upon by all his friends as his actual wife. In spite of the serious character of this connection, my father could never forgive it. It took place a few years after the marriage of my parents, and my mother told me later that Dostoevsky sobbed like a child on hearing of his niece's "dishonour." "How could she dare to disgrace our fair name?" repeated my father, weeping bitterly. He forbade my mother to have any dealings with the culprit, and I never saw that cousin.

As may be supposed, my father was not happy among people so incapable of understanding him. He was one of those men, rare enough in these days, who die brokenhearted if their sons disgrace themselves, or their daughters turn out badly. The sentiment of honour dominated all others with him. His conduct was governed by the chivalrous ideas of his ancestors, whereas his nephews and nieces had forgotten the European culture of their family, and preferred the easy morality of the semi-Oriental civilisation of Russia. They had, moreover, inherited from their mother that hardness of heart which is often to be found among the Germans of the Baltic Provinces.

Dostoevsky had not only to provide for his brother's family, but for a younger brother, Nicolai, an unhappy dipsomaniac. My father pitied him greatly, and was always good to him, though he never had the strong affection for Nicolai that he had felt for Mihail,. Nicolai was too uninteresting; he thought only of his bottle. Dostoevsky also helped his

1. My cousin was one of Anton Rubinstein's best pupils. Very often when my father was invited to read at a literary and musical party, he begged to be allowed to bring her with him, and took more pleasure in her success than in his own.
2. At this time it was very difficult to obtain a divorce in Russia. It could not be granted without the mutual consent of the parties.

sister Alexandra, the only one of his three sisters who lived in Petersburg; her invalid husband was unable to work. She showed no gratitude for his generosity, and was always quarrelling with him. Indeed, the behaviour of the whole family was abnormal. Instead of being proud to have a genius for their brother, they hated him because he had made his name famous. My uncle Andrey was the only one who was proud of his brother's literary gifts; but he lived in the country and very rarely came to Petersburg.

Odious as Dostoevsky's relations were, he forgave them much in memory of his mother, and of their common recollections of childhood and youth. He found it harder to endure the malice and perversity of his stepson, Paul Issaïeff, to whom he was bound by no tie of blood. Idle and stupid, Paul had never worked at the military school where Dostoevsky had placed him, and the school authorities had finally sent him away. This grandson of a slave fell a victim to his stepfather's literary glory; his head was turned by the success of Dostoevsky's novels. His arrogance and conceit were no less marked than my father's modesty and simplicity. He treated every one superciliously, and talked unceasingly of his "papa," the famous novelist, though he was very insolent to his stepfather. He thought it unnecessary to study and exert himself; his "papa" would give him money, and he had no hesitation in asking for it. Dostoevsky had not brought up his stepson judiciously.

Absorbed in his novels and his journalistic work, he was unable to give much time to little Paul, and seeing that Maria Dmitrievna was cruel and unjust to the child, he felt a great pity for the fatherless boy, and spoilt him. He gave him too many dainties and toys, and, later, much more pocket money than was usual for boys of his age. He thus accustomed him to idleness and luxury, and Paul Issaïeff was never able to correct his faults. Dostoevsky now recognised that he had brought the boy up unwisely. "Another stepfather would have been stricter, and would have made Paul a man capable of serving his country," he would say sadly to his friends, and he kept the good-for-nothing lad with him as a punishment sent by heaven for a neglected duty.

When his Petersburg relatives tried him too severely, Dostoevsky would go to Moscow to rest in the home of his sister Vera, who had married a native of Moscow, and had a large family. These children were simpler and less overbearing than the nephews and nieces at Petersburg. They did not understand their uncle's genius, but they loved him for his gaiety and freshness of mind. He has described these young people under the name of the Zahlebin family in his novel *The Eternal Husband*. He himself figures in it as Veltshaninov, a man of forty, who loves the young and enjoys playing games, dancing and singing with them. Dostoevsky took a special interest in his young nieces. Marie was the favourite pupil of Nicolas Rubinstein, the Director of the Moscow Conservatoire. "If she had a head to match her fingers, what a great musician she might be!" he would often say of her. "The head" seems to have always kept her back, for Marie never became famous, though she was an accomplished pianist, and my father was never tired of listening to her brilliant playing. He was even fonder of his niece Sophie, an intelligent and serious girl. He believed, on what grounds I know not, that she had inherited his literary talent. My cousin Sophie talked a great deal about the novel she intended to write, but she could never find a subject to her taste. A few years after the marriage of my parents Sophie also married and gave up her literary ambitions.

This somewhat mediaeval love for all the members of my father's large family distressed my mother considerably. Brought up in the Russian tradition, she thought that all the money her husband earned should be devoted to his wife and children, the more so as she did her utmost to help him in his literary labours. She could not understand why my father would deprive her of necessaries in order to help some member of his family who did not love him and who was jealous of his fame. It was not until later, when my brothers and I were growing up, that all Dostoevsky's love was at last concentrated upon us. But even to the day of his death he helped his brother Nicolai and the worthless Paul Issaïeff.

XIII

My Mother's Family and Its Origin

D ostoevsky soon learned what it was to have debts. Scarcely had he signed the papers taking over his brother's liabilities when the creditors, who ought to have been grateful to him for recognising obligations which the law declared null and void, became extremely insolent, insisting on the immediate payment of their claims, and threatening to throw him into prison. To satisfy the most inexorable of them, Dostoevsky in his turn got into debt, undertook to pay interest at a very high rate, and fell into the clutches of an unscrupulous publisher, one Stellovsky, who bought the right to bring out a complete edition of his works for an absurdly small sum. Stellovsky further stipulated that my father should add to this edition a new novel of a certain number of pages. This was to be delivered on the 1st of November of the same year; if it should not be finished by that date, Dostoevsky would lose his copyright and his works would become the property of Stellovsky. Harassed by his brother Mihail's creditors, my father was forced to accept these barbarous conditions. He laid aside *Crime and Punishment*[1] the epilogue of which was not yet finished, and set to work feverishly to write *The Gambler.* He worked night and day till his eyesight was affected. He was obliged to consult an oculist, who forbade him to work, telling him that if he persisted in doing so he would become blind.

1. Stellovsky, who was a regular usurer, threatened to send my father to prison, and the police despatched one of their officers to inform him of these threats. My father received the man pleasantly and talked to him with so much candour of his unfortunate financial position that the police officer was deeply touched. Instead of helping Stellovsky to get my father imprisoned, he placed all his legal knowledge at Dostoevsky's service, to enable him to escape from the usurer's toils. He conceived a great admiration for my father, came to see him often and related to him many of the strange experiences he had had in the course of his career. It was thanks to this man that Dostoevsky was able to treat the police element in *Crime and Punishment* in so masterly a manner. This episode illustrates my father's manner of making friends, and shows us why he was able to transform the most savage convicts into faithful servants. It also indicates that the character of Prince Mishkin in *The Idiot*, who had the same faculty of transforming his enemies into friends, was really Dostoevsky's own portrait.

My father was in despair. It was then the beginning of October, and there was nothing but a rough copy of the novel. Dostoevsky's friends were very anxious about him, and tried to hit upon some way of helping him. "Why don't you engage a stenographer?" said A. Milinkoff to him. "You could have dictated your novel to him, and he could have written it for you." At this time stenography was still a novelty in Russia. A certain Ohlin had studied it abroad and had just started some courses, in which he hurriedly prepared the first Russian stenographers. My father went to see him, explained his case, and asked Ohlin to send him a good stenographer. "Unfortunately," said Ohlin, "I cannot recommend any of my pupils. I only began my classes in the spring, I had to close them for the summer holidays, and in these three months my pupils forgot the little they had learnt. I have only one good pupil, but she does not want money, and has taken up stenography rather as a pastime than as a means of livelihood. She is still quite a girl, and I don't know if her mother would allow her to go and work for a man. In any case, I will offer her your work tomorrow, and I will let you know what she says."

The young girl of whom Ohlin spoke became in time my mother. Before relating Dostoevsky's romance, I should like to say a few words about the family of his second wife, who was his guardian angel for the last fourteen years of his life.

My maternal grandfather, Grigor Ivanovitch Snitkin, was of Ukrainian origin. His ancestors were Cossacks who settled on the banks of the Dnieper near the town of Krementshug. They were called Snitko. When Ukrainia was annexed by Russia, they came to live in Petersburg, and to show their fidelity to the Russian Empire, they changed their Ukrainian name of Snitko into the Russian Snitkin. They did this in all sincerity, with no thought of flattery or servility. To them Ukrainia always remained Little Russia, the younger sister of the Great Russia which they admired with all their hearts. In Petersburg my great-grandparents continued to live after the Ukrainian tradition. At this time Ukrainia was under the influence of the Catholic priests, who were reputed the best instructors of youth in the country. Accordingly, my great-grandfather, although he belonged to the Orthodox Church, placed his son Grigor in the Jesuits' College which had just been opened in Petersburg.[1]

My grandfather received an excellent education there, such as the Jesuits generally give, but throughout his life he was the least Jesuitical of men. He was a true Slav: weak, timid, kind, sentimental and romantic. In his youth he had a grand passion for the celebrated Asenkova, the only clas-

1. It was subsequently closed by order of the Russian Government.

sical tragic actress we have had in Russia. He spent all his evenings at the theatre, and knew her monologues by heart. At this period the managers of the Imperial theatres used to allow the admirers of the artists to go and visit them behind the scenes. My grandfather's timid and respectful boyish passion pleased Asenkova, and she distinguished him in various little ways. It was to him she would hand her bouquet and her shawl when she went upon the stage to recite Racine and Corneille's beautiful verses; it was his arm she would take to return, trembling and exhausted, to her dressing-room, while the delighted audience applauded the beloved artist frantically. Other admirers sometimes begged for these privileges, but Asenkova always declared that they belonged to Grigor Ivanovitch. Poor Asenkova was very ill and weak; she was consumptive, and died very young. My grandfather's despair was unbounded; for years he could not enter the theatre, of which he had been a devotee. He never forgot the great actress, and often visited her grave. My mother told me that one day, when she was still a child, her father took her and her elder sister to the cemetery, made them kneel down by Asenkova's tomb, and said to them: "My children, pray to God for the repose of the soul of the greatest artist of our age."

I had supposed that this passion of my grandfather's was known only to our own family. I was therefore much astonished to find it in an historical journal, related by an old theatre-goer. He asserted that my grandfather's passion was not the love of a young man for a pretty woman, but admiration for the talent of a great artist. We must suppose that such a passion is very rare in Russia, or it would not have so impressed the old chronicler. He added a detail which was unknown to me. Shortly after the death of Asenkova one of her sisters made her *début* as a tragic actress. On the evening of her first performance, my grandfather reappeared in the theatre where he had not been seen since the death of his idol. He listened attentively to the young *débutante,* but her acting did not please him and he disappeared once more.

My grandfather was of a type which ages very early. When he was thirty-five he had lost all his hair and most of his teeth. His face was lined and wrinkled, and he looked like an old man. It was, however, at this age that he married under somewhat strange circumstances.

My maternal grandmother, Maria Anna Miltopeus, was a Swede of Finland. She said that her ancestors were English, but that in the seventeenth century they had left their country as a result of the religious troubles there. They settled in Sweden, married Swedes, and subsequently migrated to Finland, where they bought land. Their English name must have been Miltope—or perhaps Milton!—for the termination "us" is Swedish. In Sweden men belonging to the learned professions—writers, scientists, doctors and clergymen—habitually added the syllable to their names. I do not know what was the calling of my great-grandfather Miltopeus; I only know that he had rendered such services to his country that he was buried in the Cathedral of Abo, the Westminster Abbey of Finland, and a marble tomb was raised to his memory.

My grandmother lost her parents while she was still very young, and was brought up by her aunts, who did not make her happy. As she grew up, she became very beautiful, quite in the Norman style. Tall and slender, with features of classic regularity, a dazzling complexion, blue eyes, and magnificent golden hair, she was the admiration of all who saw her. Maria Anna had a lovely voice; her friends called her "the second Christine Nilsson." Their compliments turned her head, and she determined to become a professional singer. She went to Petersburg, where her brothers were serving as officers in one of the regiments of the Imperial Guard, and disclosed her project to them.

"You must be mad!" exclaimed they. "Do you want to have us turned out of our regiment? Our brother officers would not allow us to remain in it if you were to become a professional singer." There has always been a very severe etiquette on such points in Russia: an officer was obliged to resign before marrying an *artiste*. Very probably in my grandmother's time no Russian officer had any relations on the stage. Maria Anna sacrificed her artistic ambitions to the military career of her brothers. She did so the more readily because, soon after her arrival in Petersburg, she fell in love with one of their comrades, a young Swedish officer. They became engaged and were about to be married, when war broke out; the Swede was sent to the front, and was one of the first to fall. Maria Anna was too proud to show her grief, but her heart was broken. She went on living with her brothers, but was perfectly indifferent to men; they had ceased to exist for her. Her sisters-in-law found the presence of this beautiful girl, who was extremely headstrong and masterful, most irksome. In those days no single woman of good family could live alone; she was obliged to make her home with her relatives. The only way of getting rid of her was to marry her. Her sisters-in-law accordingly set to work; they gave parties and invited young men. The beautiful Swede, who sang with so much feeling, was greatly admired. Several suitors presented themselves. Maria Anna rejected them all. "My heart is broken," she said to her relations. "I cannot love any one." The sisters-in-law were annoyed at such speeches, which seemed to them absurd, and they tried to make their romantic kinswoman listen to reason. One day, when they were urging her to accept an advantageous offer, Maria Anna lost her temper and exclaimed: "Really your *protégé* disgusts me so, that if I were absolutely obliged to marry someone, I would rather take poor old Snitkin. He at least is sympathetic." Maria Anna attached no importance to these imprudent words. Her sisters-in-law fastened upon them eagerly. They sent devoted friends to my grandfather, who spoke to him eloquently of the passion he had inspired in the heart of Mlle. Miltopeus. My grandfather was greatly astonished. He certainly admired the fair Swede, and listened with delight to her operatic airs, but it had never entered his head that he could possibly find favour with a beautiful girl. Maria Anna took no notice whatever of him; she would smile abstractedly as she passed him, but rarely spoke to him. However, if she really loved him as they said, he was quite ready to marry her.

Maria Anna's sisters-in-law laid my grandfather's proposal triumphantly before her. The poor girl was greatly alarmed. "But I won't marry that old gentleman," she said. "I mentioned him by way of comparison, to make you realise how odious the other suitor was to me." This explanation came too late. Maria Anna's relatives told her severely that a well-brought-up girl should never utter imprudent words; that it was permissible to refuse a suitor who made an offer without knowing how it would be taken, but that to refuse an offer after actually inviting it was to insult a worthy man who by no means deserved such treatment; that Maria Anna was twenty-seven years old, that her brothers could not keep her indefinitely with them, and that it was time to think seriously of her future. My grandmother saw that her sisters-in-law had laid a trap for her, and resigned herself to the inevitable. Fortunately, "poor M. Snitkin" was not antipathetic to her.

The marriage of these two dreamers did not turn out badly. My grandfather never forgot the famous Asenkova, and my grandmother cherished the memory of her fair-haired lover who had fallen on the field of honour; notwithstanding, they had several children. Their characters suited each other; my grandmother was masterful, her husband was timid; she ordered, he obeyed. Nevertheless, in matters he considered really important, he managed to enforce his will. He wished his wife to change her religion, for he thought their children could not be brought up as good Christians if their parents professed different creeds. My grandmother became Orthodox, but continued to read the Gospel in Swedish. Later, when the children began to talk, my grandfather forbade his wife to teach them her native tongue. "It is unpleasant to me to hear you talking Swedish together, when I can't understand it," he said. This embargo was very disagreeable to my grandmother, who could never learn to speak Russian correctly. All her life she expressed herself in a picturesque idiom which made her friends smile. When something important had to be said, she preferred to speak German to her children.

After their marriage my grandparents lived at first in lodgings, as people often did in Petersburg. But this manner of life did not please my grandmother, who had been accustomed to a more spacious existence in Finland. She persuaded her husband to buy a piece of land which was for sale on the other side of the Neva, in a lonely quarter not far from the Smolny monastery. There she had a large house built, and surrounded it with a garden. In the middle of Petersburg she lived as if she were in the country. She had her own flowers, fruit and vegetables. She did not like her husband's Ukrainian relatives, and received them only on family festivals. On the other hand, all the Swedes who came to Petersburg, and *who* were acquainted with one or the other of her numerous cousins in Finland, came to see her, lunched, dined, and sometimes stayed the night. The house was large and contained several guest-chambers. When they returned to Sweden, my grandmother's friends invoked her good offices for their children, whom they had placed in the various Crown establishments: sons who were to become officers in the Russian army. On the festivals of Christmas and Easter the house and garden echoed with the laughter and the Swedish chatter of little schoolgirls, pupils of the Cadet Schools, and shy young officers who could not as yet speak Russian fluently and were happy to find a bit of Finland in the strange capital. Like all the women of Germanic origin, my grandmother cared very little for her new country, and thought only of the interests of those of her own race.

This Finland which invaded the house of her parents found no favour with my mother. The Swedish ladies, with their severe profiles, stiff, ceremonious manners and unknown language, frightened her. The little Anna would take refuge with her father, whom she resembled, and whose favourite she was. He took her to church, and visited the religious houses of Petersburg with her. Every year she accompanied him on a pilgrimage to the famous monastery of Valaam, on the islands of Lake Ladoga. My mother had all her life tender memories of this kind, simple, sentimental soul. She became religious like him, and remained faithful to the Orthodox Church. The new religious ideas, which her friends eagerly adopted, gained no hold over her; my mother thought more highly of the wisdom of the early Fathers than of the fashionable writers. Like her father, she loved Russia passionately, and could never forgive her mother the indifference, verging on scorn, displayed by her towards her husband's country. My mother considered herself a thorough Russian. And yet she was but half a Slav; her character was much more Swedish. The dreamy idleness of the Russian woman were unknown to my mother; she was very active all her life; I never saw her sitting with folded hands. She was always taking up fresh occupations, becoming absorbed in them and generally turning them to good account. She had nothing of the large-mindedness of Russian women, which they generally increase by wide reading; but she had the practical mind which most of her countrywomen lack. This disposition made a great impression upon her women friends; later, during her widowhood, they habitually consulted her in difficulties, and the advice she gave them was generally good. Together with the good qualities of her Swedish ancestors, my mother had inherited some of their faults. Her self-esteem was always excessive, almost morbid; a trifle would offend her, and she easily fell a victim to those who flattered her. She was something of a mystic, believed in dreams and presentiments, and had to some extent the curious gift of second sight possessed by many Normans. She was always predicting in a jesting manner, without attaching any importance to what she was saying, and was the first to be astonished and almost alarmed when her predictions, often of a fantastic and improbable kind, were realised, as if by magic. This second sight left her completely towards her fiftieth year, together with the hysteria which ravaged her girlhood. Her health was always poor; she was anæmic, nervous and restless, and often had hysterical attacks. This neuroticism was aggravated by the characteristic indecision of the Ukrainians, which makes them hesitate between half a dozen possible courses, and leads them to transform the most trivial circumstances into dramas, and sometimes into melodramas.

XIV

My Mother's Girlhood

A s their children grew up, two hostile camps were established in the house of my grandparents, as often happens when the father and the mother are of different races. The Swedish camp was composed of my grandmother and her elder daughter, Maria, a very overbearing young person; the Ukrainian camp contained my grandfather and his favourite child, Anna. The Swedes commanded and the Ukrainians obeyed grudgingly. My uncle Jean served as a link between the opponents. He had inherited the Norman beauty of his mother with the Ukrainian character of his father, and was equally beloved by both parents.

My aunt Maria was a beautiful creature, tall and slender, with blue eyes and magnificent golden hair. She had a great success in society and innumerable suitors. She made a love-match in marrying Professor Paul Svatkovsky, to whom the Grand-Duchess Maria had confided the education of her orphan children, the Dukes of Leuchtenberg. At the time of my aunt's marriage the young princes had finished their studies, but M. Svatkovsky continued to live in the palace of the Grand Duchess as a friend. My aunt made her home there; she had aristocratic friends, beautiful dresses and fine carriages. When she visited her relations, her tone was more arrogant than ever. She treated her younger sister as a little schoolgirl, which was, perhaps, not to be wondered at, for my mother was still at the High School. Her morbid self-esteem was wounded by the authoritative tone of her elder sister. She was proud, and resented patronage, dreaming of independence. A great wave of liberalism was passing over Russia at the time. Young Russian girls, who had hitherto been brought up more or less on French lines, now refused to accept the husbands their parents chose for them, and to go into society. Their mothers had danced to excess; the daughters despised balls, and preferred literary gatherings or scientific lectures. They laughed at novels and were full of enthusiasm for the works of Darwin. They became careless in their dress, cut their hair short to save time, put on spectacles, and wore black dresses and men's blouses. It was their dream to go and study at the University. When parents opposed this wish, they ran away with idealistic students, who married them in order to save them from "the odious despotism of parents." These marriages were generally platonic; the couple lived apart and rarely met. But by way of compensation, the young wife would choose a lover among the students of the University and live with him in "civil marriage." Free love seemed the ideal love to these reckless young creatures. Some of them even went farther. Male and female students subscribed to hire large dwellings and found communes in which all the women belonged indiscriminately to all the men. They were very proud of this grotesque institution, which they ingenuously assumed to be the last word in human civilisation. They were not aware that they were, in fact, retrograding to the condition of those antediluvian tribes among whom marriage was unknown.

Brought up as she had been, my mother could not, of course, participate in these follies. An obedient daughter of the Orthodox Church, she looked upon free love as a mortal sin. Short hair and spectacles seemed to her very ugly. She loved pretty clothes and graceful coiffures. She tried to read Darwin, but found him very wearisome; the idea of simian descent did not attract her. Her young imagination was fired only by the poems and novels of the Russian authors. She had no desire to be carried off by a student; she preferred to quit her parental home on her husband's arm, with the blessing of her father and mother. In all the new movement towards liberty, my mother chose only what was really good in it—work, and the independence it offers to all who take to it seriously. She studied diligently at school, and on leaving received a silver medal of which she was very proud. For a time she followed a course of higher studies, organised by the parents of her school-friends. The behaviour of the girl-students at the University was becoming so scandalous that many parents in alarm subscribed to form private classes, at which the professors gave lessons to their daughters, thus inducing them to continue their studies, while saving them from contamination. My grandmother was one of the subscribers; but higher studies had no attraction for my mother. She cared nothing for science, and did not see how it was to benefit her. Young Russians incline to vagueness in their aspirations: they study to develop their minds, to understand life better, to appreciate literature more fully. These abstract aims did not appeal to my mother's practical mind. What she wanted was to learn some craft by which she could earn money to buy books and theatre tickets, and later to travel. My grandmother, who controlled the purse-strings, was not fond of spending money on what she considered unnecessary things; my mother, for her part, disliked having to ask for every cent; she preferred to earn for herself. She saw in the papers M. Ohlin's advertisement, in which he promised those who made good progress in his courses of stenography posts in the law-courts, at the meetings of learned societies, at congresses, and, in short, everywhere where rapid reporting was a desideratum. The idea pleased my mother. She joined the new classes and worked industriously. This purely mechanical science would have been distasteful to a girl of lively imagination; my mother, who had singularly little, found it very interesting. At this time her father was seriously ill, and had been in bed for some months. When she came back from her lessons, she would go at once to see him. He would lie propped up on pillows, turning over her notebooks with trembling fingers, and asking her the meaning of all the mysterious signs. The poor invalid was delighted that his favourite had at last found a congenial occupation. He died a few weeks later; my mother mourned him passionately, and devoted herself more than ever to her stenography to divert her thoughts from her sorrow. The interest her father had shown in her studies was a further incentive. When the holidays came and the classes ceased, my mother was afraid she might forget her stenography during the summer. She therefore proposed to M. Ohlin that she should make transcriptions from books and send them to him to correct. Ohlin, who had already begun to distinguish her from the other students, consented willingly. My mother worked a great deal throughout the summer, and in the autumn was at the top of her class. Thus she was the only stenographer Ohlin could recommend to Dostoevsky. He rightly feared the opposition of my grandmother, who, like all the Swedes of her day, was a strict upholder of the proprieties. However, my father's literary fame saved the situation.

Dostoevsky, as it happened, was the favourite author of my grandfather, who had become one of his devotees on the appearance of his first novel, and had followed his literary career with great interest. When Dostoevsky was condemned to penal servitude, my grandfather thought he had disappeared for ever. He remained faithful to his memory and often spoke of him to his children. "The modern authors are worthless," he would say. "In my young days they were much more serious. Young Dostoevsky, for instance! What a magnificent talent, what a sublime soul he had! What a pity that his literary career was cut short so soon!" When Dostoevsky began to write again, my grandfather's admiration revived. He subscribed to all the periodicals in which my father's works appeared, and read them with enthusiasm. His children, who had been infants at the time of Dostoevsky's first works, now shared their father's admiration. *The Insulted and Injured* made a deep impression on their young imaginations. When the new number of the periodical was due, all the family watched feverishly for the arrival of the postman. My grandfather seized the review first of all, and carried it off to read it in his study. If he laid it down, my mother would creep in, and hiding it under her schoolgirl apron, would run off to read it in the garden, under the shade of her favourite tree. My aunt Maria, who was not yet married at the time, sometimes caught her sister in the act, and would take the book from her, invoking her rights as the elder of the two. The whole of my grandfather's family fought over *The Insulted and Injured*, weeping at the sorrows of Natalia and little Nelly, and following the evolution of the drama with anguish. My grandmother alone showed no interest. She disliked novels and never read them; politics absorbed her entirely. I remember her later, when she was seventy years old, reading the newspaper through her spectacles. She followed the course of political events throughout Europe and talked of them continually. The marriage of Prince Ferdinand of Coburg occupied her thoughts a good deal. Would Princess Clémentine find a good match for him among the princesses of Europe? This grave question disturbed my poor grandmother greatly...

My grandfather had always talked of Dostoevsky as the writer of his youth, and my grandmother was convinced that his favourite author was a very old gentleman. When Ohlin proposed to my mother that she should work for Dostoevsky, she was much flattered and agreed joyfully. My grandmother, looking upon the novelist as a distinguished old man, raised no objections. The day when the work was to begin, my mother dressed her hair demurely, and for the first time regretted that she had no spectacles to put on her nose. On her way to her employer's house, she tried to imagine what this first session would be like. "We shall work for an hour," she thought, "and then we shall talk of literature. I will tell him how I admire his genius, and which are my favourite heroines. I must not forget to ask him why Natalia does not marry Vania, who loved her so deeply... Perhaps it would be well to criticise some of the scenes, so as to show Dostoevsky that I am not a little goose, and that I know something about literature..." Unhappily, the event dispelled all my mother's artless day-dreams. Dostoevsky had had an epileptic attack the night before; he was absent-minded, nervous and peremptory. He seemed quite unconscious of the charms of his young stenographer, and treated her as a kind of Remington typewriter. He dictated the first chapter of the novel in a harsh voice, complained that she did not write fast enough, made her read aloud what he had dictated, scolded her, and declared she had not understood him. Feeling tired after his attack, he sent her away unceremoniously, telling her to come back the next day at the same hour. My mother was much hurt; she had been accustomed to very different treatment from men. Without being pretty, she was fresh, gay and amiable, and very attractive to the young men who frequented my grandmother's house. At nineteen she was, indeed, still a child. She did not realise that a woman who works for money will never be treated in the same manner as an *ingénue* flirting with the guests in her mother's drawing-room. She went home in a rage, and resolved that evening to write a letter to Dostoevsky next day, explaining that her delicate health would prevent her from continuing her stenographic work. After sleeping on the matter, she came to the conclusion, however, that when one has begun a task one ought to finish it; that her teacher might be annoyed if for mere caprice she refused the first post he had found her, and might not recommend her again; that *The Gambler* had to be finished by the 1st of November, and that after this she would be under no obligation to continue working for the captious author. She got up, carefully copied what Dostoevsky had dictated on the preceding day, and presented herself at his house at the appointed hour. She would have been very much alarmed if anyone had predicted on that day that she would transcribe Dostoevsky's novels for fourteen years.

XV

The Betrothal

My mother owned one of those albums with pink, blue and green pages to which young girls confide the great events of their days each evening. My mother opened hers the more readily because she could record her impressions in shorthand, and thus write a good deal in a limited time. She kept this artless journal of her youth, and this enabled her later to recall the story of her betrothal and of her honeymoon almost day by day. These interesting souvenirs of hers were about to be published when the great war broke out, and it was necessary to put off their appearance to a more propitious season. I will not deprive my mother of the pleasure of describing this important period of her existence. I will content myself with tracing this phase of Dostoevsky's life in broad outlines, and painting the romance of my parents from my own point of view, and from my own estimate of their characters.

Having recovered from the first wound to her vanity, my mother set to work valiantly, and went every day to take down *The Gambler* from my father's dictation. Dostoevsky gradually became conscious that his Remington machine was a charming young girl, and an ardent admirer of his genius. The emotion with which she spoke of his heroes and heroines pleased the novelist. He found his young stenographer very sympathetic, and got into the habit of confiding his troubles to her, telling her of the manner in which his brother's creditors were harassing him, and of the complicated affairs of his large family. My mother listened in surprise and consternation. Her girlish imagination had pictured the distinguished writer surrounded by admirers who formed a kind of bodyguard about him, preserving him from all dangers that might threaten his health or interfere with the creation of his masterpieces. In the place of this agreeable picture she saw a sick man, weary, badly fed, badly lodged, badly served, hunted down like a wild beast by merciless creditors, and ruthlessly exploited by selfish relatives. The great writer had only a few friends, who were content to give him their advice, but who never took the trouble to inform the Russian public or the Russian Government of the terrible straits to which this man of genius was reduced, and of the abyss which threatened to engulf his splendid talents. My mother's generous spirit was filled with indignation when she realised the neglect and indifference surrounding the great Russian. She conceived the idea of protecting Dostoevsky, of sharing the heavy burden he had taken upon his shoulders, saving him from his rapacious relatives, helping him in his work, and comforting him in his sorrows. She was not, indeed, in love with this man, who was more than twenty-five years her senior. But she understood Dostoevsky's beautiful soul as quickly as her father had formerly understood the pure soul of Asenkova, and reverenced his genius as her father had reverenced that of the young *tragédienne*. Just as my grandfather had considered Asenkova the greatest artist of our century, so my mother would never admit that there was any novelist equal to Dostoevsky, not only in Russia, but in the whole world. In these two devotions, which were so closely akin, there was something of the Greek love of art, a rare sentiment in Russia, and one which the Ukrainians perhaps inherited from Greek colonists on the shores of the Black Sea. But my mother was only half an Ukrainian; she had also the Russian sense of pity, and she felt this holy pity of our race for this man of genius who was so kindly, so confiding, who never thought of self, and was so ready to give all he had to others. Young and strong, she desired to protect the famous writer, who was approaching his decline. His debts and his numerous obligations might have frightened a timid spirit. But my mother's Norman blood braced her for conflict; she was ready to do battle with her whole world.

A Russian girl in my mother's position would have lost herself in the clouds, and would have passed her time dreaming of all the heroic circumstances in which she could give her life to Dostoevsky. My mother, instead of dreaming, set to work energetically, and began by saving him from the clutches of his publisher. She begged Dostoevsky to prolong their hours of dictation, spent the night copying out what she had taken down in the day, and worked with such goodwill that *The Gambler* was ready on the date fixed by Stellovsky, who was much chagrined to see that his prey had escaped from the trap he had prepared. Dostoevsky was fully sensible that he could not have written his novel so quickly but for my mother's help, and he was deeply grateful to her for the passionate interest she showed in his affairs. He could not bear the thought of parting with her, and proposed that they should work together at the last chapters of *Crime and Punishment*, which were not yet written. My mother agreed willingly. To celebrate the happy conclusion of their first undertaking, she invited my father to come to tea, and presented him to her mother. My grandmother, who read her daughter's heart like an open book, and had long foreseen how her stenographic activities would end, received Dostoevsky as a future son-in-law is received. That corner of Sweden transported to Russia attracted my father; it must have reminded him of the Lithuanian corner transported by his father to Moscow in which he had spent his childhood. Dostoevsky saw in what an austere atmosphere his little stenographer had been reared, and how greatly she differed from the young girls of the day, who were leading the lives of prostitutes under the pretext of liberty. He began to think of marrying his young assistant, although he, again, was no more in love than was my mother. Like many Northerners, he had a somewhat cold temperament; it required the African devices of Maria Dmitrievna or the effrontery of Pauline to kindle passion in him. A well-brought-up young girl who never overstepped the limits of an innocent coquetry did not, of course, stir his senses. But he thought that this severely nurtured girl would be an excellent mother of a family, and it was this he had long been seeking. And yet he hesitated to make his proposal. The fact was that my mother seemed very childish to my father. She was about the same age as Anna Kronkovsky, but she was much less mature and self-confident than the young anarchist. Mlle. Korvin-Kronkovsky's political, moral and religious ideas were all clearly defined. She was a severe critic of a world God had conceived so badly and executed so defectively, and was quite ready to correct the mistakes of the Creator. My mother bowed in reverence to God's will, and had no fault to find with His works. Her ideas of life were still very vague; she acted rather by instinct than by reflection. When she was talking to Dostoevsky, she laughed and jested like the child she was. My father smiled as he listened to her, and thought to himself in alarm: "What should I do with such a baby to look after?" This young girl, who only a year ago was still wearing a schoolgirl's apron, did not seem to him mature enough for marriage. It is probable that Dostoevsky would have hesitated long, if a prophetic dream had not hastened his decision. He dreamed that he had lost some valuable object; he was seeking for it everywhere, turning out cupboards, impatiently throwing aside useless things, which were strewn on the floor of his room. All of a sudden he saw in the bottom of a drawer a very small diamond, which sparkled so brilliantly that it lighted up the whole room. He stared at it in amazement: how could the gem have got into that drawer? Who had put it there? Suddenly, as often happens in dreams, my father understood that the little diamond which shone with such lustre was his little stenographer. He woke up very happy and deeply moved. "I will ask her in marriage today," he said. He never regretted his decision...

After his betrothal to my mother, Dostoevsky went to see her every day, but did not hasten to announce his approaching marriage to his relatives. He knew too well how they would receive the news. His stepson was the first to discover the secret. He was filled with consternation at the "treachery" of his stepfather! The idle rascal had arranged his life so satisfactorily! His stepfather would work and he would amuse himself; later he would inherit Dostoevsky's works and would live on the income they yielded. And now a young girl, whom his stepfather hardly knew, had upset all these agreeable plans! Paul Issaïeff was most indignant. He put on spectacles, as he always did when he wanted to look important, and told his stepfather that he wished to speak to him seriously. He warned him against the disastrous passions of old men,[1] pointed out all the unhappiness this marriage with a young girl would bring upon him, and admonished him severely as to the duties of a stepfather. "I, too, am thinking of marrying some day," he said; "I shall probably have children; it will be your duty to work for them." My father was enraged, and turned the idiot out of the house. This was the usual ending to discussions between the stepfather and the stepson.

Paul Issaïeff hastened to warn the family of the danger which threatened their parasitical security. Dostoevsky's nephews and nieces were greatly alarmed; they, too, had counted on living all their lives at their uncle's expense; they, too, had looked forward to becoming his heirs. Dostoevsky's sister-in-law, in her turn, wished to talk to him seriously. "Why do you want to marry again?" she asked. "You had no children by your first marriage, when you were a young man. How can you hope to have any at your present age?" This marriage with a young girl of nineteen seemed an absurdity, almost a vice, to my father's relatives. His literary friends were also somewhat surprised. They could not understand why Dostoevsky, who, at the age of thirty-three, had married a woman of his own age, or perhaps older, now, when he was past forty, cared only for quite young girls. Anna Kronkovsky and my mother were about the same age when he asked them in marriage. I think this peculiarity may be explained by the treachery of Maria Dmitrievna, which produced a profound and ineradicable impression on my father's mind, and made

1. My father was then forty-five.

him distrust all women of mature age. He could now only believe in the innocence of a young heart and a pure spirit, which a man of character would always be able to mould as he wished.[1] Dostoevsky, after marrying my mother, carried on her moral education very carefully. He superintended her reading, keeping erotic books from her, took her to the museums, showed her beautiful pictures and statues, and tried to kindle in her young soul the love of all that is great, pure and noble.

He was rewarded by the absolute fidelity of his wife, both during his life and after his death.

Like most Lithuanians, Dostoevsky was pure and chaste. "The Lithuanian despises indecency and debauchery," says Vidûnas. "There is no obscenity in his folk-songs, and in Lithuania one does not find on walls and fences those pornographic scrawls so common in other countries." When he visited Paris, Dostoevsky frequented the *cafés*, and went to see the dancing in the casinos of the Champs Élysées. The gross songs he heard and the erotic dances he witnessed filled him with indignation; he spoke of them with disgust to his Russian friends. This was, perhaps, the reason why my father, when he took his young wife to Germany, Switzerland, Italy and Austria, did not visit France with her. Nevertheless, the disgust which Dostoevsky had felt when studying Parisian life did not affect his admiration for French literature. He was one of the rare travellers who distinguish between the France that works and the France that amuses itself.

---

1. *The Eternal Husband*, it will be remembered, was also attracted only by young girls after the death of his unfaithful wife.

XVI

Dostoevsky's second marriage

In spite of the opposition of his relations, Dostoevsky married my mother on February 12th of that winter, five months after their first meeting. As he had no money, he could not take his young wife on a honeymoon journey. The couple took up their quarters in a lodging which my grandmother had furnished for them. Their decision to spend their honeymoon in Petersburg was very imprudent, and nearly brought about the wreck of their happiness.

Having failed to prevent the marriage, Dostoevsky's relations conceived the idea of estranging the husband and wife. They changed their tactics; the enemies of my mother became her friends and feigned an unbounded admiration for her. They invaded her home, and rarely left her alone with her husband. These people who had hitherto neglected my father, and had visited him but rarely, now spent the entire day with the newly married couple, lunching and dining at their table, and often staying till midnight. My mother was greatly surprised at this behavior, but she did not venture to complain; she had been taught from childhood to be amiable and polite to all her mother's guests, even to those she disliked. The artful relatives took advantage of her youthful timidity; they overran her home and behaved as if it belonged to them. Pretending to give her good advice, they begged her not to disturb her husband too often, but to leave him in peace in his study. "You are too young for him at present," said these perfidious counsellors; "your girlish talk cannot interest him. Your husband is a very serious man, he wants to think over his books a great deal." On the other hand, they would take my father aside and tell him that he was much too old for his young wife and that he bored her. "Listen how prettily she chatters and laughs with her young nephews and nieces," his sister-in-law would whisper. "Your wife needs the society of young people of her own age. Let her amuse herself with them, or she will begin to dislike you." My father was hurt when he was assured that he was too old for his wife; my mother was indignant at the thought that the great man she had married considered her silly and tiresome. They sulked, too proud to speak frankly to each other of their grievances. If my parents had been in love, they would have ended by quarrelling and reproaching each other, and would thus have exposed the machinations of the mischief-makers; but they had married on the strength of a mutual sympathy. This sympathy could become ardent love under favorable circumstances; but it was also capable of turning to profound aversion. My mother saw with alarm how rapidly the admiration she had felt for Dostoevsky before their marriage was diminishing. She began to think him very weak, very simple and very blind. "It is his duty as a husband to protect me from all these schemers, and to turn them out of the house," thought the poor bride. "Instead of defending me, he allows his relations to lord it over me in my own house, to eat my dinners and to make fun of my inexperience as a housekeeper." While my mother was crying in her bedroom, her husband was sitting alone in his study, and instead of working, was thinking sadly that his hopes of a happy married life were not very likely to be realized. "Can she not understand what a difference there is between me and my foolish nephew's?" he would say to himself in mute rebuke of his wife's supposed levity. His relations were delighted. Everything was going on as they wished...

The spring was approaching, and people began to make plans for the summer exodus. My father's sister-in-law proposed that they should take a large villa at Pavlovsk, in the neighborhood of Petersburg. "We could all be together," she said to Dostoevsky, "and we should have a delightful summer. We will make excursions and take your wife out with us all day. You can stay at home and work at your novel without any interruptions." These plans were not very attractive to my father, and still less so to his wife. She told her husband that she would prefer to go abroad; she had long wished to visit Germany and Switzerland. My father, too, was eager to see once more the Europe he remembered with so much pleasure. He had already made three visits to foreign countries, the third mainly for the purpose of playing roulette. He thought he was now cured of the fatal passion, but he was mistaken. During his travels in Europe with my mother, he had several fresh attacks of the malady. It gradually weakened, however, and completely lost its hold upon him when he was approaching his fiftieth year. Like his passion for women, his passion for roulette lasted altogether only ten years.

My father began to look about for money for the projected journey. He would not apply to his aunt Kumanin, for only a few months before she had given him ten thousand roubles, which were spent in publishing the newspaper *Epoha*. He preferred to go to M. Katkov, the publisher of an important Moscow review, in which Dostoevsky's novels now appeared. My father went to see him at Moscow, described the plan of the new novel he was about to begin, and asked for an advance of a few thousand roubles. Katkov, who looked upon Dostoevsky as the great attraction of his review, readily complied with his request. My father then announced to his family that he was shortly going abroad with his young wife. The schemers clamoured that if he intended to desert them for three months, he must at least leave them some money. Each produced a list of things required, and when my father had satisfied them all he had so little money left that he was obliged to give up the projected journey.

My mother was in despair. "They will make mischief between me and my husband this summer!" she cried, with tears, to her mother. "I feel it, I can see through all their schemes." My grandmother was much troubled; her younger daughter's marriage did not promise well. She, too, feared a sojourn at Pavlovsk, and wanted her daughter to go abroad. Unfortunately, she was unable to advance the funds for the journey; the money my grandfather had left her had been invested in the building of two houses close to her own, which she let. She lived on the income from these houses. She had been obliged to mortgage a part of her income in order to give her daughter a trousseau and to furnish her new home. It was therefore very difficult for her to find a considerable sum of money immediately. After careful consideration, my grandmother advised her daughter to pledge her furniture. "In the autumn, when you come back to Petersburg, I shall be able to find the money to redeem it," she said. "Just now the essential thing is to get away as soon as possible, and to remove your husband from the fatal influence of all those schemers."

Every bride is proud of her trousseau. She loves her pretty furniture, her silver, her dainty china and glass, even the resplendent pots and pans in her kitchen. They are the first things of her very own she has possessed. To ask her to part with them after three months among them as a model housekeeper is positively cruel. But to do my mother justice she did not hesitate for a moment and hastened to follow my grandmother's wise advice. Her conjugal happiness was more to her than all the silver plate in the world. She begged her mother to carry out the transaction and send the money to her abroad. With the small sum my grandmother was able to give her at once, my mother hurried away her husband, who was also very glad to go. They started three days before Easter, which was contrary to all my mother's religious habits. She was so afraid of some fresh manœuvre on the part of the Dostoevsky family that she could only breathe freely when they had crossed the frontier. My mother would have been very much startled if someone had told her that day that she would not cross it again for four years.

XVII

Travels in Europe: First Part

The wedding journey of my parents is described in detail in my mother's journal. I refer my readers to this book, which will be published at no distant date, and I will say but a few words concerning their life abroad.

After resting at Vilna and Berlin, my parents went to Dresden, and stayed there for two months. They left Petersburg in one of those snow-storms which are so frequent in Russia in April; at Dresden they found the spring awaiting them. Here the trees were in blossom, the birds were singing, the sky was blue, all Nature seemed in holiday mood. This sudden change of climate made a great impression on my parents. They dined in the open air on the verandah at Bruhl's, listened to the music in the Grossen Garten, and explored the picturesque landscape of Sax-on Switzerland. Their hearts expanded. Now that there were no longer any schemers to come between them, they understood each other much better than before. The sympathy they had felt for each other before marriage soon became love, and their real honeymoon began at last. My mother never forgot those enchanted months. Later, in her widowhood, when she was often obliged to go to Karlsbad or Wiesbaden to take the waters, she always completed her "cure" by spending a few weeks in Dresden. She visited all the places where she had been with my father, went to look at the pictures he had admired in the famous gallery, dined at the restaurants where they had taken their meals, and dreamed of the past, listening to the music in the Grossen Garten. She said that the weeks at Dresden were the happiest of all those spent in Europe.

I could never understand this love of a young girl of nineteen for a man of forty-five, and I often asked my mother how she could have loved a husband more than double her age. "But he was young!" she replied, smiling. "You can't imagine how young your father still was! He would laugh and joke, and find amusement in everything, like a boy. He was much gayer, much more interesting than the young men of that period, among whom it was the fashion to wear spectacles and to look like old professors of zoology."

It is true that the Lithuanians preserve their youthfulness of mind till late in life. When they are past fifty they will often amuse themselves like children; looking at them one says that in spite of years they will never grow old. This was the case with Dostoevsky. He was fifty-nine when he died, but he was young to the end. His hair never turned grey, but always kept its light brown colour. On the other hand, my mother inherited the Swedish character of her ancestors. Now Swedish women have one quality which distinguishes them from all the other women of Europe: they cannot criticise their husbands. They see their faults and try to correct them, but they never judge them. It seems to me that the Swedish women are, so far, the only ones who have realised the beautiful ideal of S. Paul, that husband and wife are one flesh. "How can one criticise one's husband?" Swedes have answered indignantly when I have discussed this national peculiarity. "He is too dear to be criticised." This was just my mother's point of view; her husband was too dear to be criticised. She preferred to love him, and after all this was the surest way of being happy with him. All her life she spoke of Dostoevsky as an ideal man, and when she became a widow she brought her children up to worship their father.

In July, when it began to get very hot in Dresden, my parents left for Baden-Baden. It was an unfortunate idea, no sooner did my father see the roulette-tables again, than the gambling fever seized him like a disease. He played, lost, went through crises of exultation and of despair. My mother was greatly alarmed. When she had transcribed *The Gambler* she had not known that her husband had depicted himself in it. She wept and implored him to leave Baden-Baden; finally she succeeded in getting him away to Switzerland. When they arrived at Geneva the madness left my father, and he cursed his unhappy passion. My parents liked Geneva, and decided to spend the winter there. They did not wish to return to Petersburg; they were happy abroad, and they thought with horror of the intrigues of their relatives. My mother, moreover, was no longer able to take long journey; he was *enceinte*, and this first pregnancy was not easy. She took a dislike to noisy hotels, and my father rented a small flat from two old maids, who were very kind to my mother. She spent most of her time in bed, only getting up to go and dine at the restaurant. After the meal she would come home and go to bed again, while her husband stayed to read the Russian and foreign newspapers.

Now that he was living in Europe, he took a passionate interest in all European questions.

My parents led a very solitary life in Geneva. At the beginning of their stay in Switzerland they met a Russian friend, who often came to see them. When he left for Paris they did not seek any further acquaintances; they were preparing for the great event which was to transform their lives.

My little sister was born in February, and was named Sophie after my father's favourite niece, my Aunt Vera's daughter. Dostoevsky was very happy; at last he tasted the delights of fatherhood, of which he had so long dreamt. "It is the greatest joy a man can know here on earth," he wrote to a friend. He was immensely interested in the baby, observed the soul which looked at him through the child's dim eyes, and declared that she recognised him and smiled at him. Alas! his joy was short-lived.

My mother's first *accouchement* had caused her unusual suffering, and her anaemia had been much aggravated by it. She was unable to nurse the baby herself, and it was not possible to find a wet nurse at Geneva. The peasant women would not leave their homes, and ladies who wished to have their infants nursed were obliged to send them up into the mountains. My mother refused to part with her treasure, and determined to bring up little Sophie by hand. Like many first-born children, Sophie was very fragile. My mother knew little about the rearing of infants; the kind old maids who helped her with her charge knew even less. The poor baby vegetated for three months, and then left this troublous world for another.

The grief of my parents was overwhelming. My grandmother, who had just arrived from Petersburg to make the acquaintance of her new grandchild, comforted them as far as she could. Seeing that my mother spent all her time in the cemetery, sobbing on the little grave, my grandmother proposed that she should be taken away to Vevey. There the three spent a most melancholy summer. My mother was constantly escaping from the house, and going by steamer to Geneva, to take flowers to her little lost one. She would come back in tears; her health became worse and worse. My father, for his part, was uneasy in Switzerland. A denizen of the plains, he was accustomed to vast horizons; the mountains round Lake Leman oppressed him. "They crush me, they dwarf my ideas," he would say; "I cannot write anything of value in this country."

My parents accordingly decided to spend the winter in Italy; they hoped the southern sun might restore my mother's health. They went away alone; my grandmother remained in Switzerland with her Svatkovsky grandchildren, who were to spend the winter in Geneva by the doctor's orders.

My parents travelled across the Simplon by the diligence. My mother always recalled this journey with pleasure. It was the month of August and the weather was magnificent. The diligence went up slowly; the passengers preferred to walk, taking short cuts. My mother walked, leaning on my father's arm; it seemed to her that she had left her sorrow on the other side of the Alps, and that in Italy life would smile upon her once again. She was barely twenty-one, and at that age the thirst for happiness is so great that the loss of a baby of three months old cannot darken one's days for very long.

My parents' first sojourn in Italy was at Milan. My father was anxious to see the famous cathedral which had so greatly impressed his imagination on his first visit to Europe. He examined it thoroughly, stood lost in admiration before the façade, and even went up on the roof to see the view which extends over the wide Lombard plain. When the autumn rains began, my parents left for Florence, and settled there for the winter. They knew no one in the city, and spent several months *tête-à-tête*. Dostoevsky never cared for casual acquaintanceship which leads no further. When a man pleased him, he gave him his heart, and remained his friend for life, but he could not offer his friendship to every passer-by.

My father was busily occupied in Florence; he was writing his novel, *The Idiot*, which he had begun at Geneva. My mother helped him, taking down the scenes he dictated to her in shorthand. She was careful, however, not to disturb him in his hours of meditation, and set herself to make a thorough study of Florence, its beautiful churches and its magnificent art collections. She habitually arranged to meet her husband in front of some famous picture; when he had finished his writing, Dostoevsky would join her in the Pitti Palace. He did not like to study pictures Baedeker in hand; on his first visit to a gallery he would single out certain pictures which pleased him, and would often come back to admire them, without looking at any others. He would stand for a long time before his favourites, explaining to his young wife the ideas these pictures evoked in him. Then they would take a walk along the Arno. On their way home they would often make a *détour* to see the doors of the Baptistry, which enchanted my father. In fine weather they would stroll in the Cascine or the Boboli Gardens. The roses blooming there in the month of January struck their northern imaginations. At that time of the year they were accustomed to see rivers covered with ice, streets full of snow, and passers-by muffled in furs; the January blossoms seemed to them incredible. My father speaks of the Boboli roses in his letters to his friends, my mother speaks of them in her reminiscences.

My parents were very happy in Florence; I think this was the most perfect moment of their wedding journey. Dostoevsky loved Italy; he said the Italians reminded him of the Russians. There is, indeed, a good deal of Slav blood in Northern Italy. The Venetii who built Venice were of Slav origin and belonged to the same Slav tribe as the Russians, a tribe whose home was in the Carpathians. Intermarrying with Italians, the Venetii gave their Slav blood to the inhabitants of northern Italy. This blood flowed all over the plain of the Po, and descended along the Apennines. Russians travelling in Italy are often surprised to find in the depths of Tuscany or Umbria peasant-women of the same type as those they have seen at home. They have the same soft and patient look, the same endurance in work, the same sense of self-denial. The costume and the manner of knotting the handkerchief about the head are similar. Thus the Russians love Italy, and look upon it as to some extent their second country.

XVIII

Travels in Europe: Second Part

Towards the spring my mother became *enceinte* for the second time. The news delighted my father; the birth of little Sophie had made him more eager than ever to be a father. As the climate of Florence suited my mother, my parents at first proposed to spend another year in Italy. But they changed their minds as the time for my mother's confinement approached. The fact was that in those days the hotels and furnished flats in Florence did not yet possess any of those polyglot servants who speak all languages equally badly. The humble Florentine servants were content to speak good Italian. My mother soon learned to talk this language after a fashion, and acted as interpreter to my father, who was too busy with his novel to study Italian. Now that she was about to take to her bed, and perhaps be dangerously ill, how, she wondered, would her husband be able to manage among Italian servants and nurses. My father wondered also and told his wife he would prefer to winter in a country where he could speak the language. Dostoevsky at this time was beginning to feel an interest in the Slav question, which eventually absorbed him so entirely. He proposed to my mother that they should go to Prague, where he wished to study the Czechs. My parents left Florence at the end of the summer and travelled by easy stages that my mother might not be tired, stopping at Venice, Trieste and Vienna. At Prague they had a great disappointment; there were no furnished apartments to be had in the town.

Dostoevsky wanted to go back to Vienna, hoping to find there some Czech societies, literary or otherwise; but my mother disliked Vienna. She proposed that they should return to Dresden, of which she had such happy memories. My father agreed; he, too, remembered their stay in Dresden with pleasure.

My parents arrived in Dresden a fortnight before my birth. Dostoevsky was very happy to have a little daughter to love once more. "I saw her five minutes after her arrival in the world," he wrote to one of his friends.

"She is a beauty, and the image of me." My mother laughed heartily when she heard this. "You flatter yourself," she said to her husband. "Do you think you are handsome?" Dostoevsky was never handsome, nor was his daughter; but she was always proud of being like her father.

The landlord of the furnished rooms occupied by my parents came to warn Dostoevsky that by the laws of the town of Dresden he must go at once to the police office to announce the birth of his daughter to the Saxon authorities.

Dostoevsky hastened to the office and declared to the officials that he was the happy father of a little girl called Aimée. The Saxons were not content with this, but made my father state his name, age, social position, date of birth. Having satisfied their curiosity on the subject of my father, they passed on to his wife, and asked what her maiden name was.

Her maiden name! The devil! Dostoevsky could not remember it! He racked his brains in vain!—he could not recall it. He explained matters to the police officers and asked leave to go and consult his wife. The worthy Saxons looked at him with amazement; never had they encountered such an absent-minded husband! They allowed Dostoevsky to go. He came home in dudgeon.

"What is your name?" he asked his wife severely.

"My name? Anna," replied my mother, much surprised.

"I know your name is Anna. I want to know your maiden name."

"Why?"

"Oh! it is not I who would know it, but the police here. These Germans are so inquisitive. They insist on knowing what you were called before your marriage, and I have completely forgotten!"

My mother instructed her husband, and advised him to write the name on a bit of paper. "Otherwise you will forget it again," she said laughingly. Dostoevsky took her advice, and went off to show his bit of paper triumphantly to the Saxon authorities.[1]

My mother's health had improved greatly in the Italian climate, and she was able to nurse me herself. She also engaged a German nurse for me, distrusting her own inexperience. My grandmother came to be with her daughter during her confinement, and watched over me carefully,

1. My Russian name is Lubov. As it is rather difficult for foreigners to pronounce, we got into the habit of translating it by Aimée, which means very nearly the same thing. My father used to call me Liuba, which is the Russian diminutive of Lubov, and I figure in the Dresden letters under this name. As I grew older, I preferred the pet name of Lila, which my grandmother gave me, and which was easier for my childish tongue. To please me, my parents also called me Lila, and it is thus that Dostoevsky writes of me in all his later letters.

fearing a second domestic calamity. However, I was not at all like my elder sister. I was a sturdy Slavo-Norman, determined not to leave this planet until I had studied it thoroughly.

My grandmother had not returned to Russia after the death of little Sophie. When she quitted Petersburg for a few months, she had left the management of her house property in the hands of one of her relatives. Being much occupied with other business, he let all the houses on a long lease, without taking the trouble to consult my grandmother. As she could not return to her own house at Petersburg, my grandmother elected to stay near her daughter Anna, all the more willingly because her favourite daughter Marie was also spending the greater part of her time in Europe. Marie's husband managed the affairs of one of his former pupils, the Duke of Leuchtenberg, who lived abroad, and constantly visited the Duke either at Geneva or in Rome. My aunt, who was very intimate with the morganatic wife of the Duke, always accompanied her husband, and often took her children with her. My grandmother went from one daughter to another, and was very happy in Europe, which to her Swedish mind was much more interesting than Russia. But she felt the separation from her son, who at this time was studying agriculture at the Petrovskoë Academy near Moscow. My mother was very fond of her brother Jean, and she, too, longed to see him after years of separation. They both wrote to my uncle and begged him to come and see them. He got leave, and arrived in Dresden, intending to stay only two months, but he was obliged to remain there over two years. A strange fatality seemed to pursue my mother's family in this connection: whenever any of them visited Europe intending to stay a few months, it always became necessary for them to remain several years. My Aunt Marie, indeed, never returned to Russia. She died in Rome two years after the time of which I am writing, and was buried there.

My uncle Jean had at the Academy a friend whom he greatly loved and admired, called Ivanov. He was older than my uncle, whom he protected and looked after as if he had been a younger brother. When Ivanov heard that my grandmother washed to see her son, he urged my uncle strongly to accept the invitation of his relatives. Knowing the somewhat vacillating character of his young comrade, Ivanov went himself to see the Director of the Academy, persuaded him to grant my uncle leave of absence for two months, took steps to hasten the issue of his passport, and saw him off at the station. My uncle was somewhat surprised at this eagerness for his departure, but he attached no importance to it. When he arrived in Dresden he talked enthusiastically of his dear Ivanov, wrote him letters and awaited his answers impatiently. A few weeks later Ivanov was found murdered in the park surrounding the Academy. The police set to work to track the murderer, and finally discovered a political plot, in which most of the students were implicated. These young fanatics had been working to overthrow the Government, instead of attending to their agricultural studies. Ivanov was one of the chief agitators; he thought better of it, however, began to have doubts, and finally gave notice to his comrades that he intended to leave the secret society. The young revolutionaries were furious at his defection, and determined to punish it by death; they enticed him into a lonely part of the park one night, and there one of his comrades, named Netchaïeff, killed him while the others held his arms. This political affair, which was known as the Netchaïeff Case, made a great sensation in Russia; it is still remembered there.

The curious part of this story is that my uncle, who was almost inseparable from Ivanov, knew nothing at all of the plot. It is probable that Ivanov, who was really attached to him, prevented his companions from drawing him into this dangerous business. My poor uncle felt his friend's death bitterly; he understood now why Ivanov had been so anxious for him to go abroad. He knew, no doubt, the fate he had to expect from his comrades, and wished to place his young friend out of danger. My grandmother was greatly alarmed when she heard of the murder of Ivanov, and forbade her son to return to Russia, more especially as the Academy of Agriculture was closed by order of the Government. Throughout the proceedings, my uncle settled at Dresden with his mother. He afterwards married a young girl of the Russian colony in Dresden.

The Netchaïeff Case made a deep impression on Dostoevsky, and provided the subject for his famous novel, *The Possessed*. His readers at once recognised the Netchaïeff affair, though the action took place in different surroundings. The critics argued that my father, who was living abroad at the time of the Netchaïeff Case, had not at all understood it. No one knew that he had had an opportunity of forming a very clear idea of the plot by questioning my uncle Jean, who was intimately connected with the victim, the murderer, and the other revolutionaries of the Academy, and was able to reproduce their conversation and their political ideas.[1]

1. My uncle was very brave and very intelligent. He had inherited his father's religious and monarchical ideas and was not afraid to profess them openly. It was probably on this account that his comrades concealed the plot from him. If our revolutionaries were merciless to those who forsook them after sharing their faith, they did not molest those who had the courage of their opinions.

Schatov, Verhovensky, and many other characters in *The Possessed* are portraits. Of course, Dostoevsky could not tell his critics of his sources, for fear of compromising his brother-in-law. My uncle's relations were truly thankful that the police had forgotten his existence and had not ordered him to attend the trial as a witness. He might have been bewildered and have said something imprudent that would have endangered him. It is probable that his fellow-students followed Ivanov's example, and were careful not to commit my uncle, who was a general favourite. He was a delightful creature, a true Christian. He treated all men as his brothers. People began by laughing at him and ended by loving him. Dostoevsky was always much attached to his brother-in-law.[1]

When the Russian colony heard that the famous novelist Dostoevsky was living in Dresden with his family, many people wished to make his acquaintance. They came to see him and invited him to their houses. My mother might have led a much more cheerful life at Dresden than at Geneva or Florence, but she was very unhappy there. She was now suffering from homesickness, that curious malady which often attacks young creatures who have been torn too abruptly from their native soil. She hated Germany, hated foreigners. Dresden, which she had thought so charming, now seemed odious to her. She had moments of despair, thinking that she would perhaps never see her dear Russia again. She suffered the more acutely because, now that her health was restored, her Norman nature asserted itself, and made her long for action and struggle. She pined in her furnished flat, between her husband and her child. She thought that at Petersburg she would certainly find a means of paying off the debts which were crushing her life. Moreover, her family affairs were causing her much anxiety. One of the houses belonging to my grandparents was to come to my mother, according to her father's will. The Russian law did not allow her to sell it before her brother was of age. Jean was now just on the verge of his majority, and my mother hoped to sell her house and pay her husband's debts. The house-agent, who had taken all my grandmother's property on lease, paid her regularly for the first few months; then he had ceased to pay, and did not answer the letters she wrote him. My mother wrote to friends at Petersburg

1. A curious thing happened to the novel *The Possessed*. When Dostoevsky began it, he had taken Nicolai Stavrogin for the hero, but when he had nearly finished the book, he realised that Verhovensky was much more interesting, and decided that he must be the hero. He had to rewrite almost the whole of the book, and cut out several chapters in which he had developed his study of Stavrogin. My mother wanted to publish one of these chapters in the last edition, at the beginning of this century. But she asked the advice of several old friends of my father's, and they were opposed to its inclusion.

and begged them to go and see him and inquire into the matter. They did so, but could never find him at home; the neighbours whom they questioned declared that his business was in a bad way, and that the police had paid him visits. All this alarmed my mother, and she implored my father to return to Russia. She no longer feared the machinations of his relatives; she knew that she had now her husband's entire confidence. Her character, moreover, had changed greatly; her school-friends scarcely recognised their gay companion. Privations, exile, the influence of Europe, where life is more serious and difficult than the childish life of Russia, had prematurely aged her.

Dostoevsky was not home-sick, and felt very comfortable abroad; his health had improved, his epileptic attacks occurred only at long intervals. Yet he, too, wanted to return to Petersburg; he feared that he would cease to understand Russia if he stayed any longer in Dresden. All his life he had this fear, in Germany as in Siberia. Probably Dostoevsky was conscious that there was very little of the Russian in him. Turgenev and Count Alexis Tolstoy spent their whole lives abroad, yet this did not prevent them from giving their readers admirable types of Great Russia. They nearly always spoke French, yet they wrote most excellent Russian. These writers carried Russia with them in their blood, and remained eternally Russian, though they naïvely accounted themselves perfect Europeans. My father, who, on the other hand, gloried in being a Russian, was really much more European than they. He was capable of being absorbed by Europe; it was therefore more dangerous for him to go away from Russia. His mastery of the Russian language was also imperilled. It has often been made a reproach to my father that his style is heavy, incoherent and careless; this has been explained by the fact that he was obliged to work for his daily bread, and had not time to correct his manuscripts. But those who have a good style know that it is easy to write well at the first attempt. I think Dostoevsky's faulty style may rather be accounted for as follows: he wrote Russian badly because it was not his ancestral tongue.

During the second part of her stay in Dresden my mother became *enceinte* for the third time. She proposed at first to stay at Dresden for her confinement; then, fearing illness might keep her another year in Germany, she changed her mind, and made her husband start for home at once. We arrived at Petersburg a few days before the birth of my brother Fyodor.

XIX

The Return to Russia

It was the month of July, and my parents found the city deserted;
all their friends had left for the country. The first to return was my
father's stepson, Paul Issaïeff, who had lately married a pretty mid-
dle-class girl. As my mother was still weak after her recent confinement,
and could not run about looking for a flat, he offered his services. In
the evening he would come and show my mother sketch-plans of the
various places he had inspected during the day.

"But why do you look at such large flats?" she said to him. "Until our
debts are paid, we must be content with four or five rooms at most."

"Four or five rooms! Then where will you put me and my wife?"

"Were you thinking of living with us?" asked my mother, greatly surprised.

"Of course. Would you have the heart to separate father and son?"

My mother was exasperated. "You are not my husband's son," she said
severely. "You are not even related to him, as a fact. My husband took
care of you when you were a child, but his duty now is to look after his
own children. You are old enough now to work and to earn your own
living."

Paul Issaïeff was overwhelmed by this plain speaking. He was not to
consider himself the son of the famous Dostoevsky! Others had better
claims than he on his "papa"! What an infamous plot had been hatched
against him! He was furious, and so was his young wife.

"He promised me," she told my mother ingenuously, "that we should
all live together, that you would keep house, and that I should have
nothing to do. If I had known that he was deceiving me, I certainly
would not have married him."

This selfish little creature became, under the discipline of years and
sorrows, an excellent wife and mother, respected by all who knew her.
Poor woman! her married life was a long martyrdom.

Seeing that nothing could shake my mother's determination, and that Dostoevsky was of one mind with his wife on the subject, Paul Issaïeff turned for sympathy to my father's relatives, complaining bitterly of the dark intrigues of his "stepmother," and her efforts to separate "father and son." Dostoevsky's family had more sense than he. They realised that my mother's character had developed, that the timid girl-bride had become the energetic wife, able to protect her home from intruders. They made a virtue of necessity, and ceased to harass her. Their position, moreover, had greatly improved during the past four years. The sons had grown up and were able to work for their living; the girls had married, and their husbands helped their mother. My aunt Alexandra, now a widow, married a rich man. The only members of the family dependent on my father were my unhappy uncle Nicolai and the worthless Paul Issaïeff.

As soon as my mother's health was restored, she took a small flat and furnished it cheaply. Her own pretty furniture had all been sold. Paul Issaïeff, who had undertaken to pay the interest of the loan on the furniture during my grandmother's absence, spent the money my parents had sent him for this purpose on himself. Another disappointment, of a more serious nature, awaited my mother on her return to Petersburg. My grandmother's house-property was sold by auction by order of the police, and changed owners several times. Thanks to a badly worded lease, the agent had been able to pass it off as his own. The only hope was in a lawsuit, and lawsuits are very expensive in Russia. My mother preferred to give up her share of the inheritance; my grandmother followed her example, although she was now utterly ruined as a result of her unlucky sojourn in Europe. Fortunately, her son had made a rich marriage at Dresden. With his wife's fortune he bought a fine estate in the Government of Kursk, and set to work to apply the theories he had learnt at the Academy of Agriculture. My grandmother went to live with him and his family, and soon became absorbed in his agricultural experiments. Now that her favourite daughter was dead, she rarely came to Petersburg. Her relations with Dostoevsky were always cordial, but she played a very small part in his life.

When my uncle Mihail's creditors heard that Dostoevsky had returned to Petersburg, they at once presented themselves, and again threatened him with imprisonment. My mother then entered upon the struggle, for which she had been bracing herself at Dresden. She lectured them and argued with them, and borrowed from money-lenders to pay off the most rapacious. Dostoevsky was amazed at the facility with which his wife manipulated figures and talked the jargon of notaries. When publishers came to make proposals to him, he listened to them quietly, and said: "I cannot decide anything for the moment. I must consult my wife." People soon began to understand who it was that managed the business of the Dostoevsky household, and they addressed themselves directly to her. Thus my father was relieved of all wearisome details, and was able to devote himself entirely to his works.

With a view to paying off the debts quickly, my mother introduced a rigid economy in her home. For many years we had to live in very modest dwellings; we had only two servants, and our meals were extremely frugal. My mother made her own dresses and her children's frocks. She never went into society, and very rarely to the theatre, in which she delighted. This austere life was unnatural at her age, and made her unhappy. She was often in tears; her melancholy disposition, which painted the future in the darkest colours, conjured up visions of an old, infirm husband, sick children, a poverty-stricken household.[1] She could not understand my father's serenity. "We shall never be without money," he would say, in tones of conviction. "But wdiere is it to come from?" she would ask, vexed at his confidence. My mother was still young. There are certain truths we only grasp after the age of forty. My father knew that we are all God's workers, and that if we perform our task faithfully, the Heavenly Master will not forsake us. Dostoevsky had perfect faith in God, and never feared for the future of his family. He was right, for after his death we lacked nothing.

To comfort his wife and lighten her heavy burden, my father accepted the post of sub-editor of the newspaper, *The Citizen*, edited by Prince Mestchersky, an absurd person who was the laughing-stock of all the other journalists. Mestchersky, who had been brought up by English nurses and French tutors, could not even speak Russian correctly; my father had to be always on the watch to prevent him from publishing something ridiculous in the paper. His journalistic work exhausted him terribly, and directly the most pressing of the debts were paid, my father hastened to leave *The Citizen* and its fantastic editor to their fate.

My mother, for her part, did not spend all her time in weeping. She prepared my father's novels which had appeared in reviews for publication in book form, which brought in a little money. Moreover, it gave her experience; she became an excellent editor in time, and after my

1. My father's Aunt Kumanin could no longer help him. She died while we were in Europe, leaving her affairs in great disorder. Her heirs quarreled over her property for years. We did not receive our share till after my father's death.

father's death published several complete editions of his works. She was the first Russian woman to undertake work of this nature. Her example was followed by Countess Tolstoy, who came to Petersburg to make my mother's acquaintance and ask her advice. She gave all the necessary information, and thenceforward all Tolstoy's works were published by his wife. Long afterwards, when at Moscow, my mother showed the countess the musuem she had organised in memory of her husband in one of the towers of the Historical Museum at Moscow. The idea appealed to Countess Tolstoy, and she asked the directors of the Museum to let her have a similar tower for a Tolstoy Museum. These two Europeans[1] were not content to be merely wives and mothers; they aspired to help their husbands to propagate their ideas, and they were anxious to place all relics of their great men in safe custody. Another friend of my mother's, Madame Shestakov, asked her advice in the organization of a museum in memory of her brother, the famous composer, Glinka. My mother helped her considerably, and thus was the founder of one museum, and the inspirer of two others.

My father lived a very retired life during the first years of his return to Russia; he went out very little, and received only a few intimate friends. He made few appearances in public; the Petersburg students kept up their grudge against him, and rarely invited him to their literary gatherings. They had scarcely begun to forget that Dostoevsky had insulted them in the person of Raskolnikov when he offended them still more deeply. In his novel, *The Possessed*, he had plainly shown them the folly and madness of revolutionary propaganda. Our young men were stupefied; they had looked upon the anarchists as Plutarchian heroes. This Russian admiration for incendiaries, which is so amazing to Europeans, is easily accounted for by the Oriental sloth of my compatriots. It is much easier to throw a bomb and run away to a foreign country than to devote one's life to the service of one's fatherland, after the fashion of patriots elsewhere.

Dostoevsky attached no importance to the displeasure of the students and wasted no regrets on his lost popularity with them. He looked upon them as misguided boys, and a man of his calibre has no need of youthful adulation. The joy he felt in the creation of his masterpieces richly rewarded his toil; popular applause could add nothing to it. I think my father was happier in these early years of his return to Petersburg than later, in the agitated period of his great successes. His wife loved him, his children amused him with their infantine prattle and laughter; old

1. Countess Tolstoy was the daughter of Dr. Bers, a native of the Baltic Provinces.

friends often visited him, and he could exchange ideas with them. His health had improved, his attacks of epilepsy were no longer frequent, and the mortal disease which was to close his career had not yet declared itself.

XX

Little Alexey

We used to spend the four summer months at Staraja Russa, a little watering-place in the Government of Novgorod, not far from the great Lake of Ilmen. The doctors advised my parents to go there for the sake of my health the first year after our return to Russia. The baths of Staraja Russa did me a great deal of good, and my parents returned yearly. The quiet, sleepy little town pleased Dostoevsky; he was able to work in peace there. We rented a little villa belonging to Colonel Gribbe, a native of the Baltic Provinces, serving in the Russian army. With the savings he had made during his military life, the old officer had built a small house in the German style of the Baltic Provinces, a house full of surprises: cupboards concealed in the walls; planks which when lifted up revealed corkscrew staircases, dark and dusty. Everything in this house was on a small scale: the low rooms were furnished with old Empire furniture; the green mirrors distorted the faces of those who had the courage to look into them. Paper scrolls, pasted on linen, hung on the walls, presenting to our childish eyes monstrous Chinese ladies with claw-like nails and feet squeezed into tiny shoes. A covered verandah with coloured glass panes was our delight, and the Chinese billiard-table, with its glass balls and little bells, amused us on the long rainy days so frequent during our northern summers. Behind the house was a garden with comical little flower-beds. All sorts of fruits grew in this garden, which was intersected by tiny canals. The Colonel had constructed these himself to protect his raspberries and currants from the spring inundations of the treacherous Pereritza river, on the banks of which his villa stood. In summer the Colonel retired into two rooms on the ground-floor, and let the rest of the house to visitors. This was the custom at Staraja Russa in those days, when there were no villas to be let for the summer season. Later, after the Colonel's death, my parents bought the little house for a song from his heirs.[1]

1. Colonel Gribbe possessed four miniatures which he had bought from a soldier

My father spent all his summers there, except that of 1877, when we paid a visit to my uncle Jean in the Government of Kursk. The scene of *The Brothers Karamazov* is laid in the little town; when I read it in later years, I recognised the topography of Staraja Russa. Old Karamazov's house is the villa, with slight modifications; the beautiful Grushenka is a young provincial whom my parents knew at Staraja Russa; the Plotnikov establishment was my father's favourite shop. The drivers of the *troikas*, Andrey and Timofey, were our favourite drivers, who took us every summer to the shores of the Lake of Ilmen, to the point where the steamers stopped. Sometimes one had to wait there several days, and the sojourn in a big village on the lake is described by Dostoevsky in the last chapters of *The Possessed.*

My father led a very secluded life at Staraja Russa. He rarely went to the Park and the Casino, the resort and rendezvous of the visitors. He preferred to walk on the banks of the river, in the more retired places. He invariably took the same road, and passed along with downcast eyes, lost in thought. As he always went out at the same hour, the beggars lay in wait for him, knowing that he never refused alms. Absorbed in his own meditations, he distributed these mechanically, without noticing that he repeatedly gave to the same persons. My mother, however, saw through the tricks of the beggars, and was much amused by her husband's absent-minded ways. She was young and fond of practical jokes. One evening, seeing him returning from his walk, she threw a shawl over her head, took me by the hand, and stood by the roadside. When he approached, she began to whine plaintively: "Kind gentleman, have pity on me. I have a sick husband and two children to support." Dostoevsky stopped, glanced at my mother, and handed her some coins. He was very angry when she burst out laughing. "How could you play me such a trick—before the child, too?" he said bitterly.

This eternal dreaminess, so characteristic of writers and men of science, was a great annoyance to my father, who considered it humiliating and ridiculous. He wished intensely to be like others. But great minds cannot manifest themselves after the fashion of commonplace men. Dostoevsky could not live like his fellows. All his life, as at the Engineers' School, he stood apart in the embrasure of a window, dreaming, reading

in his regiment, who had no doubt looted them in some Polish palace, on the occasion of one of the numerous Polish revolts. They represented four princes and a princess of the Lithuanian dynasty of the Jagellons. My father admired these miniatures greatly; he bought them from the heirs of the old Colonel and hung them in his bedroom. He said that the young princess reminded him of his mother.

and admiring Nature, while the rest of humanity laughed, wept, played, ran, and amused itself in crowds. A great writer hardly lives on this earth; he spends his days in the imaginary world of his characters. He eats mechanically, without noticing of what his dinner consists. He is astonished when the night comes; he had supposed that the day was still young. He does not hear the trivial things that are said around him; he walks in the streets, talking to himself, laughing and gesticulating, till passers-by smile, taking him for a madman. Suddenly he will stop, struck by the look of an unknown person, which stamps itself on his brain. A word, a phrase he overhears reveals to him a whole life, an ideal which will eventually find expression in his works.

The little villa of Staraja Russa no longer exists. Built of poor wood bought at a low price by the old Colonel, it was unable to resist the annual inundations of the Pereritza, and at last fell to pieces, in spite of all efforts to save it. As long as it survived it attracted many visitors. All who came to Staraja Russa made a pilgrimage to the little house where Dostoevsky spent the last summers of his life. They looked at the table on which he had written *The Brothers Karamazov*, the old arm-chairs in which he sat to read, the numerous souvenirs of him we had kept.[1] Among these pious pilgrims was the Grand Duke Vladimir, who came one day when he was in the neighbourhood holding a review of young soldiers. He told my mother how greatly he admired Dostoevsky. "This is not the first domicile of his I have visited," he added. "Passing through Siberia, I stopped at Omsk to see the prison where he suffered so greatly. It is entirely changed now. The *Memories of the House of the Dead* effected a vast reform in all Siberian prisons. What a genius your husband was! What a power of touching the heart he had!" The Grand Duke Vladimir was the grandson of Nicholas I, who had condemned my father to penal servitude. Ideas change quickly in Russia, and grandchildren are ready to recognize the misdeeds of their grandparents.

My father liked Staraja Russa so well, that my mother proposed we should spend a winter there in order to economise and pay off the debts more rapidly.

They took another villa in the centre of the town, a larger and warmer house, and we spent several months there. In the course of this winter my brother Alexey was born. There had been some discussion as to his name. My mother wished to call him after her beloved brother, Jean. Dostoevsky suggested Stepan, in honour of that Bishop Stepan who, according to him, was the founder of our Orthodox family. My mother

1. These relics were all placed in a little museum we made in our new villa.

was somewhat surprised at this, as my father rarely spoke of his ancestors. I imagine that Dostoevsky, who felt an ever-increasing interest in the Orthodox Church, wished to show his gratitude to the first of our Lithuanian ancestors who had adopted Orthodoxy. However, my mother disliked the name Stepan, and my parents finally agreed to call the child Alexey. My mother's health had improved so much that the birth of this child caused her little suffering. Little Alexey seemed strong and healthy, but he had a curious forehead. It was oval, almost angular. His little head was like an egg. This did not make him an ugly baby; it only gave him a quaint expression of astonishment. As he grew older, Alexey became my father's favourite. My brother Fyodor and I were forbidden to go into our father's room uninvited; but this rule did not apply to Alexey. As soon as his nurse's back was turned he would escape from his nursery, and run to his father, exclaiming: "Papa, zizi!"[1]

Dostoevsky would lay aside his work, take the child on his knee, and place his watch against the baby's ear, and Aliosha would clap his little hands, delighted at the ticking. He was very intelligent and lovable, and was deeply mourned by the whole family when he died, at the age of two and a half years, at Petersburg, in the month of May, just before our annual journey to Staraja Russa. Our boxes were packed, and the last purchases were being made, when Aliosha was suddenly seized with convulsions. The doctor reassured my mother, telling her that this often happened to children of his age. Aliosha slept well, awoke fresh and lively, and asked for toys to play with in his little bed. Suddenly he fell back in another convulsion, and in an hour he was dead. It all happened so quickly that my brother and I were still in the room. Seeing my parents sobbing over the little lifeless body, I had a fit of hysterics. I was taken away to some friends, with whom I stayed for two days. I returned to my home for the funeral. My mother wished to bury her darling beside her father in the cemetery of Ohta, on the other side of the Neva. As the bridge which now connects the banks did not then exist, we had to make a long *détour*. We drove in a landau, with the little coffin between us. We all wept, caressing the poor little white, flower-decked coffin, and recalling the baby's pretty sayings. After a short service in the church, we passed to the burial-ground. How well I remember that radiant May day! All the plants were in blossom, the birds were singing in the branches of the old trees, and the litanies of the priest and the choir sounded melodiously in the poetic surroundings. Tears ran down my father's cheeks; he supported his sobbing wife, whose eyes were fixed

1. *I.e. ichassi, show.*

on the little coffin as it gradually disappeared under the earth.

The doctors explained to my parents that Alexey's death was due to the malformation of his skull, which had prevented his brain from expanding. For my part, I have always thought that Aliosha, who was very like my father, had inherited his epilepsy. But God was good to him, and took him home at the first attack.

During the winter preceding the death of Alexey, a celebrated Parisian fortune-teller had visited Petersburg, and there was a great deal of talk about her predictions and her clairvoyance. My father, who was interested in all occult manifestations, went to see her with a friend, and was surprised at the accuracy with which she told him of events in his past life. Speaking of his future, she said: A great misfortune will befall you in the spring. Struck by these words, Dostoevsky repeated them to his wife. My mother, who was superstitious, thought of them a good deal in March and April, but, absorbed in her preparations for our departure, she had entirely forgotten them in May. How often my parents recalled that prediction during the melancholy summer after the death of Alexey!

XXI

The Journal of the Writer

A t last, all the debts were paid. My father was now free to devote himself to his art—its master, and not its slave! He could now give his children some pleasures, and afford a few presents for his poor wife, who had sacrificed her youth to enable him to discharge his obligations. The first diamonds Dostoevsky offered to my mother were very small, but his joy in giving them was great.

Yet my father had no thought of enjoying the rest so hardly earned. Scarcely was he clear of debt than he threw himself into the public arena, and began to publish the *Journal of the Writer*,[1] of which he had long been dreaming. Russian novelists cannot devote themselves exclusively to art, after the manner of their European *confreres;* the moment always comes when they have to be priests, confessors and educationists. Our poor paralyzed Church and our horrible schools cannot function normally, and every really patriotic writer is obliged to take over part of their duties. After his return from abroad, Dostoevsky saw with alarm how swiftly unhappy Russia was rolling towards the abyss in which she now lies, thirty-five years after his death. He had just spent three years in Italy and Germany, in the great flowering time of their patriotism. In Petersburg he found only malcontents, who hated their native land. The unhappy Russian intellectuals, educated in our cosmopolitan schools, had only one ideal: to transform our interesting and original Russia, a land full of genius and promise, into a grotesque caricature of Europe. This state of mind was the more dangerous because our masses continued to be strongly patriotic admirers of their own country, proud of their nationality and contemptuous of Europe. Dostoevsky, who knew both worlds—that of our intellectuals and that of our peasantry—recognized the strength of the one and the weakness of the other. He realized that the intellectuals only existed by virtue of the Tsars; that on the day when they, in their blindness, pulled down the throne, the people

---

1. He also published under this title his articles for *The Citizen*.

would take the opportunity of vengeance on the *baré*,[1] whom they despised and hated for their atheism and cosmopolitanism. Dostoevsky's prophetic spirit foresaw all the horrors of the Russian Revolution.

When he began the publication of the *Journal of the Writer*, Dostoevsky hoped to reunite this handful of wrong-headed intellectuals with the great popular masses by awakening in them the sentiments of patriotism and religion.[2] His ardent voice was not lost in the wilderness; many Russians saw the danger of this moral abyss which separated our peasants from our intellectuals and tried to fill it in. The fathers were the first to respond to Dostoevsky's appeal. They came to see him, consulted him as to the education of their children, and wrote to him from the depths of the provinces, asking for advice. These conscientious fathers belonged to all classes of Russian society. Some were humble folks of the lower middle classes, who had deprived themselves to give their children a good education, and who saw with terror that they were becoming atheists and enemies of Russia. At the other end of the scale there was the Grand Duke Constantine Nicolaïevitch, who begged my father to exercise his influence on his young sons, Constantine and Dmitri. He was an intelligent man, of wide European culture; he wished to see his sons patriots and Christians. My father's affection for the young princes lasted till his death; he was fond of both, but especially of the Grand Duke Constantine, in whom he divined the future poet.[3] After the fathers came the sons. No sooner did Dostoevsky begin to speak of patriotism and religion than the boy and girl students of Petersburg flocked to him, forgetting their former grievances against him. Poor Russian youth! Is there any other in the world so abnormal, so crippled? Whereas in Europe parents try to evoke patriotism in the hearts of their children, and to make them good Frenchmen, good Englishmen, good Italians, Russian parents make their children the enemies of their fatherland. From their earliest years our little Russians hear their fathers insulting the Tsar, repeating scandalous stories about his family, laughing at priests and religion, and talking of our beloved Russia as of an offence against humanity. When at a later period our children go to school, they find their teachers professing the same hatred of their own country; whereas in

1. The name the Russian masses give to nobles and intellectuals.

2. In his *Journal* of 1876 Dostoevsky said: "The cure for our intellectual malady lies in our union with the people. I began my *Journal of the Writer* in order to speak of this remedy as often as possible." Thus my father returned to the propagation of the same idea he had formerly preached in the *Vremya*, with my uncle Mihail's help.

3. Later on, the Grand Duke Constantine published some charming poems and some dramas under the initials K. R. (Konstantin Romanov).

other countries schoolmasters endeavour to cultivate patriotism in the hearts of young citizens, Russian professors teach our students to hate our Orthodox Church, the monarchy, our national flag, and all our laws and institutions. They inculcate admiration of the Internationale, which, according to them, will one day bring justice to Russia. They talk to their pupils, with tears in their eyes, of that ideal nation which has neither fatherland nor religion, which speaks all languages equally badly, and whose leaders, the future great men of Russia, are being educated in the cafés of Paris, Geneva and Zurich! Alas! it was in vain that our Russian students waved the red flag in the streets of Petersburg and Moscow, and yelled the war-songs of the Internationale! Despair was in their hearts; death chilled their souls and urged them to suicide. Can there be any happiness for those who hate their fatherland? These poor young men and maidens came to my father weeping and sobbing and opened their hearts to him. Dostoevsky received them as if they had been his sons and daughters, sympathized with all their sorrows, patiently answered all their artless questions as to the life beyond the grave. Our students are nothing but "children of a larger growth," and when they encounter a man who commands their respect, they listen to him as a master, and carry out his instructions to the letter. My father sacrificed his art to the publication of the *Journal of the Writer*, but these years were certainly not lost for Russia.

The Russian girl-students in particular were warm admirers of Dostoevsky, for he always treated them with respect, and never gave them the kind of Oriental advice which many of our writers lavish on young girls: "What is the good of reading and studying? Marry early and have as many children as possible." Dostoevsky never preached celibacy to them; but he told them that they should marry for love, and that meanwhile they ought to study, read, and think, so that later they might be enlightened mothers, capable of giving their children a European education. "I expect much from the Russian woman," he often said in his *Journal*. He realised that the Slav woman has a stronger character than the Slav man, that she can work harder and bear misfortune more stoically. He hoped that later, when the Russian woman was really emancipated (for so far, though she had pushed open the doors of her harem, she had not emerged from it), she would play a great part in her country. It may be said of Dostoevsky that he was the first Russian feminist.

The students now renewed their invitation to my father to read his work to them at their literary gatherings. By this time the mortal disease to which he was to succumb had already declared itself. He was suffering from catarrh of the respiratory organs and reading aloud fatigued him greatly. But he never refused to attend these meetings; he knew what an influence well-chosen literature may have on young minds. He liked especially to read them the monologue of Marmeladov, a poor drunkard, who from the depths into which he has fallen always looks up to God, hoping humbly for pardon. The miserable creature dreams that at the Last Judgment God, after rewarding the good and faithful, will remember him. Humble and contrite, hiding behind others, he waits with downcast eyes for the Lord to say a word of pity to him. All the religious philosophy of our childlike people is contained in this chapter of *Crime and Punishment.*

Dostoevsky soon became a fashionable reader. He read admirably and could always touch the hearts of his listeners. The public applauded him enthusiastically and recalled him again and again. My father thanked them smilingly, but he had no illusions concerning his audience. "They applaud me, but they don't understand me," he said sadly to his collaborators at these literary evenings. He was right. Our intellectuals felt instinctively that he knew the truth, but they were incapable of changing their own mentality. The Russian people had been so strong that they had endured three centuries of tyranny without losing their dignity. Our intellectuals were so weak that they had kept up a semblance of tyranny long after the emancipation of the peasants. Their petty pride forbade them to share the ideas and traditions of the people. Unable to forget that their fathers had lorded it as masters of the serfs, they continued to treat the free peasants as slaves, trying to impose on them the Utopias they found in European literature. Just as my grandfather failed to understand the Russian people, and was killed by them, so our intellectual society lived in space, suspended between Europe and Russia, and was cruelly punished by the revolution.

The favour of the students which Dostoevsky now enjoyed again brought about an absurd, though not illogical, incident. One day when my mother was out, the maid announced that a lady had called, but had refused to give her name. Dostoevsky was accustomed to receive unknown visitors, who came to unburden themselves to him, and he told the maid to show the lady in. A figure dressed in black and thickly veiled entered and sat down without uttering a word. My father looked at her in astonishment.

"To what do I owe the honour of this visit?" he asked.

The lady replied by throwing back her veil and gazing at him with a tragic air. My father frowned. He disliked tragedy.

"Will you tell me your name, Madam?" he said drily.

"What! You don't know me?" exclaimed the visitor in the tone of an offended queen.

"No, I do not know you. Why will you not tell me your name?"

"He does not know me!" sighed the lady. My father lost patience.

"What is the meaning of this mystery?" he cried.

Please tell me the reason of your visit. I am very much occupied at present and have no time to waste." The unknown rose, pulled down her veil and left the room. Dostoevsky followed her, much perplexed. She opened the front door and ran hurriedly down the stairs. My father stood in the anteroom deep in thought. A distant memory began to dawn upon his mind. Where had he seen that tragic air? Where had he heard that melodramatic voice? "Good Heavens," he said at last, "it was she — it was Pauline!"

Just then my mother returned, and Dostoevsky dolefully described the visit of his former mistress.

"What have I done!" he repeated. "I have offended her mortally. She is so vain. She will never forgive me for not having recognised her. Pauline will know how dear the children must be to me. She is capable of killing them. Don't let them go out of the house!"

"But how was it you did not recognise her?" asked my mother. "Is she so much changed?"

"No. Now I think of it, I see that she has changed very little. But you see, Pauline had passed from my mind altogether; she had ceased to exist for me."

The brain of an epileptic is abnormal. He retains only facts that have impressed him in some way. Pauline N. was probably one of those pretty women whom men love when they are with them, but forget as soon as they are out of sight.[1]

---

1. When she was past fifty, Pauline N married a student of twenty, a great admirer of my father's. The young enthusiast, who afterwards became a distinguished author and journalist, was inconsolable because he had never known Dostoevsky, and he determined at least to marry one whom his favourite writer had loved. It may easily be imagined how this extraordinary marriage ended.

XXII

Dostoevsky in His Home

The Russian students are not very orderly in their habits. They interfered with my father's work by coming to see him at all hours of the day, and thus Dostoevsky, who never refused to receive them, was obliged to sit up at night writing. Even before this, when he had any important chapters on hand, he preferred working at them when everyone around him was asleep. This nocturnal toil now became a fixed habit. He would write until four or five in the morning, and would not get up till eleven o'clock. He slept on a sofa in his study. This was then the fashion in Russia, and our furniture-dealers used to stock Turkish sofas with a deep drawer, in which the pillows, sheets and blankets were hidden during the day. Thus the bedroom could be transformed into a study or drawing room in a few minutes. On the wall over the sofa there was a large and beautiful photograph of the Sistine Madonna, which had been given to my father by friends who knew how he loved the picture. His first glance when he woke fell upon the sweet face of this Madonna, whom he considered the ideal of womanhood.

When he rose, my father first did some gymnastic exercises; then he went to wash in his dressing-room. He made very thorough ablutions, using a great deal of water, soap and eau de Cologne. He had a perfect passion for cleanliness, though this is not a characteristically Russian virtue. It did not make its appearance in Russia before the second half of the nineteenth century.[1] Even in our own days, it was not uncommon to see authentic old princesses with their nails in deep mourning. Dostoevsky's nails were never in mourning. However busy he was he always found time to perform his manicure carefully. It was his habit to sing while he was washing. His dressing-room was next to our nursery, and every morning I used to hear him singing the same little song in a low voice:

1. Our grandmothers used to tell us how in their youth young girls who were going to a ball would send their servants to ask their mothers if they should wash their necks for a low, or only a slight *décolletage*.

"Wake her not at early dawn!
Sweetly she sleeps in the mom!
Morning breathes upon her breast,
Touches her cheeks with rose."

My father then went back to his room and finished dressing. I never saw him in dressing-gown and slippers, which Russians habitually wear for the greater part of the day. From early morning he was always carefully dressed and shod, wearing a fine white shirt, with a starched collar.[1] He always wore good clothes; even when he was poor, he had them made by the best tailor in the town. He took great care of his clothes, always brushed them himself, and had the secret of keeping them fresh for a very long time. If he happened to spill a drop of grease on them when moving his candlesticks, he at once took off his coat and asked the maid to remove the spot. "Stains offend me," he would say; "I cannot work when I know they are there. I think of them all the time, instead of concentrating on my writing." When he had finished dressing and said his prayers, Dostoevsky would go into the dining room to drink his tea. It was then we used to go and wish him good-morning, and chatter to him about our childish affairs. He liked to pour out his tea himself, and always drank it very strong. He would drink two glasses of it, and carry away a third to his study, where he sipped it as he wrote. While he was breakfasting the maid cleaned and aired his room. There was very little furniture in it, and what there was, was always ranged along the walls, and had to be kept in place. When several friends came at the same time to see my father, and displaced his chairs, he always put them back in their places himself after the visitors had left. His writing-table was also very neat. The newspapers, the cigarette-box, the letters he received, the books he consulted, all had to be in their places. The slightest untidiness irritated him. Knowing what importance he attached to this meticulous order, my mother went every morning to see that her husband's writing-table was properly arranged. She would then take up her station beside it and lay out her pencils and notebooks on a small round table. When he had finished his breakfast my father returned to his room, and at once began to dictate to her the chapters he had composed the night before. My mother took them down in shorthand and transcribed them. Dostoevsky corrected these transcriptions, often adding fresh details; my mother copied them out again and sent them to the printers. In this manner she saved her husband an immense amount of work. He

---

1. At this period only working men wore coloured shirts.

would not, perhaps, have written so many novels if his wife had never learnt stenography. My mother's handwriting was very beautiful; my father's was less regular, but more elegant. I called it "Gothic writing," because all his manuscripts were adorned with Gothic windows, delicately drawn with pen and ink. Dostoevsky traced them mechanically as he pondered on his work; it seems as if his soul had craved for these Gothic lines, which he had admired so much in the cathedrals of Milan and Cologne. Sometimes he would sketch heads and profiles on his manuscripts, all very interesting and characteristic.[1]

When dictating his works to my mother, Dostoevsky would sometimes stop and ask her opinion. My mother was careful not to criticise. The malicious criticisms in the newspapers were sufficiently wounding to her husband, and she was anxious not to add weight to them. Still, fearing that praise might become monotonous, she ventured on certain slight objections. If the heroine were dressed in blue, my mother was all for pink; if there were a cupboard on the left, she preferred to have it on the right; she would change the shape of the hero's hat, and sometimes cut off his beard. Dostoevsky always made the suggested modifications eagerly, in the ingenuous belief that it was to please his wife. He saw through her devices no more clearly than he had seen through those of the Russian convicts in Siberia when, to distract his thoughts, they would talk politics to him, and question him on the life in European capitals. Dostoevsky was so honest that it never occurred to him that anyone could wish to deceive him. He himself never said anything untrue except on one day in the year — the first of April. "April fool" was a tradition, and my father loved traditions. One spring morning he came out of his bedroom with a face of consternation. "Do you know what has happened to me in the night?" he said to my mother as he entered the dining-room. "A rat got into my bed. I strangled it... Please tell the maid to go and take it away. I can't go back into my room while the rat is there. It horrifies me!" and he hid his face in his hands. My mother called the maid and went with her into the master's room. My brother and I followed; we had never seen a rat, and we wondered what it would be like. The maid shook the sheets, pillows, and blankets — then lifted up the carpet. Nothing! The corpse of the rat had disappeared. "But where did you throw it?" asked my mother, returning to the dining-room, where my father was quietly drinking his tea. He began to laugh. "April fool!" he cried, delighted with the success of his trick.

When he had finished his dictation to my mother, Dostoevsky would

1. Drawing was very carefully taught at the Engineers' School.

send for us, and give us some dainties for our luncheon. He was very fond of such delicacies, and in a drawer of his bookcase he kept boxes of dried figs, dates, nuts, raisins, and those fruit pastes which are made in Russia. He liked to eat such things occasionally during the day, and even during the night. This "dastarhan"[1] was, I think, the only Oriental habit my father had inherited from his Russian ancestors; perhaps his delicate constitution needed all these sweet things. When we came to his study he would give us a large share of his dainties, dividing it between me and my brother. As we grew older he became more severe, but he was very tender to us when we were little. I was a very nervous child, and cried a good deal. To cheer me up, my father would propose that I should dance with him. The furniture in the drawing-room was pushed back, my mother took her son for her partner, and we danced a country dance. As there was no one to play the piano, we all sang a kind of refrain by way of accompaniment. My mother would compliment her husband on the precision with which he executed the complicated steps of the country-dance. "Ah!" he would reply, mopping his forehead, "you should have seen how I used to dance the mazurka in my youth."[2]

About four o'clock, my father went out for his daily walk. He always took the same road, and, absorbed in his thoughts, never recognised the acquaintances he met on the way. Sometimes he would pay a visit to a friend, to discuss some literary or political question that interested him. When he had money, he would buy a box of bonbons from Ballet (the best confectioner in Petersburg), or pears and grapes from one of the famous fruiterers. He always chose the best, and had a great aversion from cheap, second-class goods. He would bring home his purchases himself and have them served for dessert. At this period it was usual to dine at six, and to have tea at nine. Dostoevsky devoted the interval to reading, and did not begin to work until after tea, when everyone had gone to bed. He used to come into our nursery to bid us good-night, give us his blessing, and repeat with us a short prayer to the Virgin which his own parents had taught him to say when he was a child. He would then kiss us, return to his study, and begin to work. He disliked lamps and wrote by the light of two candles. He smoked a good deal as he worked and drank very strong tea. I do not think he could have stayed awake for so many hours without these stimulants.

The same regular, monotonous life continued at Staraja Russa. My father was no longer able to spend all the summer with us; he had to go

1. "Dastarhan" means the refreshment offered to a guest in the East.
2. The mazurka is the national dance of Poles and Lithuanians.

to Ems every year for a course of treatment. The waters there did him a great deal of good, but he disliked being in Germany. He counted the days till his return to Russia and looked forward impatiently to the time when he should be rich enough to take all his family abroad with him. He thought wistfully of us when he saw the little Germans enjoying donkey-rides and dreamed of giving his own children such pleasures. When he returned to Staraja Russa he would often tell us about the little German donkeys. There are no donkeys in Russia, and this unknown animal, which seemed to be so fond of children, had a mysterious attraction for my brother and me. We were never tired of questioning my father about the moral and physical attributes of the little, long-eared beasts.

My father used to bring us charming presents from abroad. These were generally serviceable and expensive things, chosen with much taste. He brought my mother a beautiful pair of opera-glasses, in painted china, an ivory fan very delicately carved, some Chantilly lace, a black silk dress, daintily embroidered linen; for me there would be white piqué dresses for the summer, and little silk frocks trimmed with lace for the winter. Unlike the generality of parents, who dress their little girls in blue or pink, my father chose pale-green dresses; he was very fond of this colour, and often dressed the heroines of his novels in it.

Dostoevsky was very hospitable, and on family festivals he loved to collect his own relatives and my mother's round his table. He was always very pleasant to them, talking of things in which they were interested, laughing, jesting, and even playing cards, an amusement he disliked. In spite of his exertions and my mother's amiability, these gatherings generally ended unpleasantly, thanks to that black sheep, Paul Issaïeff, who always expected an invitation to such entertainments. He had no idea how to behave in society. Although he was the son of an officer of good family, a member of the hereditary nobility, had been educated in the Corps of Cadets with well-bred boys, and had spent his holidays in the house of my uncle Mihail, who received all the most distinguished writers of the day, Paul Issaïeff conducted himself much as his maternal forefathers may have done in some oasis of the Sahara; I have rarely encountered such a curious case of atavism.

Insolent and malicious, he offended everyone by his impertinences. Our relations were indignant and complained to my father. Dostoevsky would be angry, and would show his stepson the door; but, metaphorically speaking, he always came back by the window. He clung closer than ever to his "papa," continued to live in idleness and to depend upon him for money. Dostoevsky's friends hated his stepson, and never invited him to their houses. Hoping to rid my father of this parasite, they obtained excellent situations for him in private banks.[1] Any sensible man would have tried to keep such situations, and provide for his future, but Paul Issaïeff never stayed long anywhere. He treated not only his colleagues but his superiors like dirt, was always talking of his stepfather, the famous writer, whose friends were Grand Dukes and Ministers, and threatening those who displeased him with his all- powerful vengeance. At first people laughed at his megalomania; when they got tired of it, they turned Paul Issaïeff out, and he came back to Dostoevsky like a bad penny. He was now the father of a numerous family. Faithful to the Mameluke tradition, he increased the population every year. He gave his children our names: Fyodor, Alexey, and Aimée, evidently with the idea of prolonging the imaginary relationship, and making them as it were the grandchildren of Dostoevsky. A parasite himself, he proposed to make them parasites in their turn, but happily he failed here. His children, who were very well brought up by their mother, turned out greatly superior to their father. Russia has absorbed them and will gradually purge them of their "Mamelukism." Perhaps that African blood which proved so disastrous to Paul Issaïeff and his mother may bestow some great gift on one of their descendants and make him a distinguished man. Such a development is not unknown in Russia.

My mother always protested hotly against this spurious relationship. She protected our blond Slavo-Norman heads and would not allow that there was anything in common between them and the yellow skin of the unhappy mulatto. She was right, for Russian law recognises no kinship as between stepfather and stepson. On the other hand, the Orthodox Church admits a spiritual relation, and it is possible that Dostoevsky, who was always a faithful servant of our Church, accepted her ruling on this point.[2] But, in any case, he considered that the connection would

1. As he had never finished a course in any Government school, he could not get a post in a Government office.

2. My father thought himself responsible for his stepson's moral conduct more especially. Once when he had been making a long stay abroad, he suspected Paul Issaïeff of having attempted a forgery. In a letter to Maikov he describes how this had distressed him, and how he had prayed to God that it might not happen. He rejoiced greatly to find that he had been mistaken. I do not, indeed, think that Paul Issaïeff had any criminal proclivities. If he had been a rogue, he might easily have provided for himself during my father's lifetime, for Dostoevsky, always absent-minded and confiding, would sign any paper presented to him without troubling to see to what it committed him. Many others took advantage of this disposition, but Paul Issaïeff was not of the number. He was idle all his life, but

die with him, for he never exhorted us to treat Paul Issaïeff as our brother. We were forbidden to call him by his nickname, or to address him as "thou." But my brother Fyodor and I found him strangely attractive. He was never kind or amiable to us, but he amused us immensely. When he came to see his stepfather we would creep into the study, and, hiding behind the armchairs, we would note with delight his extraordinary gestures and strange attitudes, and drink in his extravagant conversation. To us he was a kind of Punch, representing the grotesque comedy that delights children of a certain age.

But though we laughed at Paul Issaïeff, Dostoevsky never ridiculed his unhappy stepson. Whenever his friends or relatives had treated Paul with contempt, my father was full of pity for him, and would do all he could to comfort him. He would go to his house, caress his children, discuss their education with Madame Issaïeff, and give her good advice by which she profited greatly later on.

Paul Issaïeff has been dead many years. On the ground that he poisoned Dostoevsky's life, the Russian intellectuals would never do anything for his children. I think myself that they would have shown their admiration for my father better by a little kindness to this family, which was dear to him. After all, Paul Issaïeff's children, who were all very young when Dostoevsky died, never did him any harm. On the contrary, they had to suffer for their father's perversity, and thus, as the victims of his defective education, had a claim to help and sympathy.

honest after his fashion.

XXIII

Dostoevsky as a Father

It was very likely the spectacle of his grotesque stepson which caused Dostoevsky to think seriously of his duties to my brother and myself. Having failed in the one instance, he was the more anxious to succeed in the other. He began our education very early, at an age when most children are still in the nursery. Perhaps he knew that his disease was mortal, and that he had little time in which to sow the good seed. He adopted to this end the same method his father had chosen before him: reading the works of great authors. In my grandfather's home the children were made to read aloud in turn, but Dostoevsky was obliged to read to us, for we could scarcely do so at all when our literary *séances* began. The first of these impressed itself indelibly on my memory. One autumn evening at Staraja Russa, when the rain was coming down in torrents and the yellow leaves lay thickly on the ground, my father announced that he was going to read us Schiller's *Robbers*. I was then seven years old, and my brother was just six. My mother came to listen to this first reading. Dostoevsky read with fervour, stopping every now and then to explain some difficult expression. We listened open-mouthed; this Germanic drama seemed very strange to our childish minds. What were we to think of that fantastic Germany, that far-off country to which my father went reluctantly every year by his doctor's orders, and where the good children rode about on little donkeys with long, long ears? Alas! there were no donkeys in *The Bobbers*. But there was a very unpleasant father, who was always quarrelling with his sons; also, a young girl who tried to reconcile them, and who was always crying. "No wonder, poor girl" I thought, as I listened to my father's passionate declamation. "It must be dreadful to live with people who quarrel all day. And yet they ought to have been happy living in Germany, where there are so many little donkeys. Why, then, were they so miserable, and why did they quarrel all the time? Germans must have very bad tempers..."

If I could not understand the works of Schiller at the age of seven,

I understood perfectly that this fantastic drama interested my father immensely, and that I must pretend to be interested in it too in order to please him. Cunning as most little girls are, I put on intelligent airs, nodded my head approvingly, and appeared highly appreciative of Schiller's genius. Feeling that sleep was getting the better of me as the brothers Moor plunged more desperately into crime, I tried with all my might to keep my childish eyes open; my brother Fyodor went to sleep unconcernedly... Seeing such an audience my father stopped, laughed, and began to reproach himself... "They can't understand, they are too young," he said sadly to his wife. Poor father! He had hoped to experience afresh with us the emotion Schiller's dramas had once aroused in him; he forgot that he must have been at least double our age when he had first enjoyed them.

Dostoevsky waited a few months before he resumed the literary evenings. This time he chose the old Russian legends which our rustic bards relate in the villages at evening gatherings. These unlettered Homers have extraordinary memories and can recite thousands of verses without hesitation. They repeat them rhythmically, with much taste and expression; they are indeed poets, and often add passages to the poems they recite. The chief subject of the legends is the life of the knights of Prince Vladimir, that Russian Arthur, who loved to assemble his warriors round him at his table. Our people, who have no idea of history, intermingle with these ninth and tenth-century legends the more ancient myths of pagan times, and the knights of Vladimir's Slavo-Norman Court have to encounter giants and dwarfs, etc. The legends are written partly in Russian, partly in the early Slav language, which adds to their poetry.[1] They suited our childish imaginations better than Schiller's tragedies. We listened entranced, weeping over the misfortunes of the errant knights, and rejoicing at their victories. Dostoevsky smiled at our emotion and was himself full of enthusiasm for the popular poets of our race. Passing on from the legends, he read us Pushkin's stories, written in admirable Russian; Lermontov's Caucasian tales; and Gogol's *Taras Bulba*, a magnificent romance of Cossack life in ancient Ukrainia. Having thus formed our literary taste a little, he began to recite to us the poems of Pushkin and of Alexis Tolstoy, two of his favourite poets. Dostoevsky recited their verses admirably. There was one poem which always brought tears to his eyes—Pushkin's *Poor Knight*, a mediaeval legend. It is the story of a dreamer, a deeply religious Don Quixote, who

1. The Orthodox liturgy, the Gospel and the prayers are said in Old Slav in our churches, so that in Russia everyone knows the ancient tongue more or less, even children, who with us begin to attend Mass at the age of two.

wanders all his life in Europe and the East, upholding the creed of the Gospels. He has a vision in the course of his wanderings; in a moment of supreme exaltation, he sees the Holy Virgin at the foot of the Cross. He lets down "a steel curtain" over his face, and, faithful to the Virgin, will never look again on any woman. In *The Idiot* Dostoevsky describes how one of his heroines recited this poem: "A spasm of joy passed over her face." This was just what happened to my father when he read it; his face was irradiated, his voice trembled, his eyes filled with tears. It was the story of his own soul. He, too, was a poor knight, without fear and without reproach, who fought all his life for great ideas. He, too, had a beatific vision; it was not the mediaeval Virgin who appeared to him, but Christ, Who came to him in his prison, and called him to follow Him.

Although Dostoevsky attached great importance to reading, he did not neglect the theatre. In Russia parents take their children very often to the Ballet. Dostoevsky did not care for the Ballet and preferred to take us to the Opera. Strange to say, he always chose the same, *Russian and Ludmilla*, which Glinka composed on a poem by Pushkin. My father seems to have wished to engrave the legend on our childish hearts. It is indeed very curious; it is a political allegory, prefiguring the destiny of the Slav nations. Ludmilla, the daughter of Prince Vladimir, represents the Western Slavs. Tchernomur, an Oriental magician, a hideous dwarf with a long beard, who personifies Turkey, arrives at Kiev when a great festival is in progress, plunges every one into a magic sleep, and carries off the fair Ludmilla to his castle. Two knights, Russian (Russia) and Farlaff (Austria), pursue the dwarf, and after many adventures arrive at Tchernomur's castle. Russian challenges him; Tchernomur accepts the challenge, but, before the combat, again plunges Ludmilla into a magic sleep. While they are fighting, the cunning Farlaff seizes the sleeping maiden and brings her back to Kiev to Prince Vladimir, who had promised her hand to the knight who should rescue her. Farlaff tries in vain to wake Ludmilla; she does not respond to his advances. Russian, having slain Tchernomur, takes his magic ring. Returning to Kiev, he puts it on Ludmilla's finger, and she at once awakes, throws herself into his arms, calls him her dear betrothed, and turns disdainfully away from Farlaff. Seeing that Ludmilla will have nothing to say to him, Farlaff leaves Kiev ignominiously.

This fine opera, very splendidly put on the stage, delights children. My brother and I admired it greatly, though we were unfaithful to it on one occasion. On a certain evening when we arrived at the theatre we learned that one of the singers had been taken ill, and that *Russian and Ludmilla* could not be performed. *The Bronze Horse*, a very popular comic opera, had been substituted. My father was vexed and proposed to go home. We protested and began to cry; he sympathised with our disappointment and allowed us to stay for this Chinese or Japanese spectacle. We were enchanted. There was so much noise, so many little bells jangling, and the great bronze horse, which figured in every act, struck our childish imaginations. Dostoevsky was not very well pleased at our admiration. He evidently did not wish us to be dazzled by the wonders of the Far East. He wanted us to be faithful to his beloved Ludmilla...

When Dostoevsky went to Ems, or was too busy to read to us himself, he begged my mother to read us the works of Walter Scott, and of Dickens, "that great Christian", as he calls him in the *Journal of the Writer*. During meals, he would question us concerning our impressions, and evoke episodes in the novels. He, who forgot his wife's name and the face of his mistress, could remember all the English names of the characters of Dickens and Scott which had fired his youthful imagination, and spoke of them as if they were his intimate friends.

My father was very proud of my love of reading. I learned to read in a few weeks, and I devoured all the books I could lay hands on. My mother protested against this inordinate reading, which was, of course, very bad for a little nervous girl. Dostoevsky, however, was indulgent to it, seeing in it a reflection of his own passion for books. He chose historical novels and the sentimental tales of Karamzin for me from his bookshelves, discussed them with me and explained the things I had not understood. I got into the habit of keeping him company while he breakfasted, and this was the happiest hour of my day. Thus, our literary conversations began, but, alas! they did not continue long.

The first book my father gave me was the *History of Russia,* by Karamzin, beautifully illustrated. He explained the pictures, which represented the arrival of Rurik at Kiev, the struggles of his son Igor against the nomad tribes who surrounded what was then the small Slav nation on every side, Vladimir introducing the Christian religion into his principality, Jaroslav promulgating the first European laws, and other descendants of Rurik, who founded Muscovy, defending the infant Great Russia against the invading Tatars. The Slavo-Norman princes became my favourite heroes. I heard their songs and war-cries as in a dream. My favourite heroine was Rogneda, daughter of the Norman prince Rogvolod; I liked to act her part in our childish plays. Later, when I began to travel in Europe, I sought the traces of my dear Normans everywhere. I was surprised to find Europeans talking always of Latin and Germanic culture and forgetting that of the Normans. At the time when Europe was plunged in mediaeval barbarism, the Normans were already protecting liberty of conscience, and allowing the practice of all religions in their realms. Instead of worshipping power and riches they reverenced poets and men of learning, invited them to their courts, and even shared their labours. Thus, in Sicily the Norman prince Roger II helped the learned Arab Edrizy to write the first geography under the artless title of *The Joy of Him Who Loves to Travel*. The civilisation of the Normans was so advanced for their period that it could not find admittance in barbarous Europe; it could only subsist in small forgotten countries such as Lithuania and Sicily. And yet this fine civilisation is not dead; it lives on in souls of Norman descent, and manifests itself from time to time in some great poet or writer.

One thing which struck me as strange at a later date, when I began to analyse this period of my life, was the fact that my father never gave me any children's books. *Robinson Crusoe* was the only work of this kind I read, and this my mother gave me. I suppose Dostoevsky knew nothing about children's books. In his youth they did not exist as yet in Russia, and he must have begun to read the works of the great writers at the age of eight or nine. Another thing, still more curious, strikes me when I recall our conversations. Dostoevsky, who spoke to me with so much pleasure of literature, never uttered a single word to me about his childhood. My mother told me of the smallest details in her life as a little girl, described her earliest impressions, and her affection for her brother, but I cannot recall a single detail of my father's childhood. He maintained the same reserve as his father before him, who would never tell his sons anything about their grandfather or their Ukrainian uncles.

Dostoevsky superintended our religious education and liked to worship in company with his family. In Russia we communicate once a year, and we prepare for this solemn event by a week of prayer. My father performed his religious duties reverently, fasted, went to church twice a day, and laid aside all literary work. He loved our beautiful Holy Week services, especially the Resurrection Mass with its joyful hymns. Children do not attend this mass, which begins at midnight, and ends between two and three in the morning. But my father wished me to be present at this wonderful ceremony when I was barely nine years old. He placed me on a chair, that I might be able to follow it, and with his arms around me, explained the meaning of the holy rites.

XXIV

Dostoevsky and Turgenev

Before passing on to my father's last years, I should like to say a few words about his relations with Turgenev and Tolstoy. In talking to Dostoevsky's European admirers, I have always noticed that they were specially interested in these relations.

My father's acquaintance with Turgenev began when they were both young, and both full of ambition, as young people beginning life generally are. They were as yet unknown to the Russian public; their talent had hardly developed. They frequented the same literary *salons*, listened to the same critics, and worshipped the same masters—their favourite poets and novelists. Turgenev attracted my father greatly; Dostoevsky admired him as one student admires another who is handsomer and more distinguished than himself, is a greater favourite with women, and seems to him an ideal man. However, as Dostoevsky learned to know Turgenev better, his admiration gradually changed to aversion. Later he called Turgenev "that *poseur*." This opinion of Dostoevsky's was shared by most of his literary colleagues. Later, when I myself questioned the older Russian writers about their relations with Turgenev, I always noted the somewhat contemptuous tone they adopted in speaking of him, which disappeared when they talked of Tolstoy. Turgenev had deserved their contempt to some extent. He was one of those men who cannot be natural, who always want to pass themselves off as something they are not. In his youth he posed as an aristocrat, a pose which had no sort of justification. The Russian aristocracy is very restricted; it is rather a coterie than a class. It is composed of the few descendants of the ancient Russian and Ukrainian boyards, some chiefs of Tatar tribes assimilated by Russia, a few barons of the Baltic Provinces and a few Polish counts and princes. All these people are brought up in the same manner, know each other, are nearly all related, and have intermarried with the European aristocracies. They give magnificent entertainments to foreign ambassadors and enhance the prestige of the Russian Court. They have very little influence on the politics of their country, which, since the second half of the nineteenth century, have been gradually passing into the hands of our hereditary nobility. This is perfectly distinct from the aristocracy and has nothing in common with the feudal nobility of Europe. I have already explained its origin in describing the Lithuanian *Schliahta*. This union, primarily a martial one in Poland and Lithuania, was in Russia transformed into an agrarian union of rural proprietors. Catherine II protected them, desiring to create a sort of Third Estate in Russia. The landed proprietors in each province combined and chose a Marshal of the nobility to superintend their affairs. He did this gratis, sometimes ruining himself by giving balls and sumptuous dinners to the nobles who had elected him. Nevertheless, the post of Marshal of the nobility was always greatly in request, for it conferred many privileges. The Emperor always bestowed the rank of Gentleman or Chamberlain on the elected Marshal, and invited him to all Court festivities. The Marshal of the nobility was quite independent of Ministers and might ask for an audience of the Emperor at any time to speak of the affairs of the nobles in his province. Our Tsars always patronised these unions, and even attempted to represent themselves as hereditary nobles. Thus Nicolas I declared that he was "the first noble of the Empire." The Grand Dukes bought estates in the provinces, fraternised with the members of the union, and signed telegrams addressed to the Marshal, "Hereditary Noble" instead of "Grand Duke." The Tsar readily accepted invitations from the nobles, and when he and his family lunched, dined, or took tea at one of the provincial Assemblies, tried to ignore his Imperial dignity and to play the part of the noble, Romanov. I have been present at some of these Imperial visits, and I was surprised at the absence of etiquette and the patriarchal simplicity that obtained. The Russian aristocrats in their turn caused their names to be inscribed in the registers of the nobility and maneuvered for election to the office of Marshal. They were by no means always successful. Very often at the elections a prince would be rejected, and a noble, more obscure, but more highly esteemed, would be chosen. The utmost equality reigned in the Assemblies; the Russian nobility had no quarterings, and a recently ennobled member had the same rights as those belonging to the noblest families. The unions became very rich in time, for unmarried or childless members often bequeathed their fortunes, their estates and their houses to the nobility of their district. After the emancipation of the serfs most of the landowners were ruined and had to sell their properties. The unions of the nobles were wise enough not to forsake them; thanks to their wealth, they were able to grant pensions to widows, and allowances for the education of orphans. Russian parents are so improvident and think so little of the future of their children, that without the union the latter, lacking the means of education, would have gradually lapsed into the state of the illiterate *moujiks*. By helping them, the unions maintained hereditary culture, the only culture which makes a man really civilised. We hereditary nobles are very proud of our union, for it has spent millions in order to introduce European culture into Russia. Better still, in introducing ᵗʰis it never dissociated itself from the Orthodox Church and was always distinguished for its patriotism. This was why the Russian nobility became strong and influential, and soon all-powerful.

Turgenev belonged to this hereditary nobility[1], as did Dostoevsky and Tolstoy, and most of the writers of this period. With the exception of Gontsharov, who was the son of a merchant, and Belinsky, who belonged to the lower middle classes, all my father's literary contemporaries — Grigorovitch, Pleschéev, Nekrassov, Soltikov, Danilevsky — were hereditary nobles. Some of them belonged to a much older nobility than Turgenev — the poet Maikov, for instance. This close friend of my father's came of such an ancient stock that he had even the honour of reckoning a saint among his ancestors — the famous Nil of Sorsk, canonised by the Orthodox Church.[2] Of course, Turgenev's pretensions to a higher degree of nobility irritated his literary colleagues and seemed ridiculous to them. On the other hand, the Russian aristocrats smiled at his claims, and refused to treat him as a great personage when he appeared in their *salons*. He was mortified and took his revenge on the Russian aristocracy by describing in his novel, *Smoke*, certain well-born adventurers, such as are to be found in all countries, but whom he represents as typical great Russian nobles.

Turgenev's megalomania, which is not uncommon in Russia, would not have prevented my father from remaining his friend. Snobbery is a malady more insidious than influenza. If we were to ostracise all the

1. The distinctive term "hereditary" is generally used in this connection, for there is in our country another nobility, known as "personal." It was introduced into Russia at the time when persons not belonging to the hereditary nobility could be condemned to suffer corporal punishment. The title of "personal nobility" was conferred on citizens who had received the higher education of the universities, in order to secure their immunity from such punishments. The "personal" nobles could not be registered with the hereditary nobles and enjoyed none of their privileges. After the abolition of corporal punishment, the distinction lost all meaning.
2. The Orthodox Church does not canonise saints until three or four centuries after their death.

snobs we know, we should live in comparative solitude. Dostoevsky would have pardoned Turgenev's weakness, as we forgive the lapses of those we love; yet my father broke with him and ceased to frequent literary *salons* some time before his arrest and his condemnation to death. To understand the situation as between Dostoevsky and his friends, the younger writers, we must go back a little.

Petersburg was never loved by the Russians. This artificial capital which Peter the Great created on the marshes, cold, damp, exposed to all the winds of the north, and plunged in darkness for three-quarters of the year, was obnoxious to my compatriots, who preferred the peaceful, sun-bathed cities of central Russia. Seeing that the Russians would not come and settle in Petersburg, our Emperors were obliged to people the new capital with Swedes and Germans of the Baltic Provinces. In the eighteenth-century Petersburg was three-quarters German, and German society led the fashion there. Towards the beginning of the nineteenth century the Schillerian tone reigned in Germany and passed thence into Russia. Everyone became lyrical; men swore eternal friendship to each other; women fell into swoons at the noble sentiments they uttered, young girls embraced each other passionately, and wrote each other long letters full of lofty sentiments. Politeness became so exaggerated that when ladies received visitors, they had to smile the whole time, and laugh at every word they uttered. This tone of exalted sentimentality is to be found in all the novels of the period.

When Moscow was burnt in 1812, many Moscowites fled to Petersburg and settled there. Other families followed their example, and Peter the Great's favourite capital soon became Russian. When my father entered the Engineers' School, Russian society was giving the tone in Petersburg. My compatriots, who are simple and sincere, thought the Schillerian pose ridiculous, and they were not altogether wrong; but unfortunately, in their reaction against this over-sentimental attitude, they fell into the opposite extreme of brutality. They declared that a self-respecting man should always speak the truth, and, under the guise of frankness, they became impudent. My grandmother, a Swede, brought up her children in the Schillerian tradition, and my mother has often told me how difficult her life became when she grew up and began to visit in Russian families. "It was no use to be polite and amiable," she said: "I received insults on every side. I could not even protest, for I should have been considered ridiculous. I could only retort by similar rudenesses." By degrees my compatriots began to enjoy these incivilities, and contests in insolence became the fashion. In drawing-rooms, at receptions, and at dinner-parties two men or two women would begin to attack each other with gross impertinence, and as they warmed to this vulgar display the spectators would listen with interest, taking sides, now for one and now for the other. At bottom of these conversational cockfights we find the Mongolian coarseness which lurks in the heart of every Russian, and emerges when he is angry, surprised, or ill. "Scratch the Russian and you will find the Tatar," say the French, who must often have noticed how a Russian of European education and distinguished manners became coarse and brutal as a *moujik* in a moment of anger.

Dostoevsky, brought up by a father who was half Ukrainian, half Lithuanian, knew nothing of this Tatar brutality. If we may judge by the lyrical letters he wrote to his brother Mihail, and the extremely respectful epistles addressed to his father, the Schillerian tone must have reigned in my grandfather's family. Russian coarseness amazed Dostoevsky when he first came in contact with it at the Engineers' School, and was, perhaps, the principal cause of his contempt for his schoolfellows. It astonished him still more when he encountered it in the literary *salons* of the period. As long as he remained obscure, he had not to suffer from it. He held his peace, and observed people; Grigorovitch, with whom he lived, had been brought up in the French tradition, and was always well-mannered.[1] But when the unexpected success of his first novel excited the jealousy of the younger writers, they avenged themselves by calumnies and insults. My father could not defend himself effectually, for he could not be insolent. He was nervous and excitable, as the children of drunkards generally are. Losing his self-control, Dostoevsky said absurd things, and excited the laughter of his unfeeling companions. Turgenev in particular delighted in tormenting him. He was of Tatar origin, and showed himself to be even more cruel and malicious than the others. Belinsky, who was a compassionate soul, sought in vain to defend my father, reproved his rivals, and tried to make them listen to reason. Turgenev seemed to find a special pleasure in inflicting suffering on his sensitive and nervous *confrère*. One evening in Panaév's house, Turgenev began to tell my father that he had just made the acquaintance of a conceited provincial, who considered himself a genius, and elaborated a caricature of Dostoevsky. Those present listened with amusement; they expected one of those cockfights which, as I have said, were

---

1. Baron Wrangel, with whom my father lived in Siberia, had been brought up in the German manner, that is to say in the Schillerian tone, which he retained till the end of his life.

so much in favour at the time. They applauded Turgenev and awaited Dostoevsky's counterattack with curiosity. My father was not a game-cock, but a gentleman; his sense of honour was more highly developed than that of the Russians who surrounded him. Finding himself thus grossly insulted, he turned pale, rose, and left the house without saying good-bye to anyone.[1] The young writers were much astonished. They sought out my father, sent him invitations, wrote to him—but all in vain. Dostoevsky refused to frequent the literary *salons*. The young writers were alarmed. They were only starting on their literary career and had as yet no position. Dostoevsky was the favourite of the public, and his young *confrères* feared that the public would take his part and would accuse them of jealousy and malice. They had recourse to calumny—a favourite device of the Russians, or rather of all societies still in their infancy. They went about clamouring against Dostoevsky as a pretentious upstart, who thought himself superior to every one, and was a mass of selfishness and ill-humour. My father allowed them to say what they would. He was indifferent to public opinion, and all his life he scorned to refute calumnies. When he cut himself off from Belinsky's advice and the literary conversation of other writers, which was so necessary to him, he consoled himself with the thought that honour and dignity are a man's best friends, and can take the place of all others. But it is very difficult for a young man to turn hermit; the youthful mind requires the interchange of ideas for its development. Having renounced literary society, Dostoevsky sought that of other intellectuals, and unfortunately became involved with Petrachevsky.

The aggressive tone of the conversational cockfights I have described have disappeared now, at least in good society. My compatriots travelled much in Europe in the second half of the nineteenth century, observed the politeness that reigned there, and introduced it into Russia. Yet in 1878, in the *Journal of the Writer*, my father confessed to his readers that when he was going on a journey, he always took plenty of books and newspapers, in order to avoid conversation with his travelling companions. He declared that such conversations always ended in gratuitous insults, uttered merely to wound the interlocutor.

My father's uncompromising attitude made a great impression on the Russian writers. They realised that his sense of honour was more highly developed than that of his contemporaries, and that consequently they could not talk to him in the disrespectful manner usually adopted by

1. "The Lithuanian is very reticent, one may indeed say modest. But when he encounters insolence, he becomes extremely haughty," says Vidûnas.

writers to each other at that period. When he returned from Siberia, his new friends, the collaborators of the *Vremya,* treated him with consideration. My father, who asked nothing better than to live on friendly terms with his colleagues, but who would not sacrifice his dignity on the altar of friendship, became their sincere friend, and remained faithful to them until his death. Turgenev imitated the other writers, and was polite, and even amiable with my father.[1] They met very rarely. While my father was undergoing his sentence in Siberia, Turgenev had the misfortune to fall in love with a celebrated European singer. He followed her abroad and was at her feet all his life. He settled in Paris, and only came to Russia for the sporting season. His unhappy passion prevented him from marrying and having a family. In his novels he is fond of depicting the type of the weak-minded Slav, who becomes the slave of an evil woman and suffers but is unable to throw off her yoke. Turgenev's character became embittered; misfortune developed his faults instead of correcting them. Seeing that the Russian aristocracy would not recognise him as the great noble he imagined himself to be, Turgenev changed his pose, and adopted the role of the European. He exaggerated the Paris fashions, took up all the manias of the French old beaus, and became more ridiculous than ever. He spoke disdainfully of Russia, and declared that if she were to disappear altogether, civilisation would not suffer in any appreciable degree. This new pose disgusted my father; he thought that if the first was ridiculous, the second was dangerous. Turgenev had, by adopting these opinions, become the leader of the *Zapadniki* (Occidentals), who had hitherto only had mediocrities in their ranks, and his incontestable talents gave them a certain prestige. Every time my father met Turgenev abroad, he tried to make him realise the wrong he was doing to Russia by his unjust contempt. Turgenev would not listen to reason, and their discussions generally ended in quarrels. When Dostoevsky returned to Russia, after spending four years in Europe, he became one of the leaders of the Slavophils, the party opposed to the Occidentals. Seeing the disastrous influence the Occidentals were exercising upon the infant society of Russia, Dostoevsky began to wage war upon them in his novel, *The Possessed.* In order to discredit them in the eyes of the Russian public, he caricatured their chief in his description of

1. Turgenev was particularly agreeable to my father at the time when the brothers Dostoevsky were publishing their paper. During one of his sojourns in Petersburg he gave a grand dinner to all the staff of the *Vremya.* Turgenev always managed his money affairs well, made friends with the rich publishers and insisted on good terms for himself, whereas Dostoevsky, who was obliged to ask his publishers for sums in advance, had all his life to take what they chose to give him.

the celebrated writer Karmazinov, and his stay in a little Russian town. The Occidentals were indignant and made a great outcry. They thought it quite legitimate for Turgenev to ridicule my father and caricature the heroes of his novels, but they declared it to be odious when Dostoevsky adopted the same attitude to Turgenev. Such is justice, as understood by the Russian intellectuals.

Although he opposed Turgenev and his political ideas, my father was all his life a passionate admirer of his contemporary's works. When he speaks of them in the *Journal of the Writer*, it is in terms of the warmest appreciation. Turgenev, on the other hand, would never admit that Dostoevsky had any talent, and all his life ridiculed him and his works. He acted like a true Mongol, maliciously and vindictively.

XXV

Dostoevsky and Tolstoy

Dostoevsky's relations with Tolstoy were very different. These two great Russian writers had a real sympathy and a real admiration for each other. They had a common friend, the philosopher Nicolas Strahoff, who lived at Petersburg in the winter and in the summer spent some months in the Crimea with his comrade Danilevsky, stopping at Moscow or at Yasnaïa Poliana[1] to see Tolstoy. My father was very fond of Strahoff and attached great importance to his criticism. Tolstoy also liked him and corresponded with him. "I have just read the *Memoirs of the House of the Dead* again," he wrote. "What a magnificent book! When you see Dostoevsky tell him that I love him." Strahoff gave my father great pleasure by showing him this letter. Later, when a new book by Tolstoy appeared, Dostoevsky in his turn said to Strahoff: "Tell Tolstoy I am delighted with his novel." These two great writers complimented each other through Strahoff, and their compliments were sincere. Tolstoy admired Dostoevsky's works as much as my father admired his. And yet they never met, and never even expressed any desire to meet. Why was this? I believe they were afraid they would quarrel violently if they ever came together. They had a sincere admiration for each other's gifts, but their respective ideas and outlook upon life were radically opposed.

Dostoevsky loved Russia passionately, but this passion did not blind him. He saw his compatriots' faults clearly and did not share their conceptions of life. Centuries of European culture separated my father from the Russians. A Lithuanian, he loved them as a man loves his younger brothers, but he realised how young they still were, and how much they needed to study and to work. European critics often make the mistake of identifying Dostoevsky with the heroes of his works.[2] My father was a great writer, who painted his compatriots from Nature. A moral chaos

---

1. The name of an estate belonging to Tolstoy, in the government of Tula.
2. Russian critics never make this mistake.

reigns in his novels, because such a chaos reigned in our Russia, a state still youthful and anarchical; but this chaos had no counterpart in Dostoevsky's private life. His heroines forsake their husbands and run after their lovers; but he wept like a child on hearing of the dishonour of his niece and refused to receive her thenceforth. His heroes lead lives of debauchery and throw their money about recklessly; he himself worked like a slave for years in order to pay the debts of his brother, which he accepted as debts of honour of his own. His heroes are bad husbands and bad fathers; he was a faithful husband, conscientiously doing his duty towards his children, and superintending their education as very few Russian parents do. His heroes are unmindful of their civic duties; he was a fervent patriot, a reverent son of the Church, a Slav devoted to the cause of the people of his race. Dostoevsky lived like a European, looked upon Europe as his second country, and advised all those who consulted him to study and acquire the culture which most of my compatriots lack.

Tolstoy's attitude was altogether different. He loved Russia as did Dostoevsky, but he did not criticise her. On the contrary! He despised European culture and considered the ignorance of the *moujiks* a supreme wisdom. He advised all the intellectuals who visited him to leave their studies, science and arts, and to return to the state of peasants. He gave the same advice to his own children. "I tell my sons that they must study, learn foreign languages, and become distinguished men, and their father tells them to leave their schools and go and work in the fields with the *moujiks*," said Countess Tolstoy to my mother. The prophet of Yasnaïa Poliana admired the faults of his compatriots and shared their absurd puerilities, their childish dreams of primitive communism. His ideal is the Oriental ideal of the Russian masses: to do nothing, to cross one's arms, and lie on one's back, yawning and dreaming. An apostle of pacifism, he advised his disciples to lay down their arms before the enemy, and not to struggle against wrong but to let it invade the world, leaving its overthrow in the hands of God. He prepared the triumph of the Bolsheviks and asserted ingenuously that he was preaching Christian ideas. He forgot that Jesus did not remain in a Yasnaïa Poliana, but that He went from place to place, eating as He journeyed, sleeping little, appealing to all hearts, awaking all consciences, sowing the seeds of truth in every town He entered, training disciples and sending them to preach His doctrine in other lands, fighting against evil to His last breath.

The difference between my father's ideas and those of Tolstoy manifested itself very clearly during the Russo-Turkish War. Dostoevsky in
his newspaper, *The Journal of the Writer*, demanded the liberation of the
Slav nationalities, their independence, and the free development of their
national ideal. He was indignant when he read how the Turks tortured
the hapless Serbs and Bulgarians, and he incited the Russians to deliver
these persecuted peoples by force of arms. He reiterated passionately
that this was the duty of Russia, that she could not abandon people of
her own race and religion. Tolstoy, on the other hand, thought Russia
had nothing to do with Balkan affairs, and that she ought to leave the
Slavs to their fate. He even asserted that the indignation of Russians
at the Turkish atrocities was merely a pose, and that a Russian was not
and could not be moved by descriptions of these cruelties. He confessed
himself that he felt no pity. "How is it possible that he should feel no
pity? It is incomprehensible to me!", wrote Dostoevsky in *The Journal of
the Writer*. Tolstoy's hostile attitude in the midst of the general enthusiasm for the Slav cause seemed so scandalous to his publisher, Katkov,
that he refused to allow the epilogue to *Anna Karenina*, in which Tolstoy
expounded his anti-Slav ideas, to appear in his paper. The epilogue was
published as a separate pamphlet. As a leading Slavophil, Dostoevsky
thought it his duty to protest in his own journal against Tolstoy's strange
attitude towards the unhappy victims of the Turks. In combating Tolstoy, he did not adopt the same method as in his conflict with Turgenev.
He had despised the cruel comrade of his youth and had not spared
him. But he loved Tolstoy and did not wish to give him pain. To take
the sting out of his criticism, he exalted Tolstoy to a giddy height, pro-
claiming him the greatest of Russian writers, and declaring that all the
rest, himself included, were merely his pupils.[1]

Such reverent criticism could not anger Tolstoy and did not affect his
admiration for Dostoevsky. When my father died Tolstoy wrote to Strahoff: "When I heard of Dostoevsky's death, I felt that I had lost a kinsman, the closest and the dearest, and the one of whom I had most need."

Tolstoy's European biographers generally describe him as a great aristocrat, and contrast him with Dostoevsky, whom, I know not why, they

1. Dostoevsky specially admired Tolstoy's powers of description and his style,
but he never looked upon him as a prophet. He thought indeed that Tolstoy did
not understand our people. Often in talking to his friends my father said that
Tolstoy and Turgenev could only paint truthfully the life of the hereditary nobility, which, according to him, was in its decline, and would soon be extinguished.
This surprised his friends very much, but Dostoevsky was right, for the Revolution has changed all the conditions of Russian life. He looked upon Tolstoy and
Turgenev as gifted *historical* novelists.

believe to be a plebeian. The better-informed Russian biographers know that both belonged to the same union of hereditary nobles. I suppose it was Tolstoy's title of Count which misled European writers. In Russia the title was nothing; it was possible there to meet titled people, bearing historic names, who belonged to the middle classes, and others, who had no titles, but were members of the aristocracy. European biographers of Tolstoy who wish to understand his position in Russia should read the history of the Counts Rostov in *War and Peace*. In this family Tolstoy describes that of his paternal grandfather. Count Ilia Rostov lives in Moscow, and receives everyone; but when he goes to Petersburg with his family he knows no one save an old Court lady, who is only able to procure them a single invitation to a ball in the great world, and even on this occasion cannot introduce any partners to the charming Natalia, because she knows no one herself. Count Rostov is very popular with the nobles of his own province who chose him as their Marshal; but when he goes to invite a travelling aristocrat, Prince Volkonsky, to dinner, the Prince receives him insolently, and refuses his invitation. When Countess Bezuhov insists that Natalia should come to her party, all the Rostov family is much flattered by the graciousness of the great lady. And yet the Countess only invites her to please her brother, Prince Kouragin, who is in love with the fair Natasha and wants to carry her off. He is already secretly married, so he cannot marry her; but he does not hesitate to compromise the girl, a villainy he would never have committed if she had belonged to his own world, for it would have ruined his career. Evidently, in the eyes of a Russian aristocrat the Counts Rostov were hereditary nobles of no importance, whom they could treat cavalierly. In contemporary times, the relations between the Russian aristocrats and the hereditary nobles were greatly modified, but in 1812 they were very cruel. In *War and Peace* Tolstoy carefully explained the position occupied by his grandfather and his father in Russia. But his mother was a Princess Volkonsky, a very ugly old maid, who, unable to find a husband in her own world, had married Count Nicolaï Tolstoy for love. She was a provincial, but she must have had relations in Petersburg, through whom Tolstoy could have gained admittance to the great world of the capital much more easily than Turgenev had been able to do. But he made no bid for such recognition. He was no snob and had all that dignity and independence of spirit which have always characterised our Moscow nobility. He made an unambitious marriage with the daughter of Dr. Bers, and spent all his life in Moscow, receiving everyone who was congenial to him without asking to what class of society his visitors belonged. Tolstoy had no love for the aristocrats. He shows his antipathy to them very plainly in *War and Peace, Anna Karénina* and *Resurrection*. He contrasts their opulent, luxurious and artificial exist-ence with the simple, hospitable life of the Moscow nobility. Tolstoy was right, for indeed the latter were very sympathetic. Their houses were not rich, but they were always open to their friends. The rooms were small and low, but there was always a corner for some old relative or invalid friend; they had a great many children, but they always managed to find a place among them for some poor orphan, who received the same ed-ucation and treatment as the children of the house. It was in this hospi-table, cheerful, kindly and simple atmosphere that Tolstoy was brought up, and it is this world that he describes in his novels. "Tolstoy is the historian and the poet of the lesser Moscow nobility," wrote Dostoevsky in his *Journal of the Writer*.

Tolstoy's European biographers, who have blamed his aristocratic luxu-ry, are strangely ill-informed; they can never have been either to Moscow or to Yasnaïa Poliana. I remember one day going with my mother when we were in Moscow to call on Countess Tolstoy. I was struck by the pov-erty of her house; not only was there no single good piece of furniture, no single artistic object, such as one might find in any Petersburg home, but there was absolutely nothing of the smallest value of any sort. The Tolstoys lived in one of those small houses between courtyard and gar-den which are so common in Moscow. Rich people build them of stone, poor people are content with wood. The Tolstoy house was of wood and was built without any architectural pretensions. The rooms of these little houses are generally small, low, and ill-lighted. The furniture is bought in cheap shops, as was the case in the Tolstoys' home, or it is made by old workmen who were formerly serfs, as was that I saw in other houses in Moscow. The hangings are faded, the carpets threadbare, the walls are hung with family portraits, painted by some poor artist, to whom a commission was given to save him from starvation. The only luxury of these houses consists of a pack of dirty, ill-tempered old servants, who show their fidelity by meddling in the affairs of their masters and speaking impertinently to them, and in a couple of clumsy ill-matched horses, brought from the country in the autumn, and harnessed to some old-fashioned carriage. Tolstoy's "luxury" was indeed far from dazzling; any prosperous European who has a pretty villa and a smart motorcar lives more sumptuously than he. I do not even know whether it would have been possible for Tolstoy to surround himself with luxuries. He owned a great deal of land, but the land of central Russia does not represent much wealth. It yields little income and absorbs a great deal of money. He could not sell it, for by Russian law, land inherited from a father must be transmitted to a son. Tolstoy had five sons; as they grew up and married, he was obliged to divide his estates between them, and it is probable that during the last years of his life he lived on the proceeds of his literary works. When Countess Tolstoy came to ask my mother's advice in the matter of publishing editions of her husband's books, it was in no rapacious spirit. She was probably in pressing need of money, and, like the honest woman she was, she wanted to work herself to increase her income.

Not only were the Tolstoys never great Russian aristocrats, they are not even of Russian origin. The founder of the Tolstoy family was a German merchant named Dick, who came to Russia in the seventeenth century, and opened a store in Moscow. His business prospered, and he decided to settle in Russia. When he became a Russian subject he changed his name of Dick, which in German means "fat," to the Russian equivalent, Tolstoy. At that period this was obligatory, for the inhabitants of Moscow distrusted foreigners; it was not until the time of Peter the Great that immigrants found it possible to keep their European names when they established themselves in Russia. Thanks to their knowledge of the German language, the descendants of Dick-Tolstoy obtained employment in our Foreign Office. One of them found favour with Peter the Great, who liked to surround himself with foreigners; he placed Peter Tolstoy at the head of his secret police. Later, the Emperor, in recognition of his services, bestowed on him the title of Count, a title Peter the Great had lately introduced in Russia, but which the Russian boyards hesitated to accept, thinking that it meant nothing.[1]

Like all Germans, the descendants of Dick-Tolstoy were very prolific, and two centuries after his arrival in Moscow there were Tolstoys in all our Government offices, in the army and in the navy. They married the young daughters of our hereditary nobility, generally choosing such as were well dowered. They did not squander the fortunes of their wives, and in many cases increased them. They were good husbands and good fathers, with a certain weakness of character which often brought them under the domination of their wives or mothers. They were industrious and useful in their various offices, and generally made good positions for themselves. I have known several Tolstoy families who were not even acquainted, and said their relationship was so distant that it was prac-

---

1. In Russia the title Count has the same value as the titles Marquis and Viscount in Japan.

tically non-existent. Nevertheless, I recognised in all these families the same characteristic traits; this shows how[7] little the Dick-Tolstoys had been affected by the Russian blood of their marriages. With the exception of Count Fyodor Tolstoy, a talented painter, they never rose above mediocrity, and Leo Tolstoy was the first star of the family.[1] Tolstoy's Germanic origin would explain many strange traits in his character, otherwise incomprehensible; his Protestant reflections upon the Orthodox Christ, his love for a simple and laborious life, which is very unusual in a Russian of his class, and his extraordinary insensibility to the sufferings of the Slavs under the Turks, which had so astonished my father.[2] This Germanic origin also explains Tolstoy's curious incapacity to bow to an ideal accepted by the whole civilised world. He denies all the science, all the culture, all the literature of Europe. *My Faith, My Confession*, he headed his religious rodomontades, evidently with the hope of creating a distinct culture, a Yasnaïa Poliana *Kultur*. Dostoevsky, when he speaks of Germany, always calls it "Protestant Germany," and declares that it has ever protested against that Latin culture bequeathed to us by the Romans and accepted by the whole world.

Tolstoy's Germanic origin may explain another peculiarity of his character, common to all the descendants of the numerous German families established in Russia. These families remain in our country for centuries, become Orthodox, speak Russian, and even sometimes forget the German language; and at the same time, they always retain their German souls, souls incapable of understanding and sharing our Russian ideas. Tolstoy is a typical example of this curious incapacity. Orthodox, he attacked and despised our Church. A Slav, he remained indifferent to the sufferings of other Slavs, sufferings which stirred the heart of every *moujik*. An hereditary noble, he never understood this institution, which has had such an immense importance in our culture.[3] A writer, he

1. The poet Alexis Tolstoy was, it is said, a Tolstoy only in name.
2. The American writers who were in Germany at the beginning of the recent war, speak of the insensibility of the Germans, not only to the sufferings of the Belgians and French, but also to those of their own compatriots. They describe the cruelty with which operations were performed on the wounded Germans, and the callousness with which the latter endured these. It is possible that the notorious brutalities of the Germans, of which so much was said during the war, were the result of a contempt for suffering produced by the severe discipline practised in Germany for centuries.
3. In *Anna Karénina* Tolstoy relates how Levin (his own portrait) is persuaded by his friends to come to a provincial town for the triennial election of a new Marshal of the nobility. While his cousins and his brother-in-law, Stiva Oblonsky, are in great excitement around him, wishing to get rid of the former Marshal and to elect another who will understand the interests of the nobility better, Lev-

did not share the admiration of all his *confrères* for Pushkin, that father of Russian literature. Dostoevsky gave up his "cure" at Ems in order to be present at the inauguration of the monument to Pushkin at Moscow; Turgenev hurried home from Paris; all the other writers, whatever their parties — Slavophils, or Occidentals — gathered fraternally round the monument to the great poet; Tolstoy alone quitted Moscow almost on the eve of the inauguration. This departure created a sensation in Russia; the indignant public asserted that Tolstoy was jealous, and that the glorification of Pushkin annoyed him. I think this was all nonsense. Tolstoy was a gentleman, and the base sentiment of envy was unknown to him. All his life he was very sincere and very honest. Pushkin's patriotic verse touched no chord in his Germanic soul, and he would not pay lying compliments to his memory. In all our vast Russia Tolstoy could only love and understand the peasants; but alas! his *moujiks* did not love and understand him! While our intellectuals were hurrying to Yasnaïa Poliana to ask the prophet for guidance, the *moujiks* of that village distrusted him and his religion. Their grandiose instinct told them, perhaps, that the good old God of Yasnaïa Poliana was only a wretched German imitation which was nothing to them.

The famous *Tolstoyism* has much in common with the tenets of the German sects which have long existed in Russia. When they settled in Russia, the German colonists at once began to attack the Orthodox Church, which they could not understand. They founded religious sects, the spirit of which was essentially Protestant, tried to propagate their ideas among our peasants, and sometimes made proselytes. The best known of these sects are: "Shtunda," "Dubohore," and "Molokané." Like a true German colonist, Tolstoy also founded a Protestant sect, the "Tolstoyans," and warred against our Church all his life. My compatriots were simple enough to take his religious ideas for Russian ideas, but foreigners were more clear-sighted. In their studies on Russia, many English and French writers have noted with surprise the affinity between Tolstoy's ideas and those of our different Germanic sects. The ignorance of my compatriots arises probably from the fact that in Russia no one attached any importance to the German origin of the Tolstoy family. Let us hope that there will yet be a biographer of the seer of Yasnaïa Poliana, who will study him from the point of view of this origin. Then we shall get a real Tolstoy.

---

in is perfectly indifferent, cannot understand their agitation and thinks only of one thing: how to get out of the town and return as quickly as possible to his village. He had evidently no inkling of his obligations to the nobles of his province.

XXVI

Dostoevsky the Slavophil

The Writer's Journal had an immense success; nevertheless, my father ceased its publication at the end of the second year, and began to write *The Brothers Karamazov*. Art claimed him, telling him that he was a novelist and not a publicist. *The Brothers Karamazov*, which many critics consider the best of Dostoevsky's novels, is one of those works which every writer bears in his heart and ponders for years, putting off the actual writing of it till the time when he shall have achieved perfection in his craft. My father did not believe he had reached this goal; he was too severe a judge to have thought so. But something told him that he had not much longer to live. "This will be my last book," he said to his friends when he told them he was going to write *The Brothers Karamazov*.

Such novels, analysed, meditated upon, caressed, so to say, for years, are generally full of autobiographical details; we find in them the impressions of childhood, youth and maturity. This was the case with *The Brothers Karamazov*. As I have said above, Ivan Karamazov, according to a family tradition, is a portrait of Dostoevsky in his youth. There is also a certain likeness between my father and Dmitri Karamazov, who perhaps represents the second period of the author's life, that between his penal servitude and his long sojourn in Europe after his second marriage. Dmitri resembles my father in his Schilleresque, sentimental and romantic characteristics, and his *naïveté* in his relations with women. Just such an one must Dostoevsky have been when he took such creatures as Maria Dmitrievna and Pauline N. for women worthy of respect. But his closest affinity with Dmitri comes out in the arrest, the interrogation, and the sentence of the young man. When he made this trial so important a part of his book, Dostoevsky evidently wished to record his own sufferings during the Petrachevsky proceedings.

There is also something of Dostoevsky in the *staretz* Zossima. The autobiography of this character was, in fact, my father's biography, at least so far as it relates to his youth. Dostoevsky placed Zossima in provincial surroundings, in a humbler rank of life than his own, and wrote his autobiography in that curious, somewhat old-fashioned language adopted by our monks and priests. Nevertheless, we recognise in it all the essential facts of Dostoevsky's childhood: his love for his mother and his elder brother, the impression made upon him by the masses he had listened to as a child; the book, *Four Hundred Bible Stories*, which was his favourite book; his departure for the Military School in Petersburg, where, according to the *staretz* Zossima, he was taught to speak French and to behave properly in society, but where at the same time he imbibed so many false ideas that he became "a savage, cruel, stupid creature." This was probably my father's opinion of the education he had received at the Engineers' School.

Although my father gave his own biography to Zossima, he was not content to create an imaginary *staretz*. He wished to study the type from nature, and before beginning *The Brothers Karamazov* he made a pilgrimage to the monastery of Optina Pustin, which is not very far from Moscow. This monastery was greatly venerated by my compatriots and looked upon as the centre of Orthodox civilisation; its monks were renowned for their scientific attainments. My father visited it in company with his disciple, the future philosopher, Vladimir Solowiev. Dostoevsky was much attached to him, and some persons supposed that he had described Solowiev in the person of Aliosha Karamazov.[1] The monks of Optina Pustin were informed of Dostoevsky's proposed visit, and they received him very cordially. They knew that he intended to describe the monastery in his new novel, and each monk wished to make him the confidant of ideas and hopes for the regeneration of the Church by the re-establishment of the Patriarchate. It is obvious that my father merely gave a literary form to the speeches of Zossima, Father Païssy and Father Iosef. In such a momentous matter as a religious question he preferred to let the monks speak, since they could speak with authority and knowledge. The personality of the *staretz* Ambrosius, who was the original of Zossima, made a great impression on Dostoevsky; he spoke of it with emotion after his return from his pilgrimage.

The success of *The Writer's Journal*, the enthusiasm with which the inhabitants of Petersburg received Dostoevsky at the literary *soirées*, the prestige he enjoyed among the students attracted the attention of people who felt more interest in the politics than in the literature of their country. These patriots saw no less clearly than Dostoevsky the abyss between

1. I think myself that Aliosha represents my father in early manhood.

the Russian masses and the intellectuals, which was widening every day. They longed to fill it; they dreamed of establishing patriotic schools, to accustom our young people to devote themselves to the great Orthodox work, our heritage from dying Byzantium, instead of allowing themselves to be carried away by the socialistic Utopias of Europe. A whole society of patriots gathered round my father, foremost among whom were Constantin Pobédonoszev and General Tcherniaev. Pobédonoszev was much liked and appreciated by the Emperor Alexander III, who kept him as his almost omnipotent Minister throughout his reign. Dostoevsky did not share all the somewhat narrow views of his new friend, but he loved him for his fervid patriotism and his honesty, an uncommon quality in Russia. It was probably this quality which made Dostoevsky choose him as the guardian of his children in the event of his premature death. Pobédonoszev accepted the responsibilities, and, in spite of his preoccupation with affairs of state, watched over us until my brother's majority, refusing to touch the money due to him as guardian. He had, however, never had any children of his own, and knew little about education, so he had not much influence upon us.

General Tcherniaev was an ardent Slavophil. Touched by the sufferings of the Slav peoples, he went to Serbia, collected an army of volunteers and fought bravely against the Turks. His chivalrous exploits produced such enthusiasm in Russia that Alexander II was obliged to declare war on the Turks, and deliver the Slavs from the Turkish yoke. This war had just come to an end, and Tcherniaev returned to Russia. Later, he was appointed Governor-General of our provinces in Central Asia; but in 1879 he was living in Petersburg with his family, and came to see Dostoevsky every day. Whenever I went into my father's study I found the General seated in his usual place on the sofa, discussing the future confederation of the Slav peoples. My father took the deepest interest in this question. A Slav Benevolent Society had just been founded in Petersburg under the presidency of a great Russian patriot, Prince Alexander Vassiletchikov. My father was offered the vice-presidency, and he accepted it eagerly. He attached so much importance to his functions that he would deprive himself of sleep in order to attend the meetings of the society, which took place in the afternoon. Dostoevsky had so accustomed himself to going to bed very late, that he was unable to sleep until five o'clock in the morning, but he always insisted on being called at eleven on the days of the meetings.

My father's biographers have often wondered why towards the end of his life he should have been so passionately interested in the Slav question, to which he had given so little thought in his youth. This ardour for the Slav cause awoke in Dostoevsky after his long sojourn abroad. When Russians go to Europe for a few months they are generally dazzled by European civilisation, but when they remain for several years and study it methodically my compatriots are struck not so much by the culture of Europeans as by their senility. How old, how worn-out all the Germanic tribes of Franks, Anglo-Saxons and Teutons seem to them! The good qualities and the vices of these people are alike those of the aged. Their very children are born old. It is painful to listen to the anaemic reflections of these little old men and women with bare legs. Europeans do not perceive this, because they are always living together, but we, who come from a youthful country, see it very plainly. It is evident that in a few centuries the trembling hands of the Germans will no longer be able to hold aloft the torch of civilisation handed to them by the dying Romans. The Slav race will pick up the fallen torch and in its turn give light to the world. The new world which all await impatiently will come from this race. True, the Germans themselves realise the urgent need of a new idea, and seek it feverishly, but they are incapable of finding it. We have lately witnessed one of these European attempts to make a new departure at last. For a whole winter we were regaled with talk of the League of Nations, which was to transform our planet into an earthly Paradise, and the result has been the conclusion of the most commonplace military treaty between France and England. The incapacity of the Germans to rejuvenate the world is easily explained; the whole of their culture is based upon the Latin civilisation of the ancient Romans, a civilisation magnificent, no doubt, but essentially pagan. Try as they may, the Germans will never free themselves from their aristocratic, feudal ideas. The Slavs, whose civilisation is more recent, knew nothing of the Latins. Their culture, received from the Orthodox Church of the East, was profoundly Christian from the beginning. We Slavs, a race of humble shepherds and modest husbandmen, have never had a feudal aristocracy. European capitalism is unknown among us. If by chance a Slav makes a great fortune, his children squander it. Their instinct tells them that capitalists are slaves, and they hasten to break the chains forged by unwise fathers. It would be easy for us to introduce into the world the new idea of Christian democracy which alone can calm the fever of socialist and anarchist agitation.

Dostoevsky, foreseeing the great mission which will some day be entrusted to the Slavs, earnestly desired their union in preparation for this solemn moment. He dreamed of a confederation of all the Slav nations, a pacific confederation, guiltless of any designs of conquest, or any desire to enslave the Germanic races. Each Slav country to keep its independence, its laws, its institutions, its government, but all to unite in ideas, science, literature and art. Whereas the Germanic nations organised Olympic games in order to show each other the strength of their mailed fists, we Slavs would organise more intelligent Olympiads, assembling in turn in our various capitals to admire the pictures and statues of our artists, listen to the music of our composers, and hear readings from our poets and men of letters. Instead of exhausting ourselves in fratricidal wars as the unhappy Germans have done, we would help, encourage, and fraternise with our fellows. Before offering the new law of Christian democracy to the world, *we* would begin by showing other nations an example of brotherhood and equality. This consummation seems very remote at present. The Slavs, but newly delivered from the yoke, are busy fixing the frontiers of their little states. They are right; before embarking on vast enterprises, it is well to consolidate one's own dwelling. But when all these houses — Russian, Serbian, Czech and others — have been solidly built, the masons will lift up their heads and begin to work out the great destiny of their race.

And yet this Slav dream may be realised sooner than we think. The League of Nations, that last refuge of feudal Imperialism, may play a great part in the organisation of the Slav Confederation. The more tactless Europeans exasperate the Slavs, meddling in their domestic affairs and trying to bend them to their will, the sooner will the Slavs begin to build up their fraternal union. The League of Nations will soon be confronted by a formidable Slav Confederation, which will be followed, logically and inevitably, by a Confederation of all the Germanic nations. The world is entering on a new phase of its civilisation. The ancient alliance between the countries of different races, the work of kings and diplomatists, has had its day. It was an anomaly, for the people in question generally hated each other the while they lavished compliments and marks of respect. The new confederations, based upon the fraternal sympathy of people of the same race, will be more durable. As they will be about equal in strength, these Slav, Germanic, Latin and Anglo-Saxon confederations will suppress war more surely than could a League of Nations, an antiquated expedient which was once adopted in Europe under the name of the Holy Alliance and lasted but a short time. When the Imperialistic countries feel the ground giving way beneath their feet, they league themselves together, hoping to arrest the popular movement by their united strength. Vain hope! We can combat men, but not ideas. The peoples of today desire above all things to be free and independent. They will suffer no tutelage, no matter under what form it may be proposed.

XXVII

Countess Alexis Tolstoy's Salon

Among the literary *salons* of Petersburg frequented by Dostoevsky in the last years of his life, the most remarkable was that of Countess Alexis Tolstoy, the widow of the poet Alexis Tolstoy. Her family was of Mongolian origin, and she had one of those incisive minds — "sharp as steel," as Dostoevsky said — which in Russia are only to be met with among persons of such descent. The Slav mind is slower, and needs long preliminary reflection before it can grasp a subject. The Countess was one of those inspiring women who are incapable of creating themselves but can suggest fine themes to writers. Her husband had a great respect for her intellect, and never published anything before consulting her. When she became a widow she settled in Petersburg. She was rich and had no children, but she was greatly attached to a niece whom she had brought up and married to a diplomatist. This diplomatist had been sent on a mission to Persia, and while awaiting his appointment to a more civilised post, the niece and her children made their home with the Countess. When Countess Tolstoy arrived in Petersburg she received all her husband's former comrades, the poets and novelists of his day, and sought to extend her literary circle. After meeting my father, she invited him to her house, and was charming to him. My father dined with her, went to her evening receptions, and was persuaded to read some chapters of *The Brothers Karamazov* aloud in her drawing-room before their publication. He got into the habit of going to see Countess Tolstoy during his afternoon walk, to talk over the news of the day with her. My mother, who was of a rather jealous disposition, made no objection to these visits, for at this time the Countess was past the age of seduction. Dressed always in black, with a widow's veil over her simply arranged grey hair, she sought to please only by her intelligence and amiability. She rarely went out, and at four o'clock was always at home, ready to give Dostoevsky his cup of tea. She was a highly educated woman, had read a great deal in all European languages, and often called my father's attention to some interesting article that had appeared in Europe. Dostoevsky, absorbed in creative work, was unable to read as much as he would have liked to do. Count Alexis Tolstoy's health had been bad, and he had spent the greater part of his life abroad, making a great many foreign friends, with whom the Countess kept up a regular correspondence. They in their turn sent their friends who were visiting Petersburg to her, and they became familiar figures in her salon. Conversing with them, Dostoevsky remained in contact with Europe, which he had always considered his second fatherland. The polished amenity that reigned in the Countess' *salon* was an agreeable change from the vulgarity of other interiors. Some of his former friends of the Petrachevsky circle had made fortunes, and were lavish of invitations to the illustrious writer. My father visited at their houses, but their ostentatious luxury was distasteful to him; he preferred the comfort and the subdued elegance of Countess Tolstoy's *salon*.

Thanks to my father, this *salon* soon became the fashion and attracted numerous visitors. "When Countess Sophie invited us to her evenings, we went if we had no other invitations more interesting; but when she added: Dostoevsky has promised to come, we forgot all other engagements and hastened to her house," said an old lady of the great Russian world (now a refugee in Switzerland) to me the other day. Dostoevsky's admirers in the higher circles of Petersburg applied to Countess Tolstoy to make them acquainted with him. She placed her good offices at their disposal, although the business was not always very easy. Dostoevsky was no worldling, and he did not care to make himself agreeable to persons who were uncongenial to him. When he met people of feeling, good and honest souls, he was so kind to them that they could never forget it, and twenty years later would repeat the words he had said to them. But when he found himself in the company of one of the numerous snobs who swarm in the drawing-rooms of a capital, he remained obstinately silent. In vain Countess Tolstoy would try to draw him out by adroit questions, my father would answer "Yes" or "No" abstractedly, and continue to study the snob as if he were some strange and injurious insect. Thanks to this uncompromising attitude he made many enemies; but this was never a matter he took very seriously.[1]

It will perhaps be objected that a great writer like Dostoevsky should

1. This haughtiness was in strong contrast to the exquisite politeness and amiability with which he would answer the letters of his provincial admirers. Dostoevsky knew that his ideas and his counsels were sacred in the eyes of all these country doctors, schoolmistresses, and obscure parish priests, whereas the snobs of Petersburg were only interested in him because he was the fashion.

have been more indulgent to stupid and ill-bred people. But my father was right to treat them with contempt, for snobbery, introduced among us by the barons of the Baltic Provinces, was disastrous to Russia. Feudal Europe has been used for centuries to bow before titled persons, capitalists and highly placed functionaries. The baseness of Europeans in this connection has often amazed me during my travels abroad. The Russian, with his ideal of fraternal equality, does not understand snobbery and is repelled by it. My compatriots look upon the haughty attitude of the snob as a provocation and an insult, which they never forget and are eager to avenge. Two centuries of Baltic snobbery brought about the disintegration of Russia. On the eve of the Revolution all our classes were at daggers drawn. The hereditary nobility hated the aristocracy, which encircled the throne like a great Wall of China; the merchants were hostile to the nobles, who despised them and would not mix with them; the clergy were impatient of the humble position they occupied in the Empire; the intellectuals, who had sprung from the people, were indignant when they found that Russian society looked upon them as *moujiks*, in spite of their superior education. If all had followed Dostoevsky's example and waged war against snobbery, the Russian Revolution might have followed a different course.

In Countess Tolstoy's *salon*, as in the *soirées* of the students, Dostoevsky had even more success with the women than with the men, and for the same reason: he always treated women with respect. The Russians have always retained their Oriental point of view with regard to women. Since the days of Peter the Great they have ceased to whip them; they bow low to them, kiss their hands and treat them as queens, trying to live up to their European civilisation. But at the same time they consider women as big children, frivolous and ignorant, who must always be amused by jests and anecdotes more or less witty. They decline to discuss serious subjects with them, and laugh at their pretensions to an interest in politics. There is nothing more exasperating to an intelligent woman than to see fools and ignoramuses posing as her superiors. Dostoevsky never adopted such a tone; he never tried to amuse or to fascinate women, but talked to them seriously, as to his equals. He would never follow the Russian fashion of kissing women's hands, he thought the practice humiliating to them. "When men kiss the hands of women they look upon them as slaves, and try to console them for their servitude by treating them like queens," he often said. "When in the future they come to recognise them as equals, they will be content to shake hands with them, as they do with their own comrades." Such speeches astonished the inhabitants of Petersburg, who could not understand them. It was one of the many ideas Dostoevsky had inherited from his Norman ancestors. The English do not kiss the hands of their women, but greet them by clasping their hands. And yet there is no country where the women have a freer and more independent position than England.[1]

Dostoevsky had a strong affection for Countess Tolstoy, who gave him that literary sympathy which all writers need; but it was not to her he entrusted his family at his death. He had another friend, whom he saw less frequently, but for whom he had a greater veneration. This was Countess Heiden, *née* Countess Zubov. Her husband was Governor-General of Finland, but she continued to live in Petersburg, where she founded a large hospital for the poor. There she spent her days tending the suffering, interesting herself in their affairs and trying to comfort them. She was a great admirer of Dostoevsky. When they met they talked of religion; my father gave her his views on Christian education. Knowing the importance he attached to the moral training of his children, Countess Heiden became my mother's friend and tried to influence me for good. After her death, which left a great blank in my life, I understood all I owed to this saintly woman.

The literary *soirées* inaugurated by the students of Petersburg soon became fashionable in the great world. Instead of getting up *tableaux vivants* or amateur theatricals, the great Russian ladies who patronised charities organised literary gatherings in their *salons*. Our writers placed themselves at their disposal and promised their help in working for a good cause. As always, Dostoevsky was the great attraction of these evenings. As the public here was a very different one to that he met at the students' gatherings, he discarded the Marmeladov monologue in favour of other fragments from his works. Faithful to his idea of bringing the intellectuals and the masses together, he chose to read to these aristocratic assemblies the chapter in *The Brothers Karamazov*, where the *staretz* Zossima receives the poor peasant women who have come on pilgrimage. One of these women having lost her son of three years old, leaves her home and her husband and wanders from convent to convent, unable to find comfort in her grief. It was his own sorrow which Dostoevsky painted in this chapter; he, too, could not forget his little Aliosha. He put so much feeling into the simple story of the poor mother that all

---

1. Dostoevsky's popularity with women may also have had another cause. According to one of his comrades in the Petrachevsky conspiracy, my father was one of those men who, "though the most virile of males, yet have something of the feminine nature," as Michelet says.

the women in his audience were deeply moved. The Hereditary Grand Duchess Marie Fyodorovna, the future Empress of Russia, was present at one of these evenings. She, too, had lost a little son and could not forget it. As she listened to my father's reading, the Cesarevna[1] cried bitterly, When the reading was over, she spoke to the ladies who had organised the evening, and told them she wished to talk to my father. The ladies hastened to meet her wishes, but they cannot have been very intelligent persons. Knowing Dostoevsky's somewhat suspicious character, they feared he might refuse to be presented to the Cesarevna, and determined to bring about the interview by a stratagem. They went to my father and told him in mysterious tones that a *very, very* interesting person wished to talk to him about his reading.

"What interesting person?" asked Dostoevsky in surprise. "Oh! you will see for yourself. Come with us!" replied the young women laughingly, and they took him to a little boudoir, pushed him in and closed the door behind him. Dostoevsky was astonished at these mysterious proceedings. The little room was dimly lighted by a shaded lamp; a young woman was quietly seated by a small table. At this time of his life my father no longer looked at young women; he bowed to the lady, as one bows to a fellow-guest, and thinking some joke was being played upon him, went out by the opposite door. Dostoevsky knew that the Cesarevna was to be at the party, but he believed, no doubt, that she had left, or perhaps, with his usual absence of mind, he had forgotten that she was among the audience. He returned to the large room, was immediately surrounded, and plunging into a discussion which interested him, entirely forgot the incident. A quarter of an hour later the two young women who had taken him to the door of the boudoir rushed up to him.

"What did she say to you?" they asked eagerly.

"Who do you mean?" asked my father.

"Who? Why, the Cesarevna, of course."

"The Cesarevna! But where was she? I never saw her."

The Grand Duchess was not content with this futile interview; knowing of the friendship between the Grand Duke Constantine and my father, she asked the former to present Dostoevsky to her. The Grand Duke at

---

1. Europeans often make a mistake in speaking of our Hereditary Grand Dukes as "Tsarevitch." This title belongs to the sons of the ancient Moscovite Tsars. The eldest son of the Emperor of Russia was the "Cesarevitch," and his wife the "Cesarevna." The word Tsar, which Europeans take for a Mongolian word, is only "Cæsar" pronounced in the Russian manner.

once arranged a reception and invited Dostoevsky, taking care to impress upon him whom he would meet. My father was rather ashamed of not having recognised the Cesarevna, whose portraits were to be seen in every shop window of the town. He went to the party bent on being amiable. He was delighted with the Cesarevna. She was a charming person, kindly and simple, who had the art of pleasing. Dostoevsky made a great impression on her; she talked so much of him to her husband that the Cesarevitch also wished to make his acquaintance. Through the intermediary of Constantine Pobédonoszev, he invited my father to come and see him. The future Alexander III interested all the Russophils and Slavophils of the Empire greatly. They expected great reforms from him. Dostoevsky wished very much to know him, and to talk to him about his Russian and Slav ideas. He went to the Anitchkov Palace, the official dwelling of our Hereditary Grand Dukes. The imperial pair received him together and were charming to him. It is very characteristic that Dostoevsky, who at this time was an ardent monarchist, disregarded Court etiquette and behaved in the palace as he was accustomed to behave in the *salons* of his friends. He spoke first, got up to go when he thought the conversation had lasted long enough, and after taking leave of the Cesarevna and her husband, left the room as he always left it, turning his face to the door. This was surely the first time in his life that Alexander III had been treated as a mere mortal. He was not in the least offended, and later spoke of my father with much esteem and sympathy. He saw so many bent backs in his life! Perhaps he was not sorry to find in his vast empire one spine less supple than the rest.

XXVIII

The Pushkin Festival

In June 1880 the inauguration of Pushkin's monument at Moscow took place. This great national festival brought all political parties together: Slavophils and Occidentals alike laid flowers at the base of the monument and celebrated the greatest of Russian poets in their speeches. Pushkin satisfied every one. The Occidentals admired his European culture and his poems, the subjects of which were of English, German and Spanish origin; the Slavophils exalted his patriotism and his magnificent Slav poems. All the Russian writers and intellectuals hastened to do him homage. Turgenev came from Paris and was given a great reception by his admirers. He had a most brilliant success at the literary *soirées* and eclipsed Dostoevsky, but the balance was redressed on the following day at the meeting of the Society of Letters, which took place in the Assembly Room of the Moscow nobility. Here Dostoevsky's success was so great that Pushkin's fête was transformed into a triumph for Dostoevsky. The leader of the Slavophils, Aksakov, declared from the tribune that my father's speech was "an event." Senator Coni, who was present, gave me an account of it later. This distinguished jurist is also a writer of talent and a brilliant lecturer. His sympathies were perhaps with the Occidentals rather than with the Slavophils, so his enthusiasm for Dostoevsky's speech is the more significant. "We were completely hypnotised as we listened to him," he said to me. "I believe that if a wall of the building had fallen away at that moment, if a huge pyre had been discovered in the square and your father had said to us, 'Now let us go and die in that fire to save Russia,' we should have followed him to a man, happy to die for our country." Extraordinary scenes took place at the close of the speech. People stormed the platform to embrace him and clasp his hand. Young men fainted with emotion at his feet. Two old men approached him, hand in hand, and said: "We have been enemies for twenty years; many attempts have been made to reconcile us, but we have always resisted. Today, after your speech, we looked at each other and we realised that henceforth we must live as brothers." Turgenev, who had hitherto vouchsafed only a chilly bow when he met Dostoevsky, was deeply moved, and, going up to my father, pressed his hand warmly. This action of Turgenev's, and the reconciliation of the two old enemies, were the two incidents of the day which impressed Dostoevsky most. He liked to talk of them at Staraja Russa on his return from Moscow.

What magic words were there in this famous speech, which was looked upon as a great event by the whole of literary Russia, those who had been unable to be present at the festival having read it in the newspapers? I give a *résumé* of what Dostoevsky said to the intellectuals of his country:[1] "You are discontented, you suffer, and you ascribe your unhappiness to the system under which you live. You think you will become happy and contented if you introduce European institutions into Russia. You are mistaken. Your sufferings are due to another cause.

Thanks to your cosmopolitan education, you are estranged from your people, you no longer understand them; you form a little clan, utterly foreign and antipathetic to the rest of the country, in the midst of a vast empire. You despise your people for their ignorance, and you forget that it is they who have paid for your European education, they who support by the sweat of their brows your universities and higher schools. Instead of despising them, try to study the sacred ideas of your people. Humble yourselves before them, work shoulder to shoulder with them at their great task; for this illiterate people from whom you turn in disgust bears within it the Christian word which it will proclaim to the old world when it is bathed in blood. Not by servile repetition of the Utopias of the Europeans, which lead them to their own destruction, will you serve humanity, but by preparing together with your people the new Orthodox idea."

These golden words went to the hearts of my compatriots, who were tired of despising their country. They were glad to think that Russia was no mere copy, no servile caricature of Europe, but that she in her turn might have a message for the world. Alas! their joy was short-lived! The curtain which hides the future, lifted by the hand of a man of genius, fell again, and our intellectuals returned to their fallacies. They worked obstinately for the introduction of the European republic into Russia, despising the people too much to ask their opinion, and believing in-

---

1. The speech, which is rather long, contains a very subtle analysis of Pushkin's poetry. The reader would do well to read the complete text. I only give my father's conception of the Russian people and its future. It was this new conception which had so fired the imaginations of our intellectuals.

genuously that eleven million intellectuals had a right to impose their will on a hundred and eighty million inhabitants. Taking advantage of the weariness produced by an interminable war, our intellectuals at last succeeded in introducing their long-desired republic into Russia. They soon realised how difficult it is to govern in Russia without the Tsar. The people at once showed their moral strength, which Dostoevsky had long ago divined, and which his political adversaries persisted in ignoring. The pride of this people of great genius and of a great future was deeply wounded by the idea that a handful of dreamers and ambitious mediocrities proposed to reign over them, and impose their Utopias upon them. They struggled against them as they continue to struggle against the Bolsheviks. The people defend their ideal, their great Christian treasure which they are keeping for the future and which they will proclaim to the world later, when the old aristocratic feudal society finally disintegrates. Have our intellectuals understood the lesson the Russian people have just given them? Not in the least. They continue to take their dream for a reality; they believe the Bolsheviks have succeeded in demonstrating to the recalcitrant *moujiks* the excellence of the European *régime* brought by them from Zurich in their sealed railway carriage. For my part, I believe that the Bolsheviks have given the death-blow to the republican idea in Russia. Our peasants have long memories, and for centuries to come the word "Republic" will be to them the synonym of disorder, robbery and murder. They will come back to the monarchic idea, by virtue of which they founded their immense empire, but the new monarchy will be much more democratic than the old. The people have realised that their *bare* are feeble folks, easily intoxicated by Utopias, incapable of weighing their actions, and they will not confide the government of the country to them again. They will, no doubt, take them into their service, because they will have need of their knowledge; but at the same time they will send to the new Duma many more of their own representatives than before. These new deputies will have no European culture; but, possessed of the good sense and knowledge of life characteristic of the Russian people, they will vote laws which would have seemed cruel and barbarous to our former government.

Russia has turned over a new page in her history. Dostoevsky, who understood and foresaw the future so clearly, will become her favourite author. Hitherto, my compatriots had been content to admire him; now they are beginning to study him.

* * *

It is curious enough that not one of the writers who gathered round Pushkin's monument and celebrated in prose and verse the great man's Russian poetry, his Russian heart, his Russian ideas and his Russian sympathies, made the slightest allusion to his negro origin, which is nevertheless of great interest.

In the seventeenth century one of the small negro principalities of Africa, on the Mediterranean coast, was conquered by its neighbours. The king was killed, his harem and his sons were sold to pirates. One of the little princes, bought by the Russian ambassador, was sent to Peter the Great as a present. The Emperor gave the little blackamoor to his young daughters, who played with him as with a doll. Noticing the intelligence of the child, Peter the Great sent him to Paris, where the young Hannibal, as the Emperor called him, received a brilliant education. Later he returned to Petersburg and served the Emperor with much devotion. Anxious to keep him in Russia, Peter the Great married him to the daughter of a *boyard*, and ennobled him. His descendants remained in our country, married Russians, and at the beginning of the nineteenth century repaid Russia's hospitality by giving her a great poet.[1] Although he was a good deal fairer than his maternal ancestors, Pushkin had many characteristics of the negro type: black frizzly hair, thick lips, and the vivacity, the passion and the ardour of the natives of Africa. This did not prevent him from being Russian in heart and mind. He formed our literary language, and gave us perfect models of prose, poetry, and dramatic art. He is the true father of Russian literature. Still, there are many things in Pushkin's life and works which are explicable by the fact of his African origin. Why, then, did none of his admirers refer to it?

Probably, because at this time the idea of race-heredity was unknown to the Russians. I do not know if it even existed at all in Europe. It was introduced later by Count Gobineau, who, I believe, discovered it in Persia. Certain French writers assimilated it, and, exaggerating it a little, made it very fashionable. It is such a basic truth that it is impossible to write a good biography without taking it into account, and we ask ourselves in astonishment how it was that it was not discovered earlier.

It was thanks to this ignorance of the idea of heredity that Dostoevsky never attached much importance to his Lithuanian origin. Although he and his brothers habitually said, "We Dostoevsky are Lithuanians," he sincerely considered himself a true Russian. This was also due to the fact that the former empire of Russia was much more united than is generally supposed. All those emigrants who at present demand the sep-

1. Pushkin's mother was a Hannibal.

aration of their country from Russia have, as a fact, no solid following. The majority of the Lithuanians established in the large Russian towns were sincerely attached to Russia. They were even more patriotic than the Russians, because they had inherited the idea of fidelity to their country from their civilised parents, whereas the sentiment has never been very strongly developed among the Russians. Our education tended to kill patriotism instead of stimulating it; its ideal was a pale and shadowy cosmopolitanism. On the other hand, the Lithuanians, with characteristic modesty, spoke so little of themselves and of their country, that Russians came to believe Lithuania had been long dead. It is only since the war that Lithuanians have begun to raise their heads timidly; but when we read the books they have published recently, we see very plainly that they know little of the history of their own country. Their intellectuals leave them year by year, migrating to Russia, Poland and Ukrainia, and the Lithuanians who have remained in the country have gradually become a rustic society of peasants and small tradespeople, who have but a dim recollection of their ancient glory and do not understand its causes. They forget their Norman culture, declare they have nothing in common with the Slavs, and pride themselves on belonging to the tribe of Finno-Turks. The Finno-Turks are a fine race; it would ill become us to disparage them, for they are the ancestors of the Russians, the Poles and the Lithuanians. But intellectually they are inferior and have never produced a single man of genius. It was not until they were crossed with superior races that they emerged from their obscurity and began to count in history. The fusion of the Finno-Turks established on the banks of the Niemen with the Slavs who came down from the Carpathians produced the Lithuanian people, who later assimilated the genius of the Normans. As long as this Norman fire continued to burn in the race, Lithuania was a brilliant and civilised state; when it began to die down, Lithuania gradually fell into oblivion, though it retained the Norman character which distinguished it from its Polish, Ukrainian and Russian neighbours. It was natural that Dostoevsky should have felt little interest in his obscure and forgotten nation, and should have attributed greater importance to his Russian antecedents. And yet those who read his letters will see that all his life he was haunted by the idea that he was unlike his Russian comrades and had nothing in common with them. "I have a strange character! I have an evil character!" he often says in writing to his friends. He did not realise that his character was neither strange nor evil, but simply Lithuanian. "I have the vitality of a cat. I always feel as if I were only just beginning to live!" he says, affirming that strength of character in himself which is natural to the Norman, but which he could not find in the Russians. "I happened to see Dostoevsky in the most terrible moments of his life," says his friend Strahoff. "His courage never failed, and I do not think that anything could have crushed him."[1] If Dostoevsky was surprised at his own strength, the childish weakness of his Russian friends was still more surprising to him. He was obliged to bring down all his own ideas to the level of their comprehension, and even so, they were often at crosspurposes. Their puerile conceptions of honour astounded him. Thus one of his best friends, A. Miliukov, anxious to save him from the trap set for him by the publisher Stellovsky, proposed that all his literary friends should help him to complete the novel *The Gambler* by writing each one chapter, and that my father should sign the whole. Miliukov, in short, proposed that Dostoevsky should commit a fraud, and was quite unconscious that he had done so. Later, when he described this incident to the public, he gloried in having tried to save his illustrious friend. "I will never put my name to another man's work," my father replied indignantly.

Another of Dostoevsky's most characteristic ideas, his passionate interest in the Catholic Church, is also only to be explained by atavism. The Russians have never shown any interest in the affairs of the Vatican. The Pope is hardly known in Russia, no one ever thinks or speaks of him, hardly any writer has mentioned him. But Dostoevsky has something to say about the Vatican in almost every number of *The Writer's Journal*, and discusses the future of the Catholic Church with fervour. He calls it a dead Church, declares that Catholicism has long ceased to be anything but idolatry, and yet we see plainly that this Church is still living in his heart. His Catholic ancestors must have been fervid believers; Rome must have played an immense part in their lives. Dostoevsky's fidelity to the Orthodox Church is merely the logical sequence of the fidelity of his ancestors to the Catholic Church. "I could never understand why your

---

1. Dostoevsky's biographers have laid too much stress on the eternal complaints in his letters to relations and intimate friends. These should not be taken too seriously, for neurotic people love to complain and to be consoled. I speak feelingly, for I have inherited this little weakness. My will is very strong; I think nothing could break my spirit or crush me, and yet any one reading my letters to my mother and my intimate friends would get the impression of a person in despair and on the verge of suicide. Doctors who specialise in nervous disorders could no doubt explain this anomaly. For my part, I think that persons may have both very strong wills and feeble nerves. In their actions they are guided by their strong wills, but from time to time they soothe their unhealthy nerves by cries and tears, and complaints to those of their friends who are indulgent to them.

father took such an interest in that old fool the Pope," said a Russian writer and friend of my father's to me one day. Now to Dostoevsky "that old fool" was the most interesting figure in Europe.

The spiritual and moral isolation in which my father lived all his life was no unique phenomenon in our country. Nearly all our great writers have been of foreign descent, and have felt ill at ease in Russia. Pushkin was of African origin, the poet Lermontov was the descendant of a Scotch bard, Lermont, who came to Russia for some reason unknown to me; the poet Yukovsky was the son of a Turk, Nekrassov's mother was a Pole; Dostoevsky was a Lithuanian, Alexis Tolstoy an Ukrainian, Leo Tolstoy of German blood. Only Turgenev and Gontsharov were true Russians. It is probable that young Russia is still incapable of producing great talents unaided. She can kindle them with the spark of her genius, but the pyre must be prepared by older or more highly civilised peoples. All these semi-Russians were never at home in Russia. Their lives were a series of struggles against the Mongolian society which surrounded and suffocated them. "The devil caused me to be born in Russia!" cried Pushkin. "It is a dirty country of slaves and tyrants," said the Scottish Lermontov. "I am thinking of expatriating myself, of escaping from the ocean of odious baseness, of depraved indolence which threatens on all sides to engulf the little island of honest and laborious life I have created," wrote the German colonist Leo Tolstoy. In fact, the more prudent of the great Russian writers left the country: the poet Yukovsky preferred to live in Germany; Alexis Tolstoy was attracted by the artistic treasures of Italy. Those who remained waged war on Russian ignorance and brutality and died young, vanquished by them, like Pushkin and Lermontov, who were killed in duels. Nekrassov lived among the Russians and died a most unhappy man; Dostoevsky himself records this in his obituary notice of Nekrassov. Tolstoy isolated himself as much as he could in his Yasnaïa Poliana, but it is difficult to isolate oneself in Russia. His disciples, stupid Mongols, ended by taking advantage of the old man's enfeebled will and estranging him from his wife, the one person who really loved and understood him; they dragged him from his home to die by the wayside... Poor great men, sacrificed by God for the civilisation of our country!

All these writers of foreign origin shared my father's ideas about Russia. They loathed our so-called cultivated society, and were only at their ease among the people. Their best types are drawn from the peasants, who in their eyes represented the future of our country. Dostoevsky acts as interpreter to all these great men when he says to the Russian intellectuals: "You think yourselves true Europeans, and at bottom you have no culture. The people, whom you propose to civilise by means of your European Utopias, is much more civilised than you, through Christ, before whom it kneels and Who has saved it from despair."

XIX

The Last Year of Dostoevsky's Life

Dostoevsky came back in the guise of a conqueror to Staraja Russa, where we were settled for the summer. "What a pity you were not at the Assembly!" he said to my mother. "How I regret that you did not see my success!" Faithful to her rule of economy, my mother had decided not to accompany my father to Moscow; she now urged him to go to Ems as soon as possible for his usual cure, but Dostoevsky had no idea of doing so. He was busy writing the single number of *The Writer's Journal* which appeared in 1880; it had an immense success. Dostoevsky wished to consolidate the theory he had just enunciated at the Pushkin festival and reply to his opponents, who, after the first intoxication was over, tried to smother the new-born idea. He hoped to go to Ems in September; then, exhausted by all the emotions of his triumph and his political struggle, he abandoned his foreign journey, thinking he should be able to do without Ems for once. Unhappily, he did not realise how worn out he was. His iron will, the ideal which was burning in his heart and filled him with enthusiasm deceived him concerning his physical strength, which was never great.

He proposed to start again with the publication of *The Writer's Journal*, for which the single number of 1880 was to serve as programme. Now that *The Brothers Karamazov* was finished, he became a publicist again and threw himself once more into the political arena. The first, and, alas! the only number of 1881, which appeared in January, contained a detailed programme. This testament of Dostoevsky's proclaims truths which no one would believe in his lifetime, but which are being realised by degrees, and will be completely realised in the course of the twentieth century. This man of genius foresaw events from afar. "Do not despise the people," he said to the Russian intellectuals; "forget that they were once your slaves; respect their ideas, love what they love, admire what they admire; for if you persist in scorning their beliefs, and in trying to inoculate them with European institutions which they cannot understand and will never accept, the time will come when the people will repudiate you in their anger, will turn against you and seek other guides. You demand a European parliament, and you hope to sit in this and to pass laws without consulting the people. This parliament will be nothing but a debating society. You cannot direct Russia, for you do not understand it. The only possible parliament in our country is a popular assembly. Let the people meet and proclaim their will. As to you intellectuals, your task will be to listen respectfully to the humble words of the peasant delegates and try to understand them, in order to give juridical form to their plain pronouncements. If you direct Russia in accordance with the desires expressed by the people you will not blunder, and your country will prosper. But if you isolate yourselves in your European debating society you will sit in darkness, knocking one against the other; instead of enlightening Russia, you will only be getting bruises on your foreheads. Increase the number of your elementary schools, extend the network of your railways, and, above all, try to have a good army, for Europe hates you and would fain seize your possessions. The Europeans know that the Russian people will always be hostile to their greedy capitalist dreams. They feel that Russia bears within her the new word of Christian fraternity which will put an end to their Philistine *regime*. Not with the Europeans but with the Asiatics should we work, for we Russians are as much Asiatics as Europeans. The mistake of our policy for the past two centuries has been to make the people of Europe believe that we are true Europeans. We have served Europe too well, we have taken too great a part in her domestic quarrels. At the first cry for help we have sent our armies, and our poor soldiers have died for causes that meant nothing to them, and have been immediately forgotten by those they had served. We have bowed ourselves like slaves before the Europeans and have only gained their hatred and contempt. It is time to turn away from ungrateful Europe. Our future is in Asia. True, Europe is our mother, but instead of mixing in her affairs we shall serve her better by working at our new orthodox idea, which will eventually bring happiness to the whole world. Meanwhile it will be better for us to seek alliances with the Asiatics. In Europe we have been merely intruders; in Asia we shall be masters. In Europe we have been Tatars; in Asia we shall be men of culture. Consciousness of our civilising mission will give us that dignity we lack as caricatures of Europeans. Let us go to Asia, to that 'land of holy miracles,' as one of our greatest Slavophils has called her, and let us try to make the name of the White Tsar greater and more venerated there than the name of the Queen of England, or the name of the Caliph."[1]

This, Dostoevsky's last will and testament, was incomprehensible to his contemporaries. His far-seeing mind had outstripped theirs. Russian society was hypnotised by Europe and lived solely in the hope of becoming entirely European some day. This idea had been greatly strengthened by the adhesion of our rulers. Like all the Slavo-Normans, the Romanovs hated the Mongols and feared Asia. Our Tsars, who owned several palaces in Europe, had none in Siberia or Central Asia, which they rarely visited. When Oriental princes came to Petersburg they were received politely but coldly. Faithful to the traditions of Peter the Great, the Romanovs worked obstinately at the introduction of European institutions into Russia. All our Imperial Councils, Senate, Duma, Ministries and Chancellories were faithful copies of the European models. Our girls' schools were imitations of French convents, and our military schools reproduced those of Germany. The Russian spirit was banished from those establishments, and my young compatriots who were educated in them preferred to talk French to each other. If our sovereigns succeeded in europeanising our nobles, they were unable to carry out the process with the people. The Russian nobles and intellectuals were weak, but the people were strong and remained faithful to their historic mission. Deprived of their European government, they immediately began to apply their Russian policy. Barely two years after the abdication of Nicholas II, Colonel Semenov was proclaimed Grand Duke of Mongolia, the Russians began to negotiate with the Emirs of Afghanistan and Kurdistan, and the Hindus were sending deputations to Moscow. The fact is that the Slav blood is decreasing more and more in the veins of the Russians, whereas their Mongolian blood increases year by year. If the Slavs of the West do not send their nationals to help us to colonise Asia, in a century more the Russians will be completely mongolised. The idea of their Slav fraternity is already waning perceptibly. In 1877-8 all Russia fought to deliver the Serbs and Bulgarians, and in 1917 our soldiers threw down their arms, indifferent to the invasion of Serbia by the enemy. Forgetting the Slavs, our people are transferring their sympathies to the Mongolians. Formerly they fought to deliver their Slav brothers from the Turkish and Austrian yoke; now they dream of de-

1. The above is only a *resume* of the last number of *The Writer's Journal*, which deserves careful study as a whole. It makes manifest Dostoevsky's Norman spirit, eager to fly to unknown regions, and to carry civilisation to the wildest places. This spirit is the more remarkable in him, because it is found in no other great Russian writer. Tolstoy, Turgenev and Gontsharov breathe nothing of this pioneer spirit. The civilisation of the Mongols does not interest them.

livering their new brothers, the Oriental peoples, from their European oppressors. The Asiatic tribes in their turn are attracted to the Russians by their Mongolian blood, which becomes ever more apparent in our people. Russia has but to hold out her hand, and it is eagerly grasped by innumerable brown paws! The Asiatics have long been awaiting this gesture. They are weary of barbarism and yearn for civilisation; they aspire to play their part in the destinies of the world. The civilisation the English offer them is too lofty for them; they cannot assimilate it, all the less because it is offered to them with scorn. The English are ready to construct canals and railways in India, but they refuse to mix with the natives and leave them to rot in their pagan superstitions. Yet nothing is so wounding to the Oriental as contempt, for nowhere is the sense of dignity so highly developed as in the East. The Oriental peoples will always be attracted to the Russians, for the bear is reputed a kindly, modest and generous beast. It is well known in the East that he is ready to give a fraternal salute to all the muzzles that offer themselves, regardless of their colour. He will gladly mate with the Mongolian and will love his yellow cubs as tenderly as his white cubs. Russia will give Mongolia her European culture, which is as yet small, and therefore easy to assimilate. She will proclaim the Gospel to them and invite the Orientals to the banquet of the Lord. In former times, the days of the Moscovite Patriarchs and Tsars, the Christian mission was considered to be the sacred duty of Muscovy. When the Russians had vanquished some Mongolian tribe, they at once sent their missionaries into the conquered provinces. They built churches and convents, they attracted the young Oriental princes to Moscow, and dazzled them with the fêtes of the Tsars, the splendour and the friendliness of the *boyards*. The young Mongolians, fascinated by the first civilisation they had encountered, embraced Orthodoxy, together with all their tribe. The majority of our aristocrats and hereditary nobles are descended from these Mongolian princes, and are distinguished by their ardent patriotism. By suppressing the Patriarchate, Peter the Great put an end to this excellent Moscovite policy. His successors followed his example, and instead of sending missionaries to Asia, patronised the mosques, adorning them with splendid carpets from the Russian palaces; they helped the Buddhists to construct their temples, to the great indignation of our clergy, who were always faithful to the Moscovite tradition. Future Russian patriarchs will renew their Christian effort in Asia. Europeans seek only mines of gold and of silver in the continent; we Russians will find in this "land of holy miracles" other mines, of greater value to humanity. We will discover treasures of faith, eloquent apostles, capable of combating the atheism of Europe, and of curing this mortal malady.

The Russian Revolution heralds the awakening of all Asia. The European phase of our history is at an end; its Oriental phase is about to begin. The Russians will gradually lose all interest in European affairs and will become absorbed in those of Asia. They will help the other Oriental nations to shake off the European yoke and will take them under their protection. Dostoevsky's dream will be realised: the name of the White Tsar will be more venerated than that of the English king or that of the Caliph.

Strange to say, the Europeans are actually promoting our conquest of Asia, which will deprive them of their rich Oriental colonies. Taking advantage of the present disorders in Russia, they are working feverishly to detach Lithuania, Ukrainia, Georgia, Finland, Esthonia and Livonia from her. They think thus to weaken our country, and do not see that as a fact they will strengthen her. The Lithuanians, the Ukrainians, the Georgians and the natives of the Baltic Provinces have always hated and despised the Mongolian blood of the Russians, and have done all they could to turn us away from Asia. More highly civilised than the Russians, they have had an immense influence on my compatriots, and have constituted the chief barrier to our fusion with the Asiatics. When there are no longer any Slavo-Norman and Georgian deputies in the Duma, the Russian deputies will agree better, and their Mongolian blood will draw them to the East. Europeans clamour for a democratic *régime* in Russia, and do not see that the more democratic Russia becomes, the more hostile will she be to Europe. Our aristocrats and nobles talked French and English to each other and looked upon Europe as their second fatherland; our middle classes and peasants do not learn foreign languages, do not read European authors, do not travel in Europe, and dislike foreigners. They will bear their new Tsars towards Asia, and these rulers, freed from the European influence of Baltic barons, Poles and Georgians, will no longer be able to oppose the will of the people. By creating a democratic *régime* in Russia, Europeans and Americans think they will prepare the way for the exploitation of our mineral and vegetable wealth. They are wrong, for our *moujiks* will be more tenacious guardians of the soil than our Europeanised nobles, who were ready to barter their possessions for the means to enjoy life on the terraces of Monte Carlo. The *moujiks* always initiate their strikes and insurrections by killing the European staff in mines and factories. The thought that foreigners are becoming millionaires by virtue of our national riches seems to them profoundly humiliating. Deceived by our *émigrés*, Europeans and Americans know nothing of the real character of our peasants, and generally take them for idiots who can be easily ruled. The Europeans hesitate to fight against Bolshevism, hoping that disorder will weaken Russia; and meanwhile the Russians are consolidating their new friendship with the Orientals, which, based as it is on mutual sympathy, may become very strong. While Europe is changing her attitude to our country daily, uncertain what policy to follow, Russia, the bird of fire, will take flight definitively to the East. The blindness of Europe and America in this connection is almost comic, yet it is in the order of things. When God is about to proclaim a new truth to the world, He begins by blinding those who cling to the old idea which has become meaningless and useless.

✳ ✳ ✳

While thus occupied with the politics of his country, Dostoevsky did not neglect his children, and he continued to read the masterpieces of Russian literature to us in the evenings. During this last winter of his life he recited to us fragments of Griboïedov's celebrated play, *The Misfortune of Being Too Clever*. This witty comedy is full of phrases which have become proverbial among us. Dostoevsky had a great admiration for this excellent satire on Moscow society, and liked to see it performed. He thought, however, that our actors misunderstood it, especially as to the part of Repetilov, in whom he saw the personification of the liberal party among the Occidentals. Repetilov does not appear until the end of the piece. He is invited to Famonsov's ball, but does not arrive till four o'clock in the morning, when all the other guests are leaving. He comes in rather drunk, supported by two footmen, and at once begins to declaim interminable speeches; the guests listen with smiles and gradually slip away, leaving their places to others. Repetilov does not notice that his audience is shifting and changing, and he talks on. Our actors represent Repetilov as a buffoon, but Dostoevsky considered the type intensely tragic. He was right, for the incapacity of our intellectuals to understand Russia and find useful work for her, their Oriental indolence which manifests itself in interminable talk, is a disease. Dostoevsky had so often declaimed and explained this comedy to us that at last he wished to play the part himself, in order to show his conception of it. He expressed this wish to some friends, who proposed that he should get up private theatricals at their house, and give the final act of Griboïedov's famous work. This interesting project was much discussed in Petersburg. My father would not appear in public until he was *well* prepared, and rehearsed constantly to his children. As usual, he was fired by his new idea and acted seriously, walked in, stumbled, gesticulated and declaimed. We followed his impersonation admiringly. We had a little friend, Serge K., the only son of a rich widow, who spoiled him a good deal. In one of the rooms of her flat she had a small stage built with a curtain and a little scenery, and there we acted for our parents, representing Krilov's fables or the poems of our great Russian writers. In spite of his many occupations, Dostoevsky never missed our performances, and would encourage the young actors by applause. We began to have a passion for the theatre, and our father's performance interested us greatly. I have always regretted that Dostoevsky's death prevented him from appearing as an actor. He would have created an original and memorable type. This, indeed, was not the first time that the Ukrainian passion for the theatre had manifested itself in Dostoevsky. When he first came out of prison he wrote a comedy, *An Uncle's Dream*, which he afterwards transformed into a novel. In one of his letters he says that he had laughed a good deal while writing this play. He declared that the hero, Prince K., was like himself, and indeed the naïve and chivalrous character of the poor prince recalls that of my father. Later, when he returned to Petersburg Dostoevsky was fond of inventing speeches "in the manner of Prince K.," and he would declaim them to his friends, assuming the voice and gestures of the poor degenerate. This amused him very much, and he was able to give life to his hero. It is curious that my father twice represented himself as a prince—in *The Idiot* and *An Uncle's Dream*—and in each instance as a degenerate.

XXX

Death of Dostoevsky

Towards the end of January my aunt Vera came from Moscow to stay with her sister Alexandra. My father was delighted to hear of her arrival, and hastened to invite her to dinner. He recalled with pleasure the numerous visits he had paid to her house and the cordial welcome he had received during his widowerhood. He looked forward to talking with her about his nephews and nieces, about his mother, and their childhood at Moscow and Darovoye. He had no suspicion that his sister was bent on a very different kind of conversation.

The fact is that the Dostoevsky had long been at daggers drawn concerning the heritage of their aunt Kumanin. When she died she left all her money to her husband's heirs; but a tract of timberland of some twelve thousand *deciatin* in the government of Riazan was to be divided between her Dostoevsky nephews and nieces, and the children of another sister, or cousin. The numerous heirs could not agree, and wasted time in interminable disputes. These discussions went on at Moscow, and my father, who was but slightly acquainted with his aunt's relatives, took no part in them, and waited impatiently for them to come to some agreement and hand over his share of the bequest, which amounted to two thousand *deciatin*. It was a very considerable property; unfortunately, it was far from a railway and difficult of access, which diminished its value. Nevertheless, Dostoevsky set great store on it, for it was the only property he could leave to his family. And this heritage was suddenly called in question by his sisters.

According to Russian law at that time, women might only inherit a fourteenth share of any real estate. My aunts, who were all rather avaricious, had counted a good deal upon their aunt's property, and were very much annoyed to find they were to receive a mere trifle. They then remembered how readily their brother Fyodor had given up his right to his parent's property in return for a small sum of ready money. They thought he would allow himself to be plundered a second time just as readily, and they asked him to resign his claim in favour of his three sisters, on the ground that he had already received much more from his aunt than any other member of the family. It is true that he was always the favourite of his aunt, who was also his godmother. But in the first place my great-aunt Kumanin had inherited her fortune from her husband, and was at liberty to dispose of it as she pleased; and secondly, my father had spent most of the money given to him by his aunt in providing for the needs of the Dostoevsky family. In a letter to a friend my father told how he had sacrificed 12,000 roubles he had received from her in an effort to save the newspaper *Epoha*, which belonged to his brother Mihail. He had helped his brother Nicolai all his life, and his sister Alexandra during her husband's illness, to say nothing of my uncle Mihail's children, *who* were dependent on him for years. Nevertheless, knowing the generosity of my father's nature, I am sure that he would have given up his share of the heritage to his sisters if he had not had to consider the superior claims of his wife and children. He had at last paid off his brother Mihail's debts, but as he had to provide for three households — that of his brother Nicolai, that of his stepson Issaieff, and his own — he spent all he made and could save nothing. It is true that he had his works to leave us; but in Russia there is no security in such a heritage. It often happens that a writer who has been widely read during his life is completely forgotten after his death. At that time no one could have foreseen the huge place Dostoevsky was destined to fill, not only in Russia but throughout the world. He himself did not suspect it. The translation of his works into foreign languages had already begun, but he attached little importance to these translations. He thought himself a Russian, and declared that Europeans were incapable of understanding Russian ideas. He was right, for our great writers — Pushkin, Lermontov, Gogol, Griboïedov, Gontsharov and Ostrovsky — never had any great success in Europe; nor, indeed, had Turgenev, though his European friends advertised him zealously. Dostoevsky was oblivious of his Norman spirit, which endeared him to the people of Europe, just as Tolstoy's Germanic spirit had ensured his fame abroad. There is scarcely any nation in Europe or America which has not some admixture of Norman blood in its veins. The passionate faith of the Normans and their prodigious perspicacity, which are manifested in Dostoevsky's works, appeal to Europeans, while his tender, generous, enthusiastic Slav soul attracts the Slavs. The Mongolian strain, which my father had inherited from his Moscovite grandfather, was, on the other hand, very weak in him; this is perhaps why the Oriental peoples, including the Jews, have never loved Dostoevsky.

My father could not reckon upon any Government pension for his wife and children. Pensions were only given to the widows of Government officials, and my father refused to serve the State, for he wished to remain free and independent. My mother was the first widow of a writer to whom the State awarded a pension,[1] and it was a surprise to everyone. My father felt that he had no right to take the bread of his children to give to his sisters, who, indeed, were better off than we were. My aunt Alexandra had a house in Petersburg, my aunt Barbara owned several in Moscow, my aunt Vera had kept Darovoye, her parents' estate, for herself. They had all married young, and at the time of which I am writing their children were grown up and able to earn their own living, while we were still very little. In vain did Dostoevsky argue thus with his sisters; they would not listen to reason. My aunt Alexandra quarrelled with her brother, and ceased to visit us; my aunt Barbara, more diplomatic, held aloof, and would not discuss the matter. Knowing how much attached Dostoevsky was to his sister Vera's family, the other two sent her to my father to make a fresh attempt.

The family dinner took place on Sunday, the 25th of January. It began gaily with jokes and reminiscences of the games and amusements of Dostoevsky's childhood. But my aunt was anxious to get to business, and she began to discuss the eternal question of the Kumanin estate which had poisoned the lives of all the Dostoevsky. My father frowned; my mother tried to turn the conversation by questioning her sister-in-law about her children. It was no use; my aunt Vera was the least intelligent of the whole family. Well coached by her cleverer and more cunning sisters, she was afraid of forgetting their instructions, and continued to talk of her business, with growing excitement. In vain Dostoevsky explained his difficult financial position, and spoke of his duties as a father; my aunt would not listen; she reproached my father for his "cruelty" to his sisters, and ended by bursting into tears. Dostoevsky lost patience, and refusing to continue the painful discussion, left the table before the meal was finished. While my mother was escorting her

1. The Government gave my mother the pension of 2000 roubles (£200) which is allotted to the widows of generals. She was further offered two nominations for us in the Corps of Pages and the Smolny Institute, aristocratic Russian schools. She accepted these, but at the time we were too young to be sent to school. When we were older, the posthumous edition of my father's works was yielding such a good income that my mother placed us in other establishments and paid for our education herself. She explained to us that according to my father's ideas parents ought to provide for their children themselves and leave the nominations to orphans.

sobbing sister-in-law, who insisted on going home at once, my father took refuge in his own room. He sat down at his writing-table, holding his head in his hands. He felt an extraordinary weariness creeping over him. He had looked forward so much to this dinner, and this cursed heritage had spoilt his evening... Suddenly he felt a strange moisture on his hands; he looked at them; they were covered with blood. He touched his mouth and his moustache and withdrew his hand in horror. He had never had any haemorrhage before. He was terrified and called his wife. My mother hurried to him, and sent at once for the doctor; meanwhile she made us come into my father's room, tried to joke, and brought in a comic newspaper which had just arrived. My father regained his self-possession, laughed at the comic illustrations, and joked with us in his turn. The blood had ceased to flow from his mouth; his face and hands had been washed. Seeing our father laughing and jesting, we could not understand why our mother had said that papa was ill and that we must try to amuse him. The doctor arrived at last, reassured my parents, declared that haemorrhage often occurred in cases of catarrh of the respiratory organs, but ordered my father to go to bed at once and to stay there for two days, keeping as quiet as possible. My father lay down obediently on his Turkish sofa, never to rise again...

The next morning he woke cheerful and comfortable. He had slept well, and only remained in bed because of the doctor's instructions. He wished to receive his intimate friends who visited him every day, and he spoke to them about the first number of *The Writer's Journal* of 1881 which was about to appear, and in which he was deeply interested. Seeing that my father attached no importance to his illness, his friends thought that it was a passing indisposition. In the evening, after they had left, my father had another haemorrhage. As the doctor had told my mother that this would perhaps happen, she was not much alarmed. She was, however, greatly distressed on the following day, Tuesday, by the extreme prostration of her husband. Dostoevsky had ceased to interest himself in his paper; he lay on his sofa with his eyes closed, astonished at the strange weakness which laid him low, for he had always been so energetic and so full of life, bearing all his sufferings without altering his daily routine or interrupting his work. The friends who came to see how he was were alarmed at his weakness, and advised my mother not to trust too much in Dr. Bretzel, our usual medical man, but to have another opinion. My mother sent for a specialist, who was unable to come till the evening. He explained that the weakness was the inevitable result of the two haemorrhages, and might pass off after a few days. But he did not conceal from my mother that the case was much more serious than Dr. Bretzel had supposed. "This night will decide everything," he said.

Alas! when my father woke in the morning after a very restless night, my mother realised that his hours were numbered. My father, too, realised it. As always in the crises of his life, he turned to the Gospel. He begged his wife to open his old prison Bible and to read the first lines on which her eyes should fall. Repressing her tears, she read aloud: "But John forbade Him, saying: I have need to be baptised of Thee, and comest Thou to me? And Jesus answering said unto him: "Hold me not back[1] for thus it becometh us to fulfil all righteousness." My father thought for a moment and then said to his wife: "Did you hear? Hold me not back. My hour has come. I must die."

Dostoevsky then asked for a priest, made his confession and received the Holy Sacrament. When the priest had left he made us come into his room, and taking our little hands in his, he begged my mother to read the parable of the Prodigal Son. He listened with his eyes closed, absorbed in his thoughts. "My children," he said in his feeble voice, "never forget what you have just heard. Have absolute faith in God and never despair of His pardon. I love you dearly, but my love is nothing compared with the love of God for all those He has created. Even if you should be so unhappy as to commit a crime in the course of your life, never despair of God. You are His children; humble yourselves before Him as before your father, implore His pardon, and He will rejoice over your repentance, as the father rejoiced over that of the Prodigal Son."

He embraced us and gave us his blessing; we left the death-chamber, weeping. Friends and relations were assembled in the drawing-room, for the news of Dostoevsky's dangerous illness had spread through the city. My father made them all come in one after the other, and said an affectionate word to each. As the day wore on his strength diminished sensibly. Towards evening he had another haemorrhage, and began to lose consciousness. The doors of his room were then opened, and his friends and relatives came in to be present at his death. They stood round without speaking or weeping, careful not to disturb his agony. Only my mother wept silently, kneeling by the sofa on which her husband lay. A strange sound like the gurgling of water came from the throat of the dying man, his breast heaved, he spoke quickly in low tones, but what he said no one could understand. Gradually his breathing became quieter, his words less audible. At last he was silent...

1. Thus in the Russian version apparently, as appears from the context. In the English version: Suffer it to be so now. — [Tr.]

I have since been present at the death of several friends and relatives, but none was so radiant as that of my father. His was a truly Christian death, such as the Orthodox Church desires for all her children — a death without pain and without shame. Dostoevsky had only suffered from weakness; he did not lose consciousness till the last moment. He saw death approaching without fear. He knew that he had not buried his talent, and that all his life he had been God's faithful servant. He was ready to appear before his Eternal Father, hoping that to recompense him for all he had suffered in this life God would give him another great work to do, another great task to accomplish.

✳ ✳ ✳

When a person dies in Russia, his body is immediately washed. He is then dressed in his finest linen and his best clothes and laid on a table covered with a white cloth until his coffin is ready. Tall candlesticks are brought from the nearest church, and a cloth of gold, which is laid over the body. Twice a day the priest comes to recite the *panikida*, or prayers for the dead, which he says accompanied by the choir of his church. The friends and relatives of the deceased attend, each holding a lighted taper. The rest of the day and all the night a lector of the church or a nun reads the Psalms aloud, standing at the foot of the coffin. The burial takes place on the third day, sometimes not until the fourth, if relations who wish to be present live in distant provinces and cannot come sooner.

When after a feverish night I got up and went, my eyes red with crying, into my father's room, I found his body lying on the table, his hands crossed on his breast, supporting an *icon* which had just been laid upon them. Like many nervous children, I was afraid of the dead, and would not go near them; but I had no fear of my father. He seemed to be sleeping on his cushion, smiling softly, as if he were looking at something beautiful. A painter was already installed by his side, drawing Dostoevsky in his eternal sleep. The papers had announced my father's death that morning, and all his friends hastened to be present at the first *panikida*. Deputations of students from the various higher schools of Petersburg followed them. They arrived accompanied by the priest attached to their school, and he recited the prayers, the students chanting the responses. The tears ran down their cheeks; they sobbed as they looked on the motionless face of their beloved master. My mother was wandering in and out like a shadow, her eyes swollen with weeping. She realised what had happened so imperfectly that when a Court official came from the Emperor Alexander II to inform her that the State proposed to allow her a pension, and provide for the education of her children, she rose joyfully to go and tell her husband the good news. "It was not until this moment," she told me later, "that I realised that my husband was dead, and that henceforth I should live alone, without that friend to sympathise with my joys and sorrows." My uncle Jean, who, by a strange coincidence, arrived in Petersburg just at the time of Dostoevsky's death, had to see to all the arrangements for the funeral. He asked his sister where she wished her husband to be buried. My mother then recalled a conversation she had had with Dostoevsky on the day of the poet Nekrassov's funeral some years before, in the cemetery of Novodevitchïe.[1] My father made a speech over the open grave of the poet and came home sad and depressed. "I shall soon follow Nekrassov," he said to my mother. "Pray bury me in the same place. I do not wish to sleep my last sleep at Volkovo among the Russian writers.[2] They hated me and persecuted me all my life and made it very bitter to me. I should like to rest beside Nekrassov, who was always good to me, who was the first to tell me I had talent, and who did not forget me when I was in Siberia."

My mother, seeing he was sad and unhappy tried to distract his thoughts by jesting, a method which she generally found successful.

"What an idea!" she said gaily. "Novodevitchïe is so dismal and lonely! I would rather bury you at the Alexander Nevsky monastery."

"I thought only generals were buried there,"[3] said my father, trying to jest in his turn.

"Well, and are you not a general of literature? You certainly have a right to lie beside them. What a splendid funeral you shall have! Archbishops shall celebrate your funeral mass, the choir of the Metropolitan shall sing it. An enormous crowd will follow your coffin, and when the procession approaches the monastery the monks will come out to salute you!"

"They only do that for the Tsar," said my father, amused by his wife's predictions.

"They will do it for you too. Oh! you shall have magnificent obsequies, such as have never been seen before in Petersburg."

My father laughed, and told the friends who came to talk about Nekrassov's funeral of this fancy of his wife's. Later, many persons recalled this strange prediction which my mother had made in jest.

1. A convent for nuns.
2. The majority of our writers are buried in the cemetery of Volkovo. There is a place in it called the Road of the Writers.
3. The monastery of Alexander Nevsky, which contains the relics of the patron saint of Petersburg, is considered the aristocratic cemetery of the city.

Remembering this conversation, my mother begged my uncle Jean to go with their brother-in-law, M. Paul Svatkovsky, to the convent of Novodevitchïe and buy a grave for my father near the tomb of the poet Nekrassov. She gave him all the money she had in the house that he might pay in advance for the grave and the funeral mass. As he was starting my uncle noticed how pale and mournful our childish faces were, and he asked his sister's leave to take us to the convent. "A drive in a sleigh will do them good," he said, looking pityingly at us.

We ran to dress and climbed joyously into the sleigh. The fresh air and the wintry sun did us good indeed, and with the happy carelessness of children we forgot for a while the cruel loss we had suffered. The convent of Novodevitchïe is on the outskirts of the city, close to the Arch of Narva. It was the first time I had ever been in a convent, and I looked curiously at the silent corridors, along which the nuns were gliding like shadows. We were shown into the reception-room; the Superior of the convent, an elderly lady dressed in black, with a long veil covering her head and her dress, entered, looking cold and haughty. M. Svatkovsky explained that the famous writer Dostoevsky had expressed a wish to be buried beside the poet Nekrassov, and, knowing that the charges were rather high, he begged that we might be allowed to have the grave for as low a price as possible, in consideration of the small means left to us by my father. The Superior made a scornful gesture. "We nuns do not belong to the world," she said coldly, "and its celebrities are nothing to us. We have fixed prices for burial in our cemetery and we cannot change them for anyone." And this humble servant of Jesus went on to name an exorbitant price, far in excess of the modest sum my mother could offer. In vain my uncle pleaded his sister's cause, asking that she might be allowed to pay the money by instalments in the course of the year. The Superior declared that the grave should not be dug until the full price had been paid. He had finally to get up and take leave of this saintly usurer.

We returned, full of indignation, to tell my mother of the ill success of our mission. "How unfortunate!" she said sadly. "I should like to have buried him in the place he himself chose. I suppose we must lay him beside our little Alexey at Ohta, but he never liked that place." It was agreed that my uncle should go to Ohta the following day to buy a grave and arrange with the priest for a funeral mass.

Towards evening my mother was told that a monk had called and wished to speak to her. He came on behalf of the community of the monastery of Alexander Nevsky, who, he said, were great admirers of

Dostoevsky. The monks wished the body of the famous writer to rest in the precincts of their monastery. They also undertook to provide the funeral mass, which they proposed to celebrate with great solemnity in their largest church. My mother joyfully accepted this generous offer. When the monk had gone, she went into her room and suddenly remembered her words to her husband some years before: "I will bury you in the monastery of Alexander Nevsky."

The next day, Friday, the crowd of Dostoevsky's admirers invaded our modest dwelling from the morning onwards. It was very varied: writers, ministers, students, grand dukes, generals, priests, great ladies and poor women of the middle classes coming in turn to salute Dostoevsky's body, and sometimes having to wait hours for their turn. The heat in the death-chamber was so great that the candles went out during the *panikida*. Magnificent wreaths of flowers adorned with ribbons bearing touching inscriptions, sent by the different ministries, societies and schools which were to figure in the funeral procession, were sent in such numbers that we did not know where to put them. The little wreaths and bouquets brought by Dostoevsky's friends were placed close to the coffin in which my father's body had just been placed. His admirers kissed his hands, weeping and begging for a flower or a leaf to keep in memory of him. Aided by our little friends who had come to watch with us beside the coffin, my brother and I distributed flowers all day long to the unknown persons who crowded round us.

On the Saturday an immense crowd filled the two streets at the angle of which our house stood. From our windows we looked down on a sea of human heads, undulating like waves, on which the wreaths and ribbons carried by the students floated. A hearse was in readiness to take the remains of Dostoevsky to the monastery. His admirers would not allow the coffin to be placed in it. They took it and carried it in relays to the burial place. In accordance with the custom the widow and the orphans followed it on foot. As the way to the Alexander Nevsky monastery was long and our childish strength was soon exhausted, friends occasionally took us out of the cortège into carriages. "Never forget the splendid funeral Russia gave your father," they said to us. When at last the procession approached the monastery, the monks came out of the great door to meet my father, who was henceforth to rest in the midst of their community. This is an honour they reserve for the Tsars; but they also paid it to the famous Russian writer, the faithful and respectful son of the Orthodox Church. Once more my mother's prediction was fulfilled.

It was too late to begin the funeral mass, and it was put off till the following day. The coffin was placed in the middle of the church of the Holy Spirit; after a short service we returned to our home, worn out with fatigue and emotion. My father's friends stayed for a time to keep watch over the crowd. Evening approached, it became dark; the crowd gradually dispersed, preparing to return the next day for the burial. Yet Dostoevsky was not left in solitude. The students of Petersburg did not forsake him; they determined to watch with their adored master during his last night on earth. We heard afterwards what had happened that night from the Metropolitan of Petersburg, who, according to custom, lived in the Alexander Nevsky monastery. A few days after the funeral my mother went to see him, to thank him for the magnificent ceremony the monks had given to my father, and she took us with her. The Metropolitan blessed us, and then began to describe his impressions of the students' vigil. "On Saturday evening," he said, "I went to the Church of the Holy Ghost to salute Dostoevsky's body in my turn. The monks stopped me at the door, telling me that the Church, which I supposed to be empty, was full of people.[1] I accordingly went up to the small chapel which is on the second floor of the adjacent church, its windows looking into the Church of the Holy Ghost. I spent part of the night there watching the students, without being seen by them. They were kneeling and praying, and as they prayed they wept and sobbed aloud. The monks began to read the Psalms at the foot of the coffin. The students took the book from them, and themselves read the Psalms in turn. Never have I heard them read in such a manner! They read in voices trembling with emotion, putting their hearts into every word they uttered. And they tell me these young men are atheists, and that they hate our Church. What magic power had Dostoevsky that he could thus bring them back to God?"

The power was that which Jesus gave to all His disciples. The unhappy Russian Church, paralysed since the time of Peter the Great, had lost that sacred power. Now that she is at length delivered from her bondage, and, since the Revolution, has been drowned in the blood of her martyrs, the priests and monks tortured and put to death by the Bolsheviks, she will rise to a new life and become as strong as in the times of the ancient Moscovite Patriarchs.

On the day of the burial, Sunday, the 1st of February, all Dostoevsky's admirers who were at work during the week took advantage of the holiday to come to the church and pray for the repose of his soul.

---

1. The Russian Metropolitans are very great personages, and only appear in public on solemn occasions.

Very early in the morning an enormous crowd invaded the peaceful monastery of Alexander Nevsky, which lies on the banks of the Neva and forms a little town of itself, with its numerous churches, its three burial grounds, its gardens, its school, seminary and ecclesiastical academy. The monks, seeing the crowd increasing every moment, filling the gardens and cemeteries, and climbing up on the monuments and iron railings, were alarmed and appealed to the police, who at once closed the great gates. Those who came later took their stand on the square in front of the monastery, and remained there until the end of the ceremony, hoping to be able to get in by some means, or at any rate to hear the funeral chants as the coffin was being carried to the grave.

Towards nine o'clock in the morning we drove up to the great gate, and were surprised to find it closed. My mother got out of the carriage, shrouded in her widow's veil, and holding us by the hand. A police officer barred the way. "No one else is to be admitted," he said severely.

"What?" cried my mother in astonishment. "I am Dostoevsky's widow, and they are waiting for me to begin the mass."

"You are the sixth widow of Dostoevsky who has tried to get in. No more lies! I shall not allow anyone else to pass."

We looked at each other in perplexity, not knowing what to do. Fortunately, friends were on the watch for us; they hastened to the gate and had us admitted. We had great difficulty in making our way through the crowd in the precincts, and still more in entering the church, which was full to overflowing. When at last we reached the place reserved for us, the mass began. It was celebrated by the Archbishop, who pronounced funeral orations, and chanted by the Metropolitan's choir. In the cemetery, it was the turn of the writers; the speeches they delivered beside the open grave, according to custom, lasted several hours. My mother's prediction was literally fulfilled. Never had there been such a funeral in Petersburg.[1]

Yet one important detail of the funeral mass had been omitted. In Russia it is customary for the coffin to remain open during the mass; towards the end, the relatives and friends approach and give the corpse their farewell kiss. Dostoevsky's coffin was closed. On the day of the funeral my uncle and M. Pobédonoszev, our guardian, went to the monastery very early in the morning. They opened the coffin, and found Dostoevsky much changed. Fearing that the sight of his altered face would be very distressing to his widow and children, M. Pobédonoszev

---

1. Dostoevsky had himself foreshadowed certain details of his death and burial when he described the death of the *staretz* Zossima in *The Brothers Karamazov*.

desired the monks not to open the coffin. My mother could never al-together forgive him for this. "What difference would it have made to me?" she said bitterly. "However changed, he would still have been my beloved husband. And he was laid in his grave without my farewell kiss and blessing."

For my part, I was later deeply grateful to my guardian for having spared me the mournful sight. I was glad to have the memory of my father lying as if sleeping peacefully in his coffin, and smiling at some beautiful sight before him. Yet it might have been better for me to see his decomposing body. It would have destroyed the strange dream that obsessed me after the funeral, at first giving me much joy and later much pain. I dreamed that my father was not dead, that he had been buried in a lethargy, that he would soon wake, call on the keepers of the cemetery for help and return to us. I imagined our joy, our laughter and our kisses. I was the child of an imaginative writer, I had a desire to create scenes, gestures and words, and this childish make-believe gave me great pleasure. However, by degrees, as the days and weeks passed, reason awoke in my youthful brain and killed my illusions, telling me that a human being could not live long under the earth without air and food, that my father's lethargy was lasting very long, and that perhaps he was really dead. Then I suffered cruelly…

And yet I was right. My childish dream was not all illusion; my father was not dead. He came back later when I was old enough to read and study his works, and has never left me. Thanks to his dear presence, I have never been afraid in my life. I know that my father watches over me, intercedes for me with God, and that our Saviour will not refuse him what he asks. As I have written, I have begged him to guide and inspire me, and above all to prevent me from saying things that would have displeased him. May he have heard my prayer!

Aimée Dostoevsky

Discovery Publisher

Discovery Publisher is a multimedia publisher whose mission is to inspire and support personal transformation, spiritual growth and awakening. We strive with every title to preserve the essential wisdom of the author, spiritual teacher, thinker, healer, and visionary artist.

www.ingramcontent.com/pod-product-compliance
Lightning Source LLC
Chambersburg PA
CBHW011343090426
42739CB00017B/3462